UNITY

TRAPPED BY
WEBNET

MATT KINDT | CAFU | BRIAN REBER

CONTENTS

Collection Cover Art: Clayton Crain

UNITY®: Trapped by Webnet. Published by Valiant Entertainment, LLC. Office of
Publication: 424 West 33rd Street, New York, NY 10001. Compilation copyright
©2014 Valiant Entertainment, Inc. All rights reserved. Contains materials
originally published in single magazine form as UNITY #5-7 Copyright ©2014,
and X-O Manowar® #5 Copyright ©2012 Valiant Entertainment, Inc. All rights
reserved. All characters, their distinctive likeness and related indicia featured
in this publication are trademarks of Valiant Entertainment, Inc. The stories,
characters, and incidents featured in this publication are entirely fictional.
Valiant Entertainment does not read or accept unsolicited submissions of ideas,
stories, or artwork. Printed in the U.S.A. First Printing.
ISBN: 9781939346346.

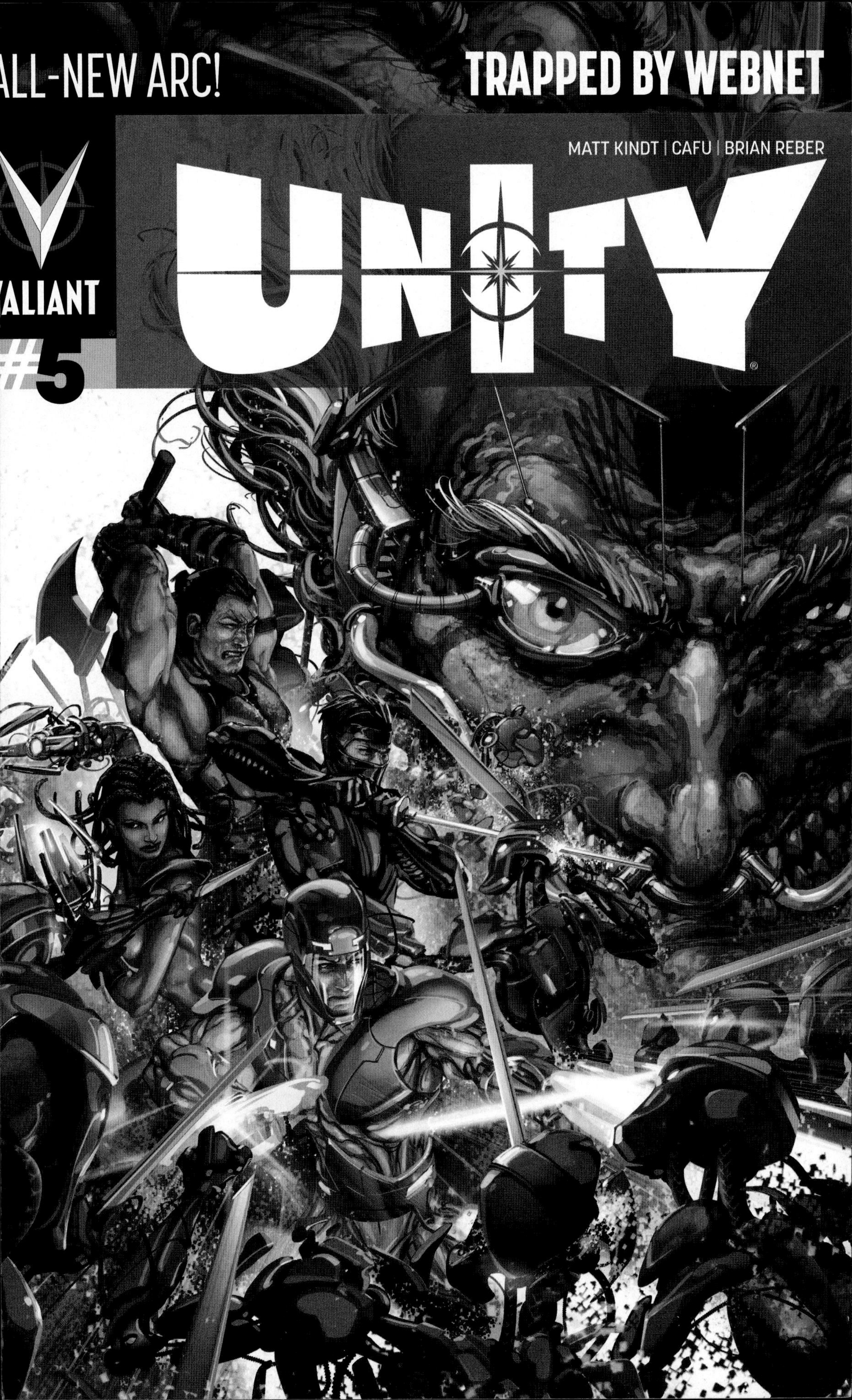
ALL-NEW ARC!
TRAPPED BY WEBNET
VALIANT
#5
MATT KINDT | CAFU | BRIAN REBER
UNITY

UNITY

OUR STORY SO FAR...

Ninjak
Weapons tech specialist and current MI-6 Operative

X-O Manowar
A displaced Visigoth Warrior who wields the most powerful weapon in all of existence, the X-O Manowar armor.

Livewire
Prized pupil of Toyo Harada. Gifted with the ability to control machinery with her mind.

The Eternal Warrior
Nearly as old as time itself, Gilad Anni-Padda wages an unending war to protect Earth.

Drawn together to stop the international crisis brought on by the arrival of the immensely powerful X-O Manowar, Ninjak, Livewire, and The Eternal Warrior have formed an elite super powered task force known only as Unity. After narrowly avoiding a global nuclear event by defeating X-O Manowar and stripping him of his unstoppable alien armor, the Unity team learned that their benefactor, Toyo Harada, had sinister intentions for the armor, and were forced into battle with the powerful psiot. The Unity team defeated Harada, and in doing so returned the armor to Aric, forging a strong ally in the process.

Now, Livewire has joined Ninjak as an agent of MI-6 in exchange for protection against Harada and his forces. Under orders to investigate a mysterious crash site Livewire begins her investigation in the jungles of Taiwan...

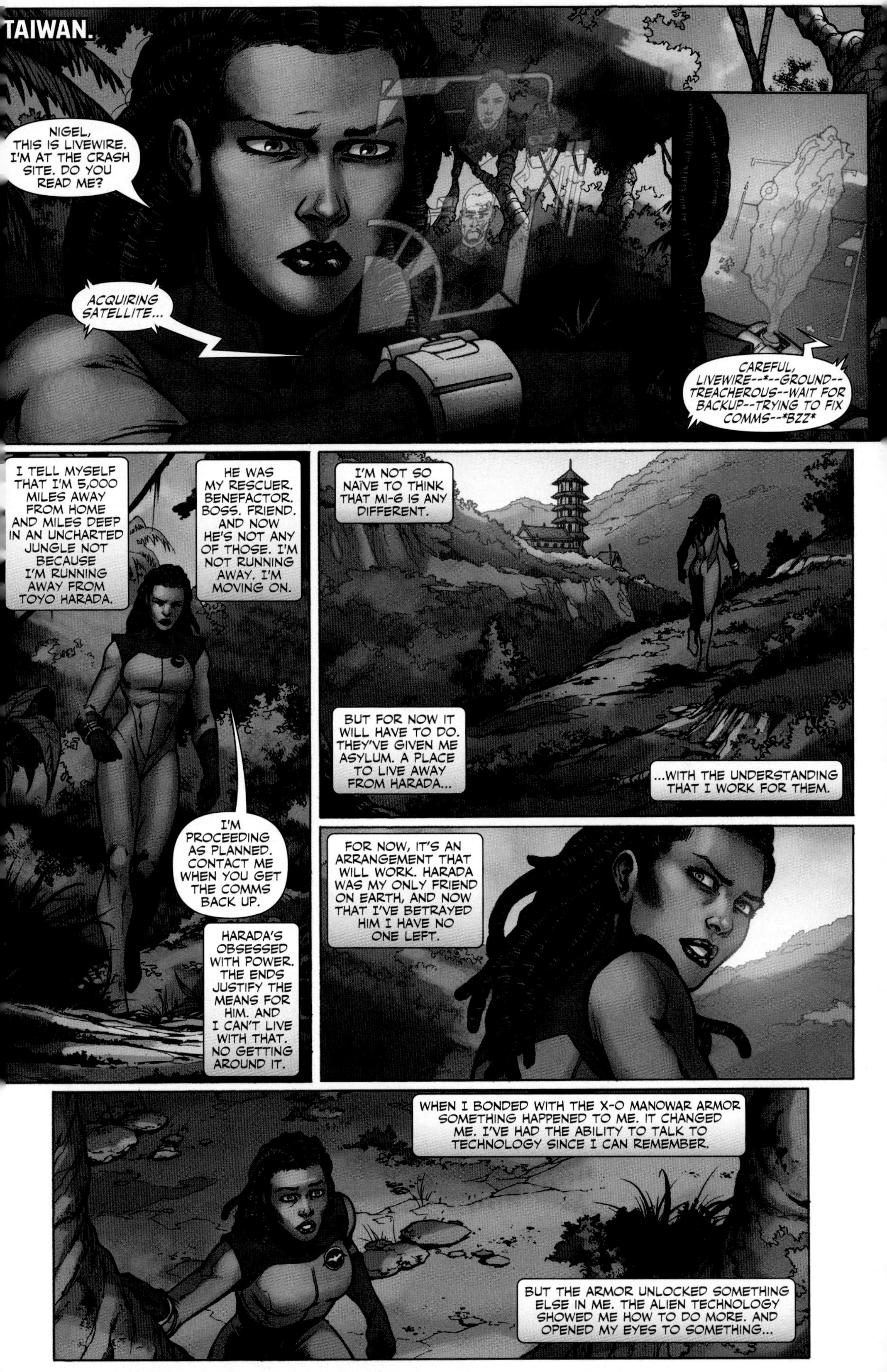
TAIWAN.
NIGEL, THIS IS LIVEWIRE. I'M AT THE CRASH SITE. DO YOU READ ME?
ACQUIRING SATELLITE...
CAREFUL, LIVEWIRE--*--GROUND--TREACHEROUS--WAIT FOR BACKUP--TRYING TO FIX COMMS--*BZZ*
I TELL MYSELF THAT I'M 5,000 MILES AWAY FROM HOME AND MILES DEEP IN AN UNCHARTED JUNGLE NOT BECAUSE I'M RUNNING AWAY FROM TOYO HARADA.
HE WAS MY RESCUER. BENEFACTOR. BOSS. FRIEND. AND NOW HE'S NOT ANY OF THOSE. I'M NOT RUNNING AWAY. I'M MOVING ON.
I'M PROCEEDING AS PLANNED. CONTACT ME WHEN YOU GET THE COMMS BACK UP.
HARADA'S OBSESSED WITH POWER. THE ENDS JUSTIFY THE MEANS FOR HIM. AND I CAN'T LIVE WITH THAT. NO GETTING AROUND IT.
I'M NOT SO NAÏVE TO THINK THAT MI-6 IS ANY DIFFERENT.
BUT FOR NOW IT WILL HAVE TO DO. THEY'VE GIVEN ME ASYLUM. A PLACE TO LIVE AWAY FROM HARADA...
...WITH THE UNDERSTANDING THAT I WORK FOR THEM.
FOR NOW, IT'S AN ARRANGEMENT THAT WILL WORK. HARADA WAS MY ONLY FRIEND ON EARTH, AND NOW THAT I'VE BETRAYED HIM I HAVE NO ONE LEFT.
WHEN I BONDED WITH THE X-O MANOWAR ARMOR SOMETHING HAPPENED TO ME. IT CHANGED ME. I'VE HAD THE ABILITY TO TALK TO TECHNOLOGY SINCE I CAN REMEMBER.
BUT THE ARMOR UNLOCKED SOMETHING ELSE IN ME. THE ALIEN TECHNOLOGY SHOWED ME HOW TO DO MORE. AND OPENED MY EYES TO SOMETHING...

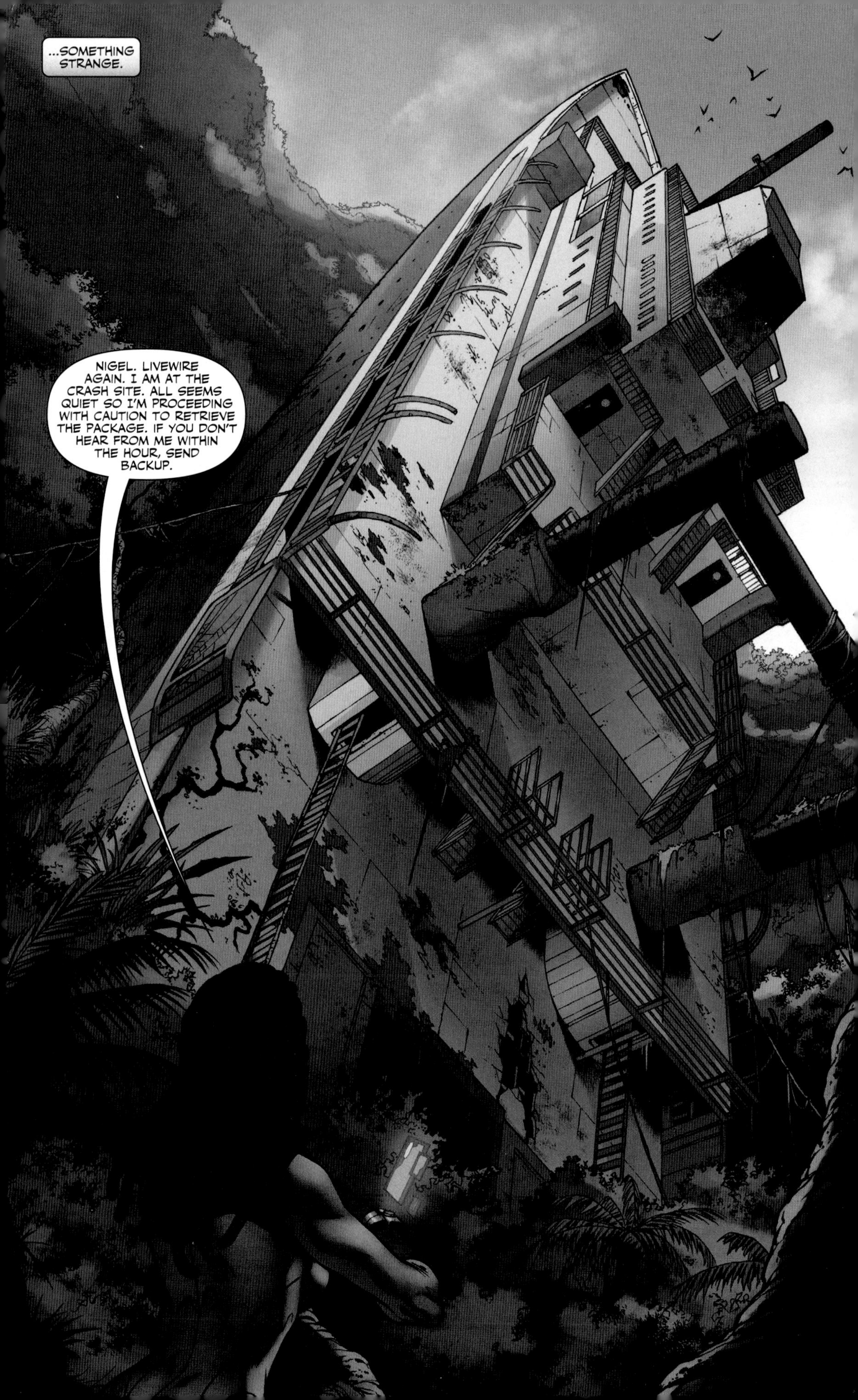
...SOMETHING STRANGE.
NIGEL. LIVEWIRE AGAIN. I AM AT THE CRASH SITE. ALL SEEMS QUIET SO I'M PROCEEDING WITH CAUTION TO RETRIEVE THE PACKAGE. IF YOU DON'T HEAR FROM ME WITHIN THE HOUR, SEND BACKUP.

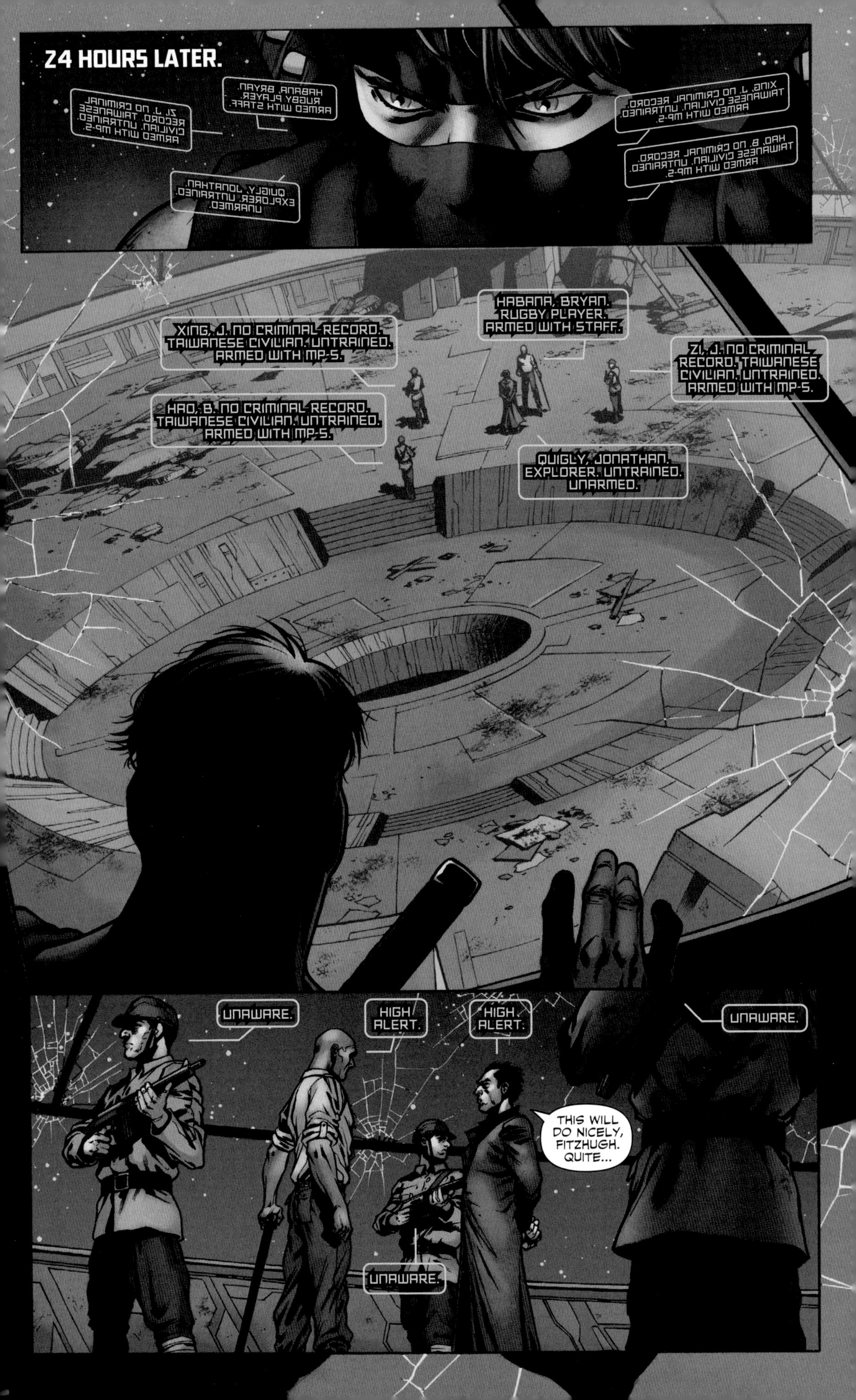
24 HOURS LATER.
XING, J. NO CRIMINAL RECORD. TAIWANESE CIVILIAN. UNTRAINED. ARMED WITH MP-5.
HABANA, BRYAN. RUGBY PLAYER. ARMED WITH STAFF.
ZI, J. NO CRIMINAL RECORD. TAIWANESE CIVILIAN. UNTRAINED. ARMED WITH MP-5.
HAO, B. NO CRIMINAL RECORD. TAIWANESE CIVILIAN. UNTRAINED. ARMED WITH MP-5.
QUIGLY, JONATHAN. EXPLORER. UNTRAINED. UNARMED.
UNAWARE.
HIGH ALERT.
HIGH ALERT.
UNAWARE.
THIS WILL DO NICELY, FITZHUGH. QUITE...
UNAWARE.

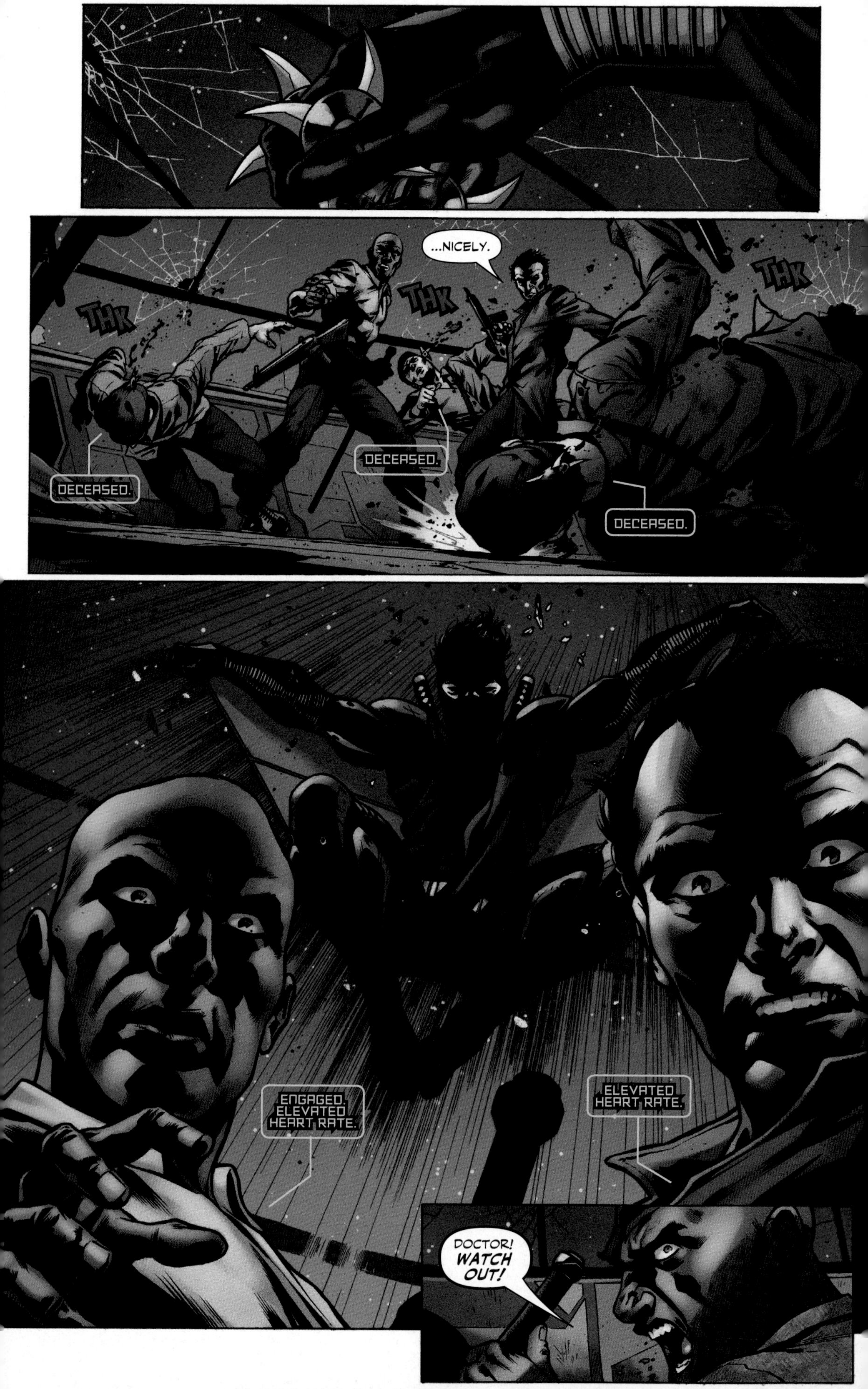

THK
...NICELY.
THK
THK
DECEASED.
DECEASED.
DECEASED.
ENGAGED. ELEVATED HEART RATE.
ELEVATED HEART RATE.
DOCTOR! WATCH OUT!

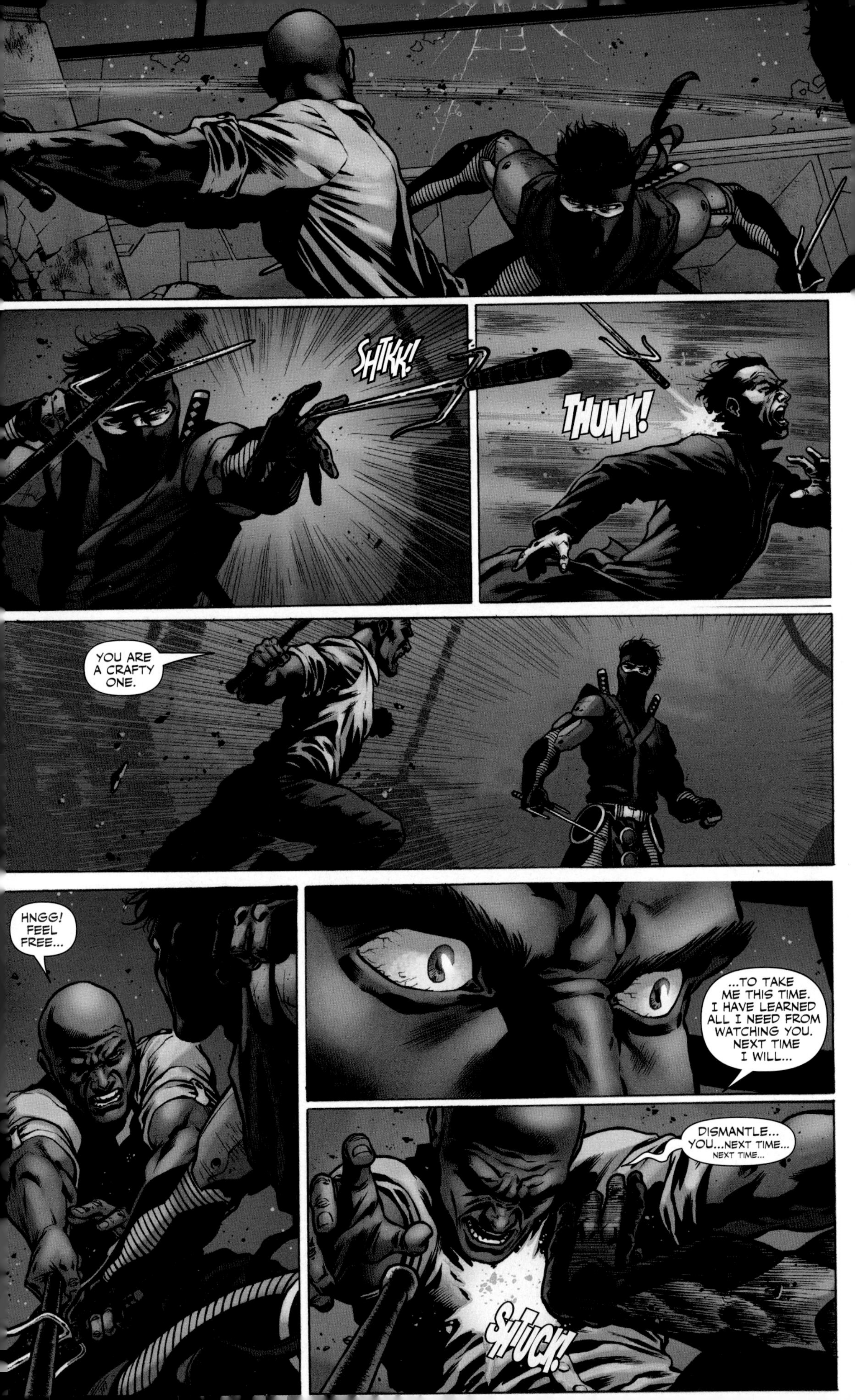
SHIKK!
THUNK!
YOU ARE A CRAFTY ONE.
HNGG! FEEL FREE...
...TO TAKE ME THIS TIME. I HAVE LEARNED ALL I NEED FROM WATCHING YOU. NEXT TIME I WILL...
DISMANTLE... YOU...NEXT TIME... NEXT TIME...
SHUCK!

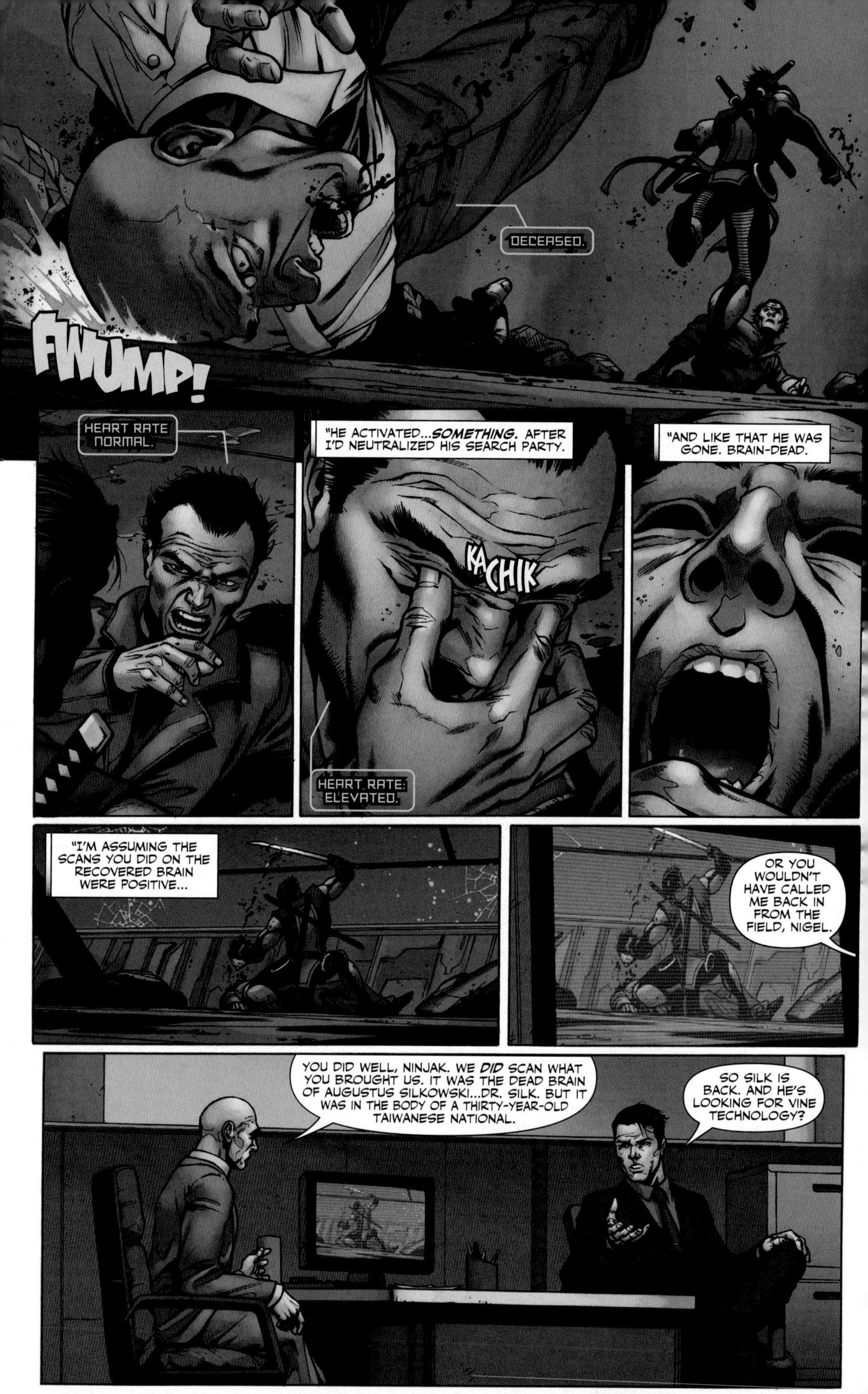
DECEASED.
FWUMP!
HEART RATE NORMAL.
"HE ACTIVATED...SOMETHING. AFTER I'D NEUTRALIZED HIS SEARCH PARTY.
KACHIK
HEART RATE: ELEVATED.
"AND LIKE THAT HE WAS GONE. BRAIN-DEAD.
"I'M ASSUMING THE SCANS YOU DID ON THE RECOVERED BRAIN WERE POSITIVE...
OR YOU WOULDN'T HAVE CALLED ME BACK IN FROM THE FIELD, NIGEL.
YOU DID WELL, NINJAK. WE DID SCAN WHAT YOU BROUGHT US. IT WAS THE DEAD BRAIN OF AUGUSTUS SILKOWSKI...DR. SILK. BUT IT WAS IN THE BODY OF A THIRTY-YEAR-OLD TAIWANESE NATIONAL.
SO SILK IS BACK. AND HE'S LOOKING FOR VINE TECHNOLOGY?

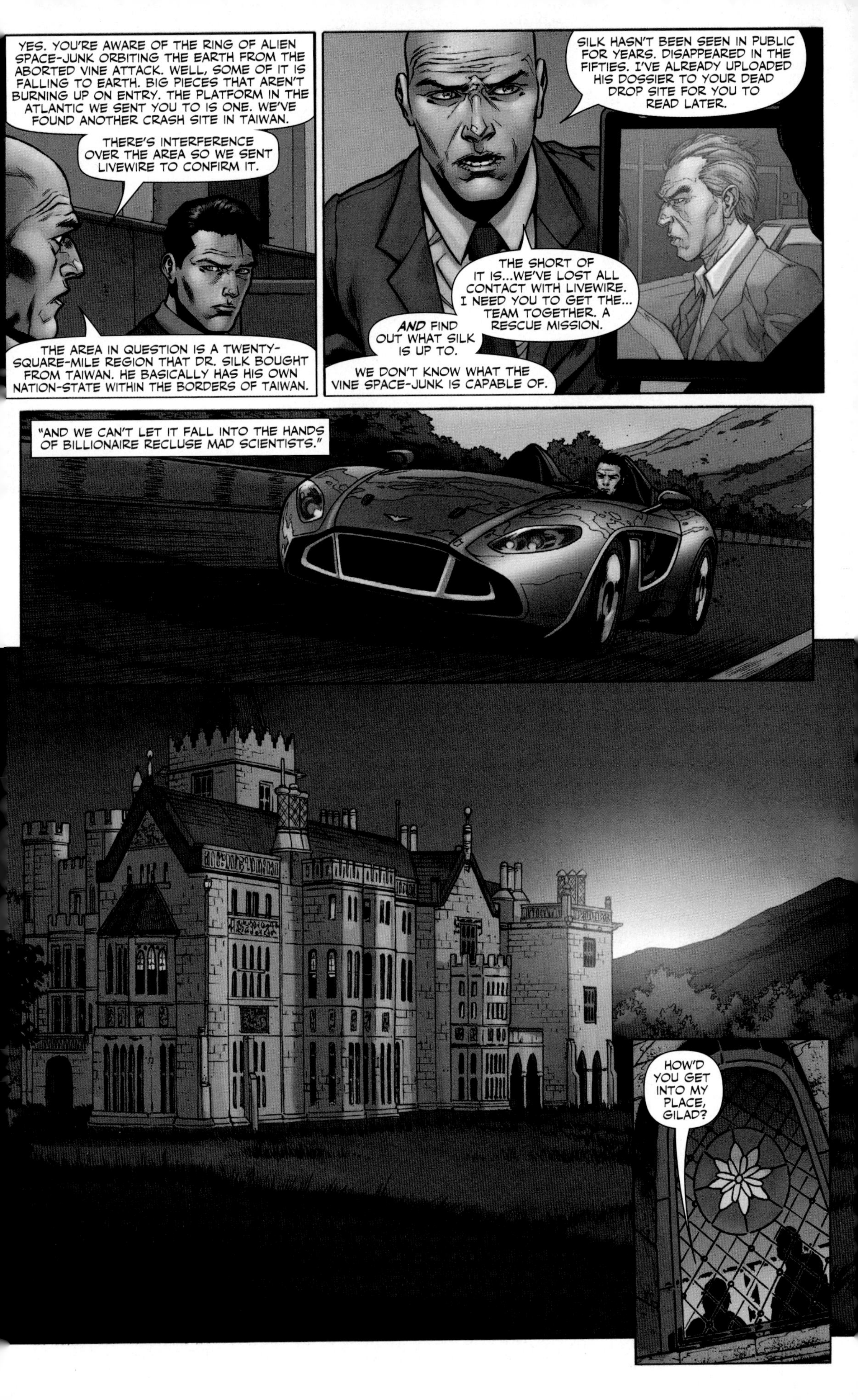
YES. YOU'RE AWARE OF THE RING OF ALIEN SPACE-JUNK ORBITING THE EARTH FROM THE ABORTED VINE ATTACK. WELL, SOME OF IT IS FALLING TO EARTH. BIG PIECES THAT AREN'T BURNING UP ON ENTRY. THE PLATFORM IN THE ATLANTIC WE SENT YOU TO IS ONE. WE'VE FOUND ANOTHER CRASH SITE IN TAIWAN.
THERE'S INTERFERENCE OVER THE AREA SO WE SENT LIVEWIRE TO CONFIRM IT.
THE AREA IN QUESTION IS A TWENTY-SQUARE-MILE REGION THAT DR. SILK BOUGHT FROM TAIWAN. HE BASICALLY HAS HIS OWN NATION-STATE WITHIN THE BORDERS OF TAIWAN.
SILK HASN'T BEEN SEEN IN PUBLIC FOR YEARS. DISAPPEARED IN THE FIFTIES. I'VE ALREADY UPLOADED HIS DOSSIER TO YOUR DEAD DROP SITE FOR YOU TO READ LATER.
THE SHORT OF IT IS...WE'VE LOST ALL CONTACT WITH LIVEWIRE. I NEED YOU TO GET THE... TEAM TOGETHER. A RESCUE MISSION.
AND FIND OUT WHAT SILK IS UP TO.
WE DON'T KNOW WHAT THE VINE SPACE-JUNK IS CAPABLE OF.
"AND WE CAN'T LET IT FALL INTO THE HANDS OF BILLIONAIRE RECLUSE MAD SCIENTISTS."
HOW'D YOU GET INTO MY PLACE, GILAD?

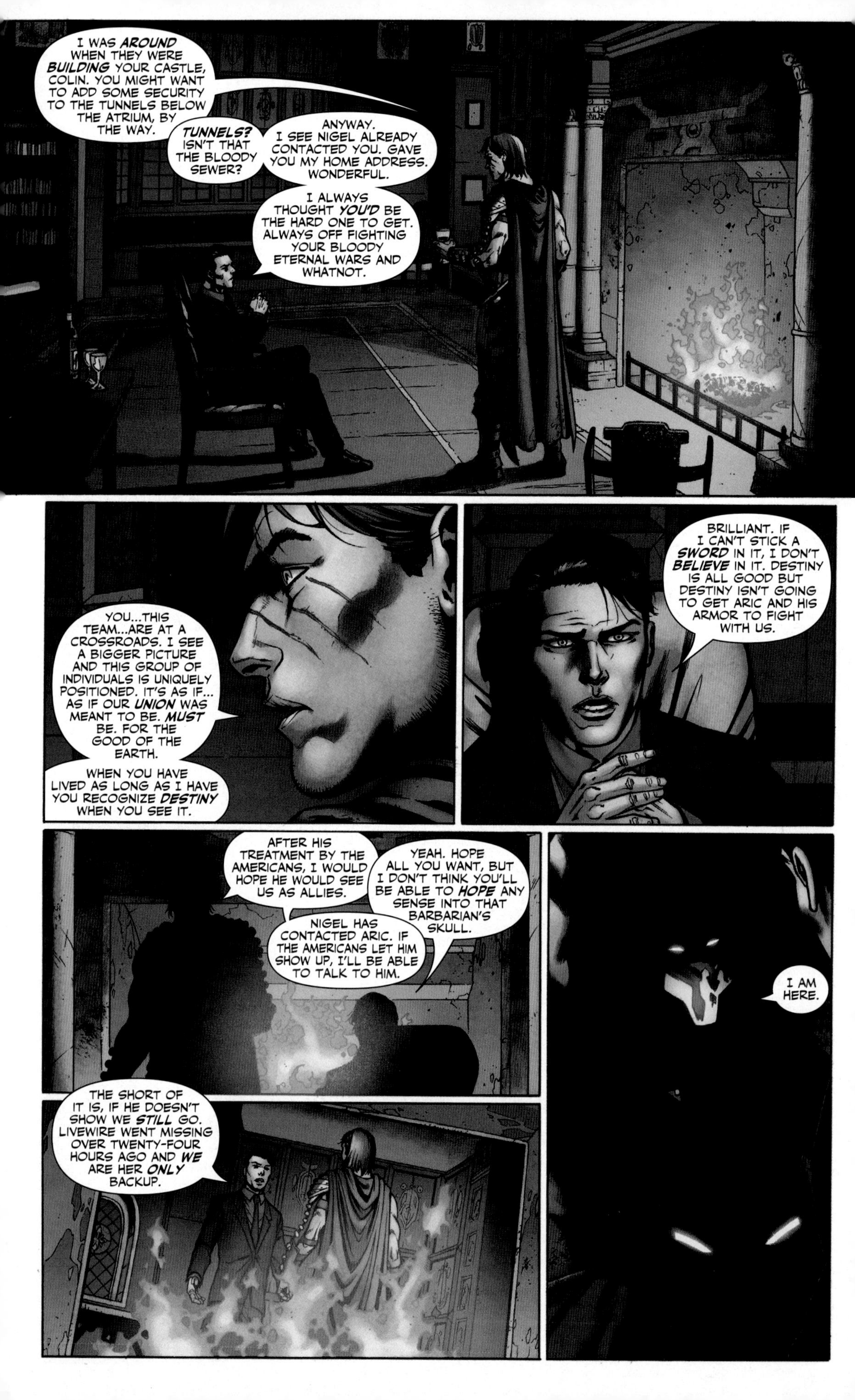
I WAS AROUND WHEN THEY WERE BUILDING YOUR CASTLE, COLIN. YOU MIGHT WANT TO ADD SOME SECURITY TO THE TUNNELS BELOW THE ATRIUM, BY THE WAY.
TUNNELS? ISN'T THAT THE BLOODY SEWER?
ANYWAY. I SEE NIGEL ALREADY CONTACTED YOU. GAVE YOU MY HOME ADDRESS. WONDERFUL.
I ALWAYS THOUGHT YOU'D BE THE HARD ONE TO GET. ALWAYS OFF FIGHTING YOUR BLOODY ETERNAL WARS AND WHATNOT.
YOU...THIS TEAM...ARE AT A CROSSROADS. I SEE A BIGGER PICTURE AND THIS GROUP OF INDIVIDUALS IS UNIQUELY POSITIONED. IT'S AS IF... AS IF OUR UNION WAS MEANT TO BE. MUST BE. FOR THE GOOD OF THE EARTH.
WHEN YOU HAVE LIVED AS LONG AS I HAVE YOU RECOGNIZE DESTINY WHEN YOU SEE IT.
BRILLIANT. IF I CAN'T STICK A SWORD IN IT, I DON'T BELIEVE IN IT. DESTINY IS ALL GOOD BUT DESTINY ISN'T GOING TO GET ARIC AND HIS ARMOR TO FIGHT WITH US.
AFTER HIS TREATMENT BY THE AMERICANS, I WOULD HOPE HE WOULD SEE US AS ALLIES.
YEAH. HOPE ALL YOU WANT, BUT I DON'T THINK YOU'LL BE ABLE TO HOPE ANY SENSE INTO THAT BARBARIAN'S SKULL.
NIGEL HAS CONTACTED ARIC. IF THE AMERICANS LET HIM SHOW UP, I'LL BE ABLE TO TALK TO HIM.
THE SHORT OF IT IS, IF HE DOESN'T SHOW WE STILL GO. LIVEWIRE WENT MISSING OVER TWENTY-FOUR HOURS AGO AND WE ARE HER ONLY BACKUP.
I AM HERE.

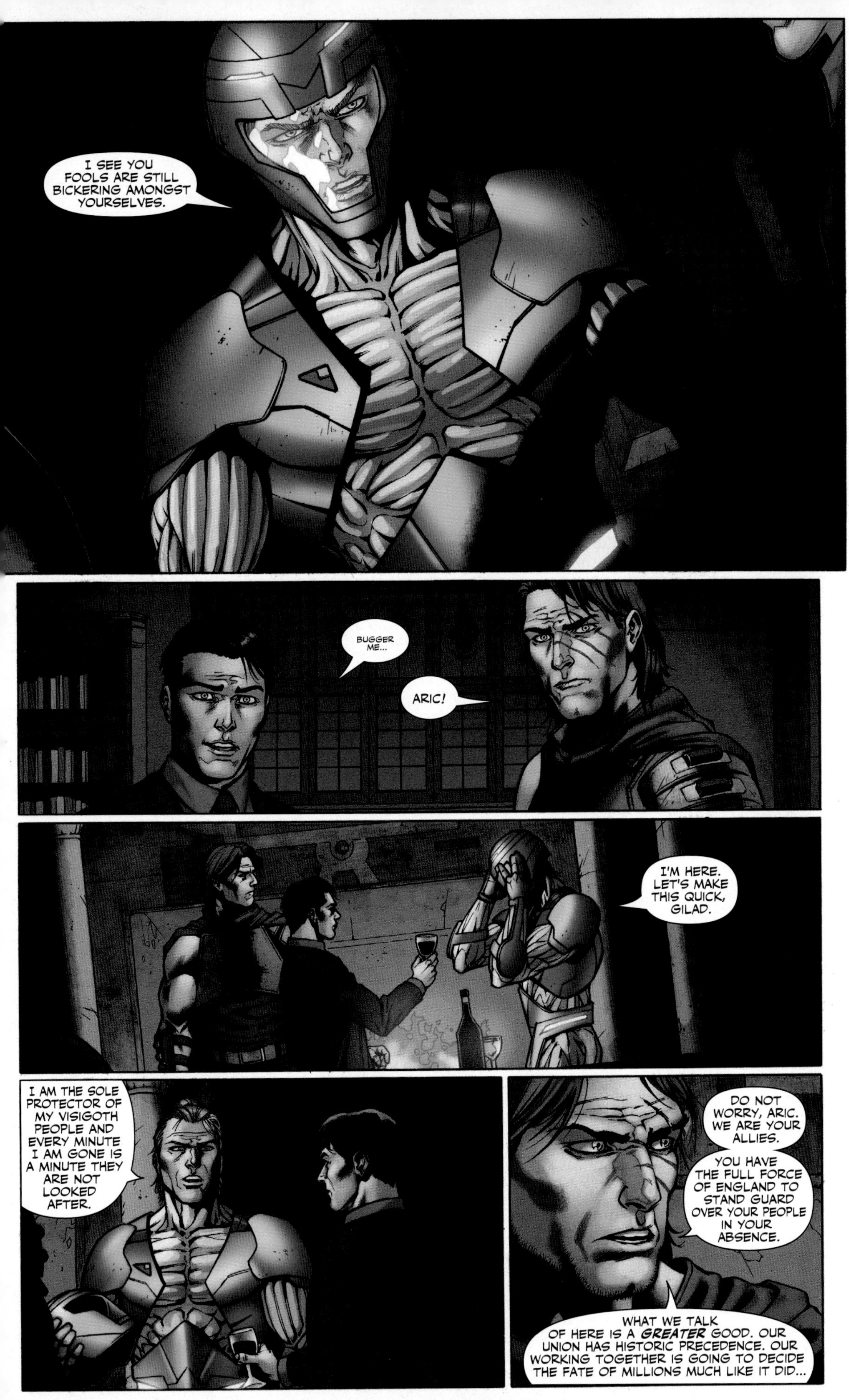
I SEE YOU FOOLS ARE STILL BICKERING AMONGST YOURSELVES.
BUGGER ME...
ARIC!
I'M HERE. LET'S MAKE THIS QUICK, GILAD.
I AM THE SOLE PROTECTOR OF MY VISIGOTH PEOPLE AND EVERY MINUTE I AM GONE IS A MINUTE THEY ARE NOT LOOKED AFTER.
DO NOT WORRY, ARIC. WE ARE YOUR ALLIES.
YOU HAVE THE FULL FORCE OF ENGLAND TO STAND GUARD OVER YOUR PEOPLE IN YOUR ABSENCE.
WHAT WE TALK OF HERE IS A *GREATER* GOOD. OUR UNION HAS HISTORIC PRECEDENCE. OUR WORKING TOGETHER IS GOING TO DECIDE THE FATE OF MILLIONS MUCH LIKE IT DID...

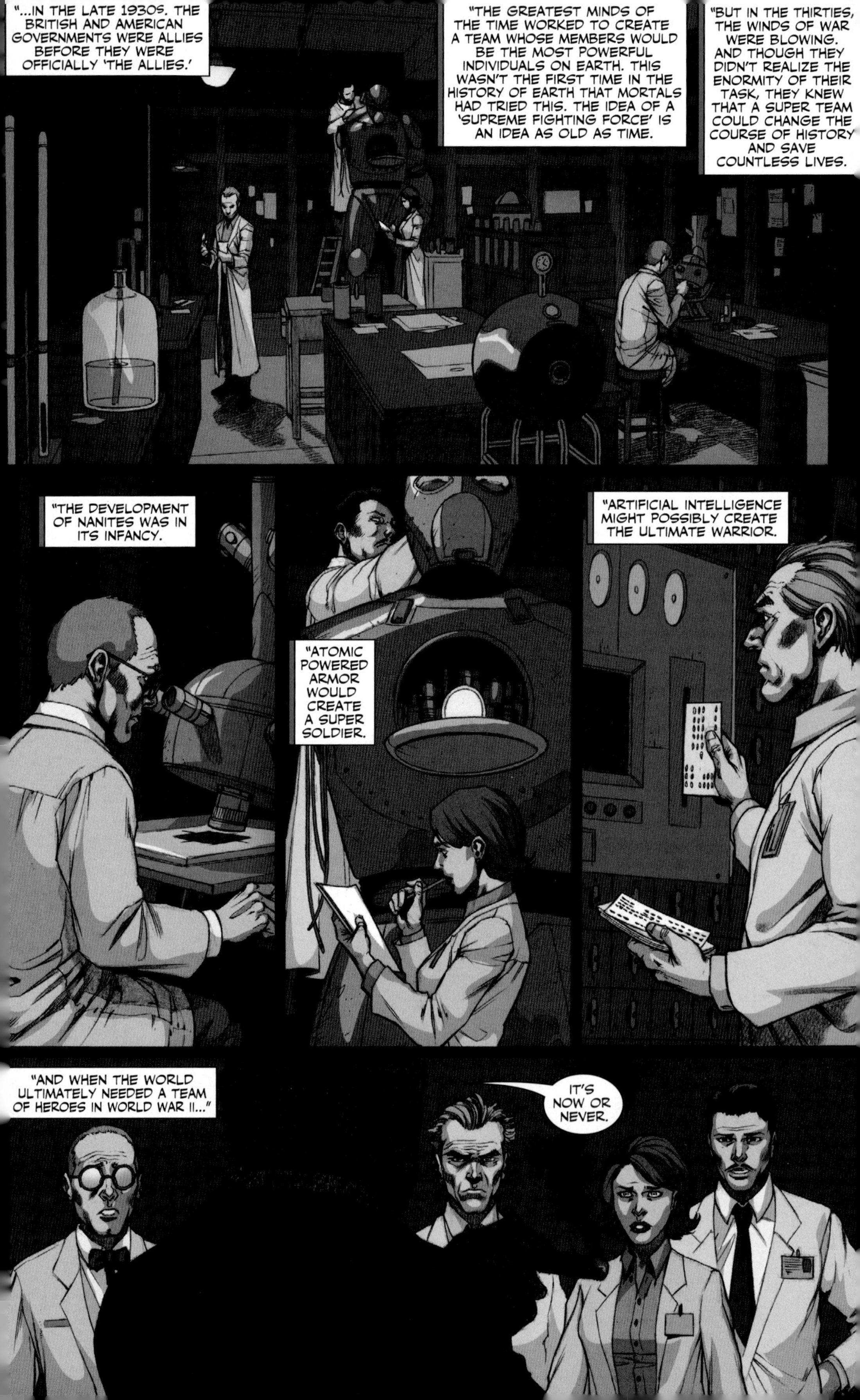
"...IN THE LATE 1930S. THE BRITISH AND AMERICAN GOVERNMENTS WERE ALLIES BEFORE THEY WERE OFFICIALLY 'THE ALLIES.'
"THE GREATEST MINDS OF THE TIME WORKED TO CREATE A TEAM WHOSE MEMBERS WOULD BE THE MOST POWERFUL INDIVIDUALS ON EARTH. THIS WASN'T THE FIRST TIME IN THE HISTORY OF EARTH THAT MORTALS HAD TRIED THIS. THE IDEA OF A 'SUPREME FIGHTING FORCE' IS AN IDEA AS OLD AS TIME.
"BUT IN THE THIRTIES, THE WINDS OF WAR WERE BLOWING. AND THOUGH THEY DIDN'T REALIZE THE ENORMITY OF THEIR TASK, THEY KNEW THAT A SUPER TEAM COULD CHANGE THE COURSE OF HISTORY AND SAVE COUNTLESS LIVES.
"THE DEVELOPMENT OF NANITES WAS IN ITS INFANCY.
"ATOMIC POWERED ARMOR WOULD CREATE A SUPER SOLDIER.
"ARTIFICIAL INTELLIGENCE MIGHT POSSIBLY CREATE THE ULTIMATE WARRIOR.
"AND WHEN THE WORLD ULTIMATELY NEEDED A TEAM OF HEROES IN WORLD WAR II..."
IT'S NOW OR NEVER.

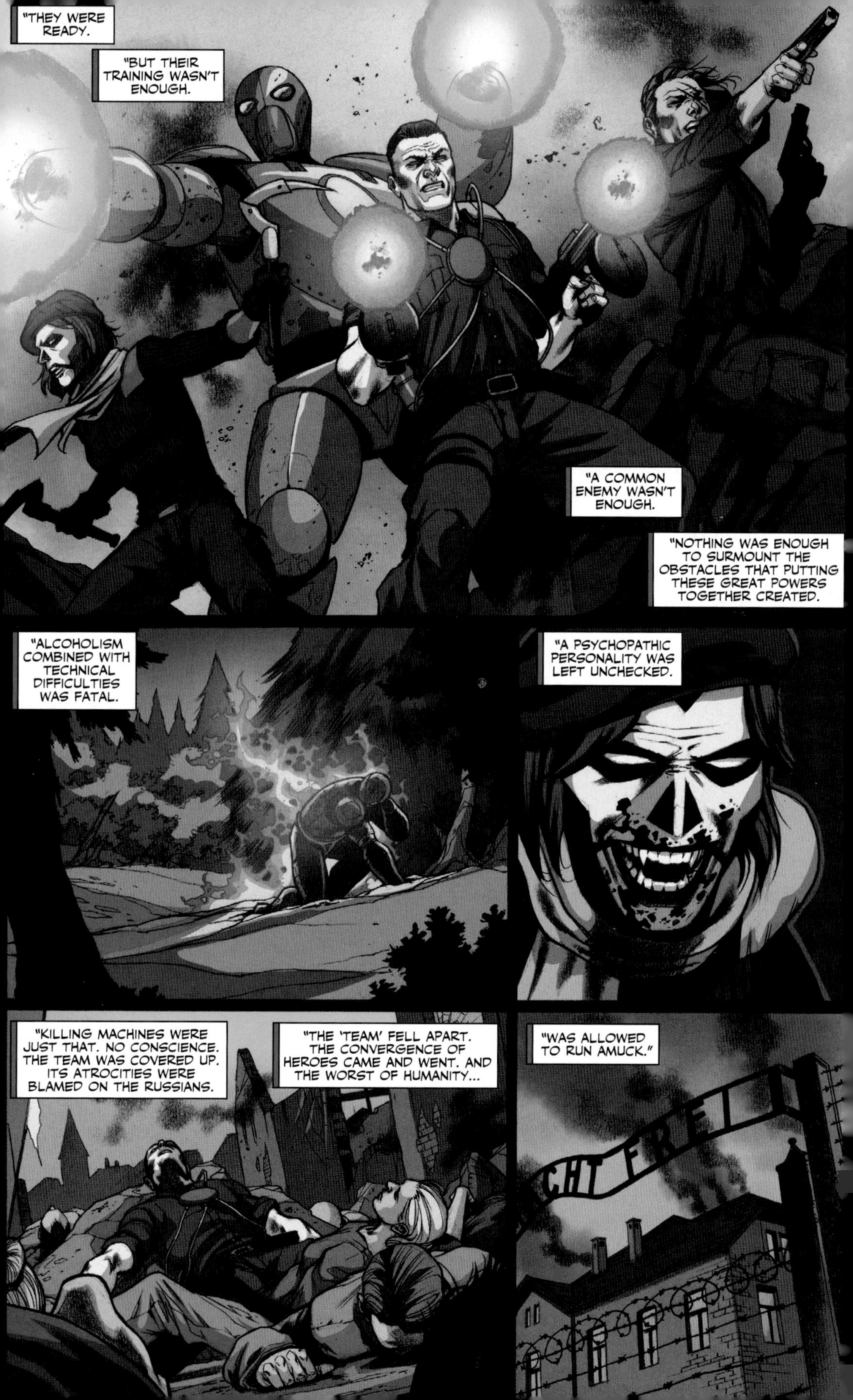
"THEY WERE READY.
"BUT THEIR TRAINING WASN'T ENOUGH.
"A COMMON ENEMY WASN'T ENOUGH.
"NOTHING WAS ENOUGH TO SURMOUNT THE OBSTACLES THAT PUTTING THESE GREAT POWERS TOGETHER CREATED.
"ALCOHOLISM COMBINED WITH TECHNICAL DIFFICULTIES WAS FATAL.
"A PSYCHOPATHIC PERSONALITY WAS LEFT UNCHECKED.
"KILLING MACHINES WERE JUST THAT. NO CONSCIENCE. THE TEAM WAS COVERED UP. ITS ATROCITIES WERE BLAMED ON THE RUSSIANS.
"THE 'TEAM' FELL APART. THE CONVERGENCE OF HEROES CAME AND WENT. AND THE WORST OF HUMANITY...
"WAS ALLOWED TO RUN AMUCK."
CHT FREI

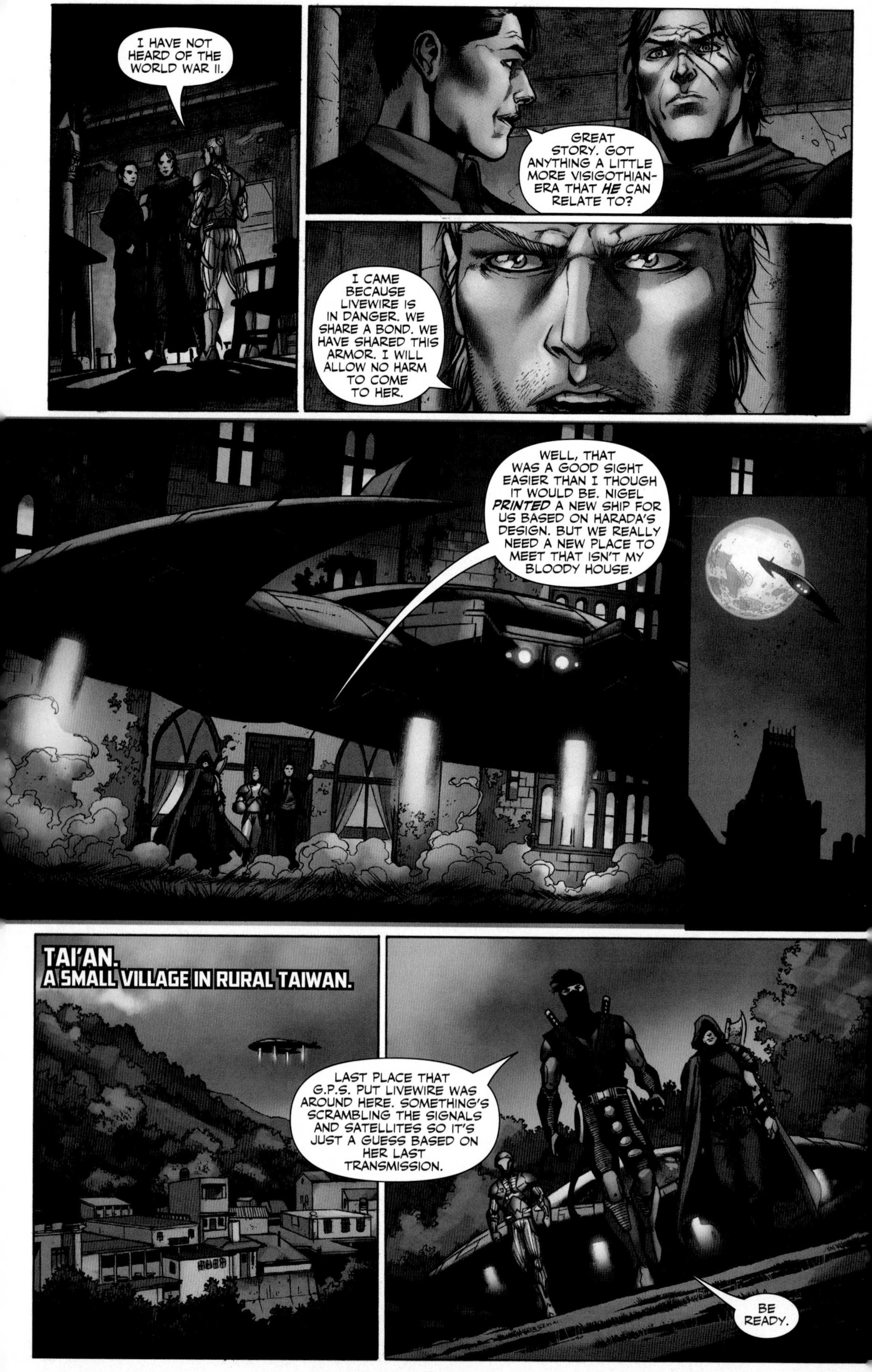
I HAVE NOT HEARD OF THE WORLD WAR II.
GREAT STORY. GOT ANYTHING A LITTLE MORE VISIGOTHIAN-ERA THAT HE CAN RELATE TO?
I CAME BECAUSE LIVEWIRE IS IN DANGER. WE SHARE A BOND. WE HAVE SHARED THIS ARMOR. I WILL ALLOW NO HARM TO COME TO HER.
WELL, THAT WAS A GOOD SIGHT EASIER THAN I THOUGH IT WOULD BE. NIGEL PRINTED A NEW SHIP FOR US BASED ON HARADA'S DESIGN. BUT WE REALLY NEED A NEW PLACE TO MEET THAT ISN'T MY BLOODY HOUSE.
TAI'AN.
A SMALL VILLAGE IN RURAL TAIWAN.
LAST PLACE THAT G.P.S. PUT LIVEWIRE WAS AROUND HERE. SOMETHING'S SCRAMBLING THE SIGNALS AND SATELLITES SO IT'S JUST A GUESS BASED ON HER LAST TRANSMISSION.
BE READY.

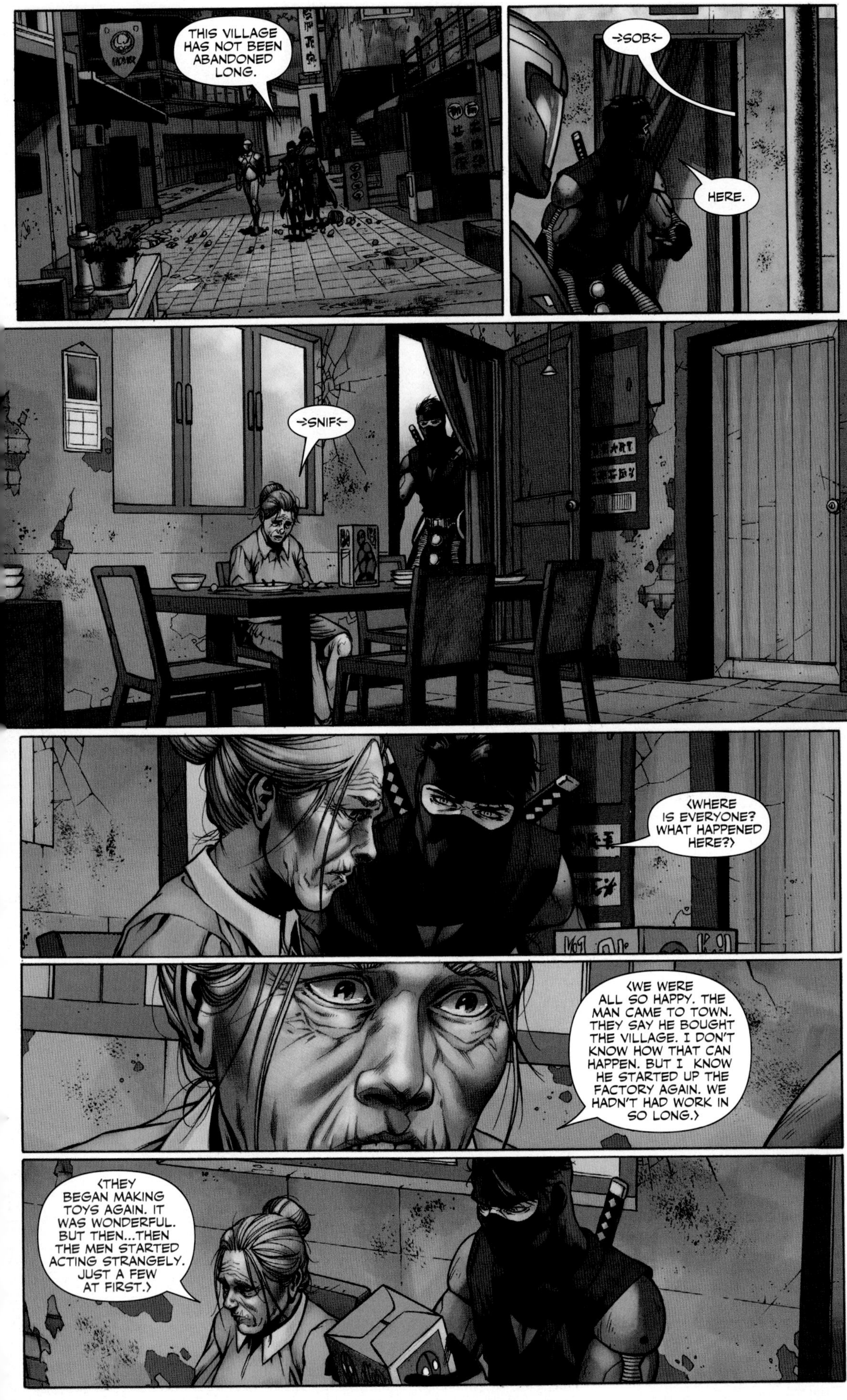
THIS VILLAGE HAS NOT BEEN ABANDONED LONG.
<SOB>
HERE.
<SNIF>
‹WHERE IS EVERYONE? WHAT HAPPENED HERE?›
‹WE WERE ALL SO HAPPY. THE MAN CAME TO TOWN. THEY SAY HE BOUGHT THE VILLAGE. I DON'T KNOW HOW THAT CAN HAPPEN. BUT I KNOW HE STARTED UP THE FACTORY AGAIN. WE HADN'T HAD WORK IN SO LONG.›
‹THEY BEGAN MAKING TOYS AGAIN. IT WAS WONDERFUL. BUT THEN...THEN THE MEN STARTED ACTING STRANGELY. JUST A FEW AT FIRST.›

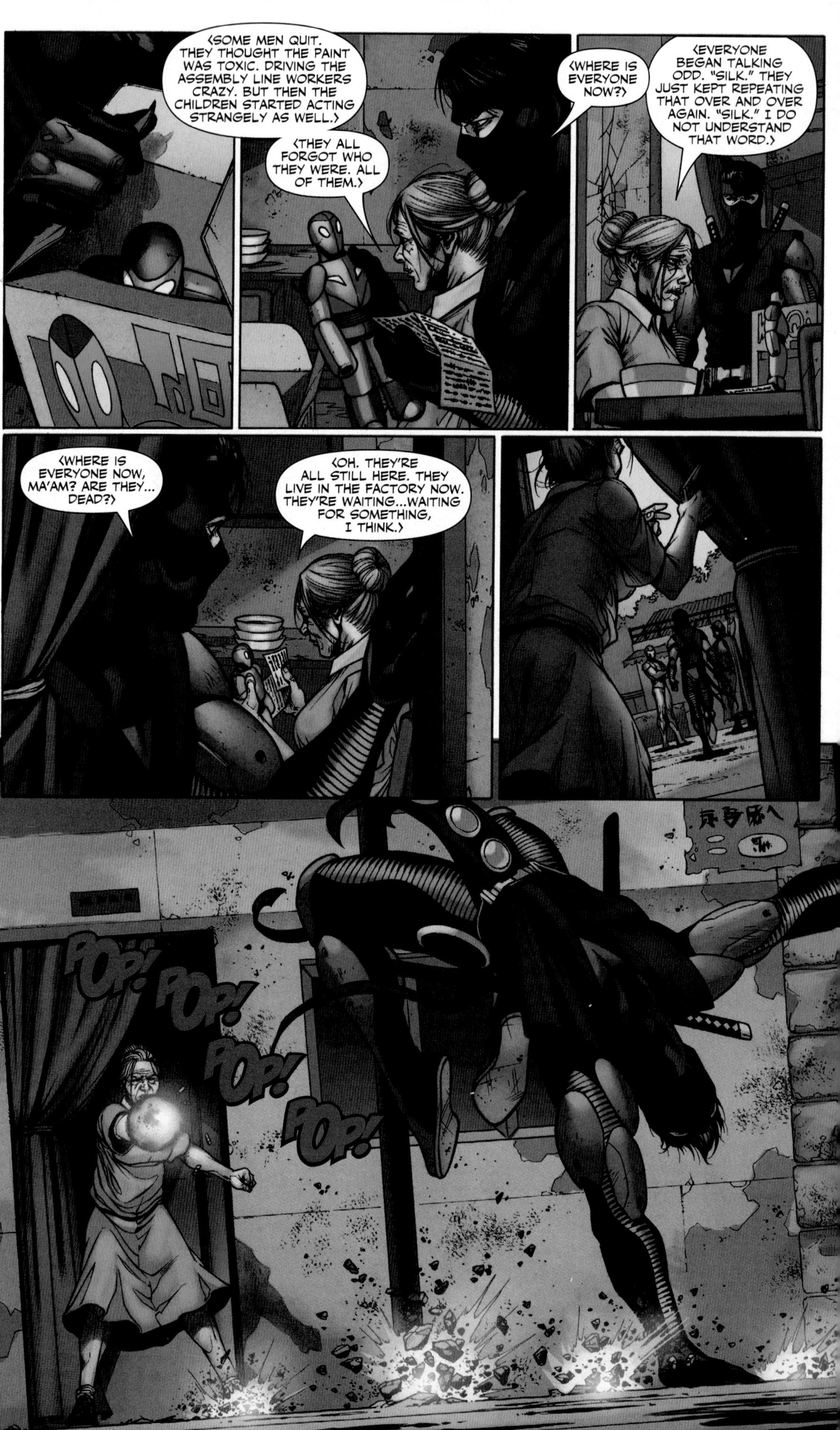
‹SOME MEN QUIT. THEY THOUGHT THE PAINT WAS TOXIC. DRIVING THE ASSEMBLY LINE WORKERS CRAZY. BUT THEN THE CHILDREN STARTED ACTING STRANGELY AS WELL.›
‹THEY ALL FORGOT WHO THEY WERE. ALL OF THEM.›
‹WHERE IS EVERYONE NOW?›
‹EVERYONE BEGAN TALKING ODD. "SILK." THEY JUST KEPT REPEATING THAT OVER AND OVER AGAIN. "SILK." I DO NOT UNDERSTAND THAT WORD.›
‹WHERE IS EVERYONE NOW, MA'AM? ARE THEY... DEAD?›
‹OH. THEY'RE ALL STILL HERE. THEY LIVE IN THE FACTORY NOW. THEY'RE WAITING...WAITING FOR SOMETHING, I THINK.›
POP!
POP!
POP!
POP!

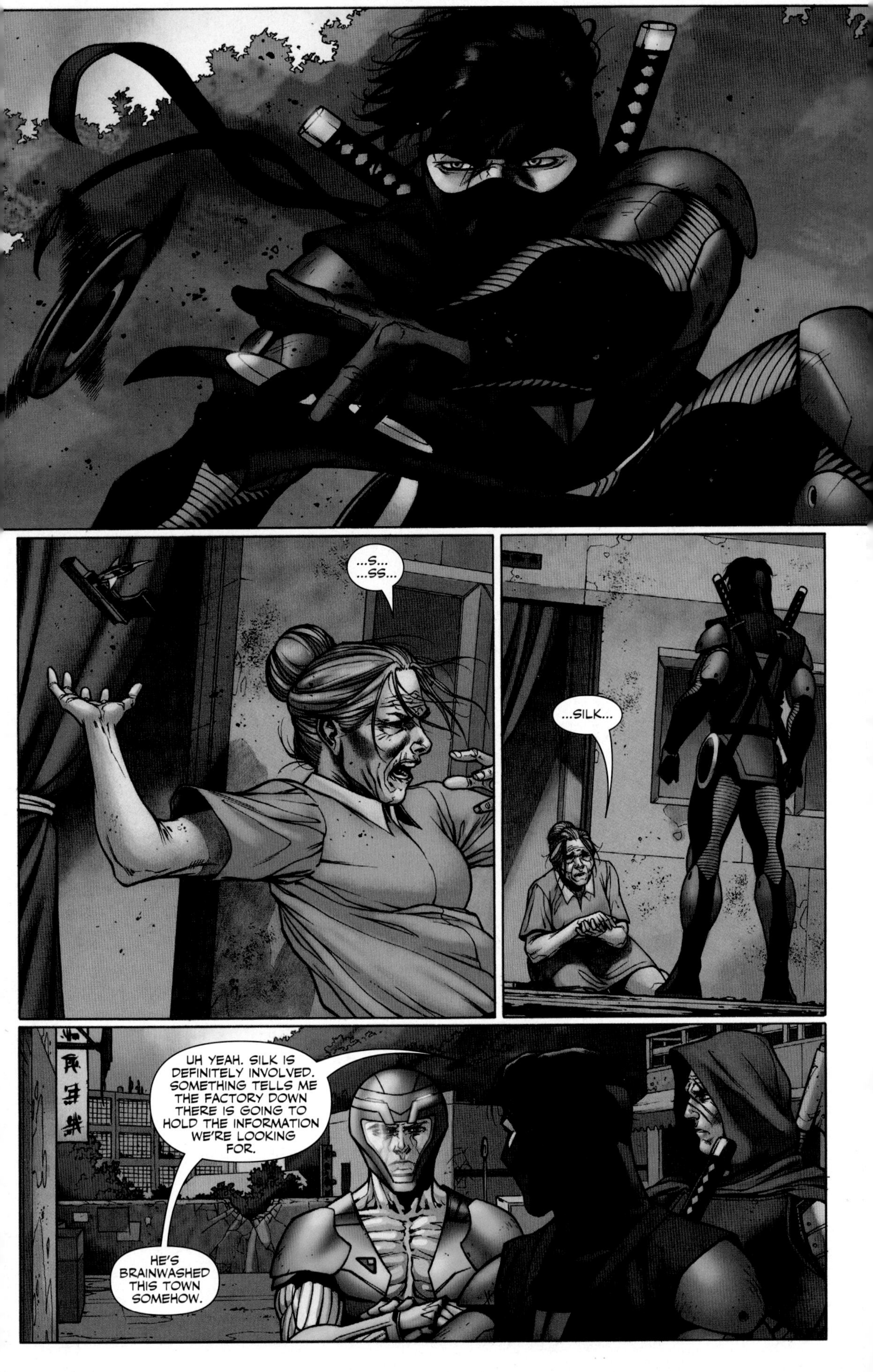

...S...
...SS...
...SILK...
UH YEAH. SILK IS DEFINITELY INVOLVED. SOMETHING TELLS ME THE FACTORY DOWN THERE IS GOING TO HOLD THE INFORMATION WE'RE LOOKING FOR.
HE'S BRAINWASHED THIS TOWN SOMEHOW.

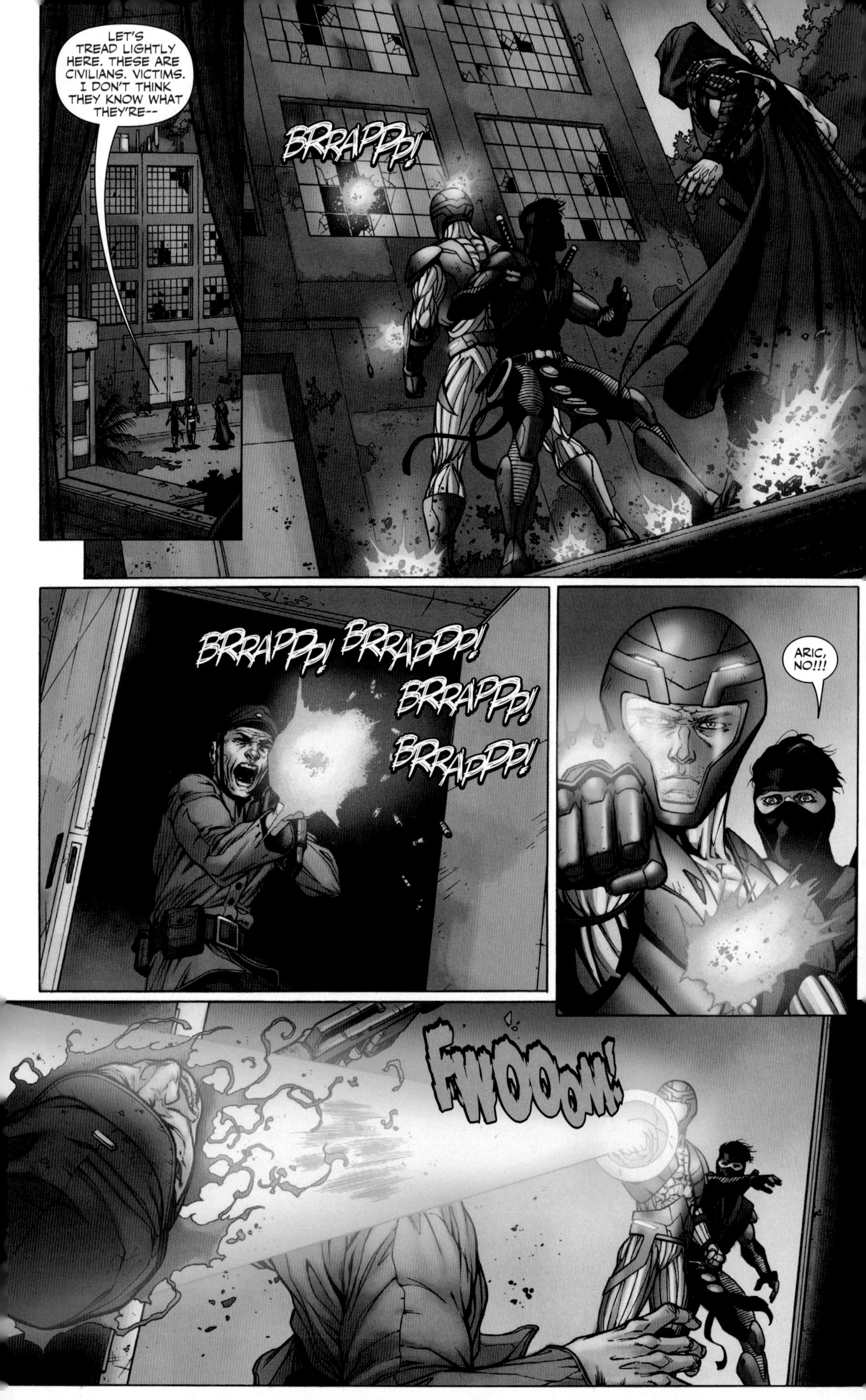
LET'S TREAD LIGHTLY HERE. THESE ARE CIVILIANS. VICTIMS. I DON'T THINK THEY KNOW WHAT THEY'RE--
BRRAPPP!
BRRAPPP! BRRAPPP!
BRRAPPP!
BRRAPPP!
ARIC, NO!!!
FWOOOM!

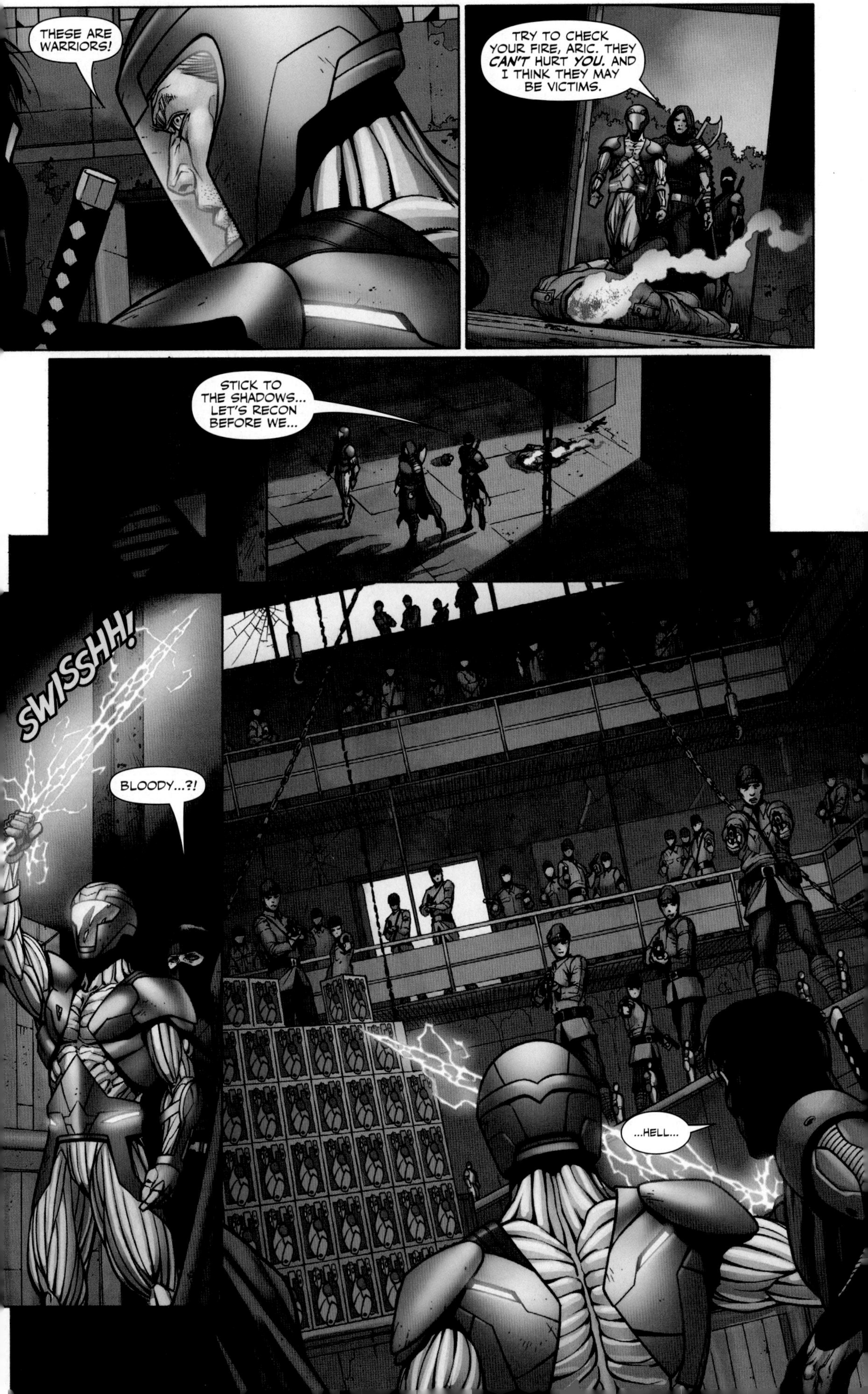
THESE ARE WARRIORS!
TRY TO CHECK YOUR FIRE, ARIC. THEY CAN'T HURT YOU. AND I THINK THEY MAY BE VICTIMS.
STICK TO THE SHADOWS... LET'S RECON BEFORE WE...
SWISSHH!
BLOODY...?!
...HELL...

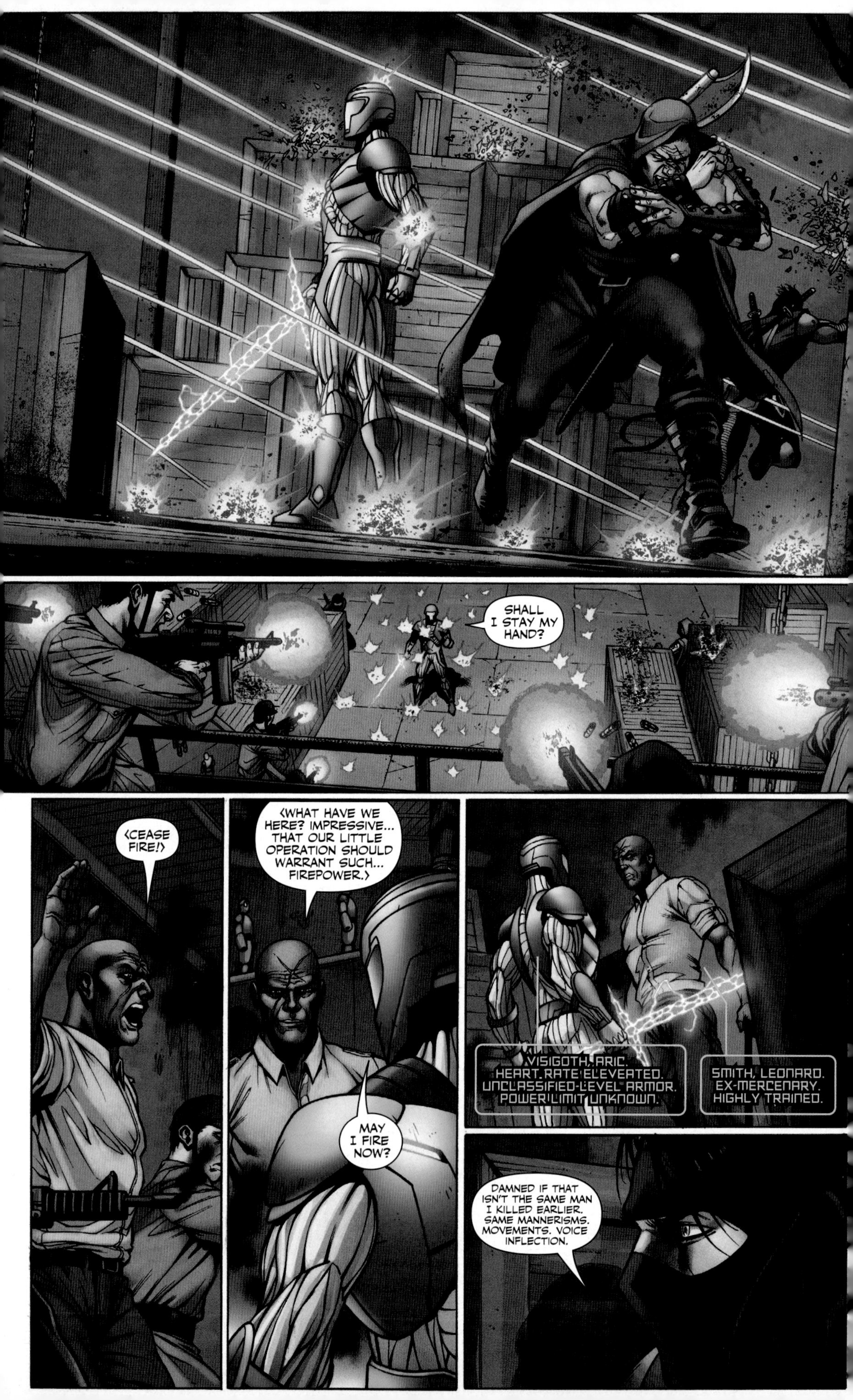
SHALL I STAY MY HAND?
<CEASE FIRE!>
<WHAT HAVE WE HERE? IMPRESSIVE... THAT OUR LITTLE OPERATION SHOULD WARRANT SUCH... FIREPOWER.>
MAY I FIRE NOW?
VISIGOTH, ARIC. HEART RATE ELEVATED. UNCLASSIFIED-LEVEL ARMOR. POWER LIMIT UNKNOWN.
SMITH, LEONARD. EX-MERCENARY. HIGHLY TRAINED.
DAMNED IF THAT ISN'T THE SAME MAN I KILLED EARLIER. SAME MANNERISMS. MOVEMENTS. VOICE INFLECTION.

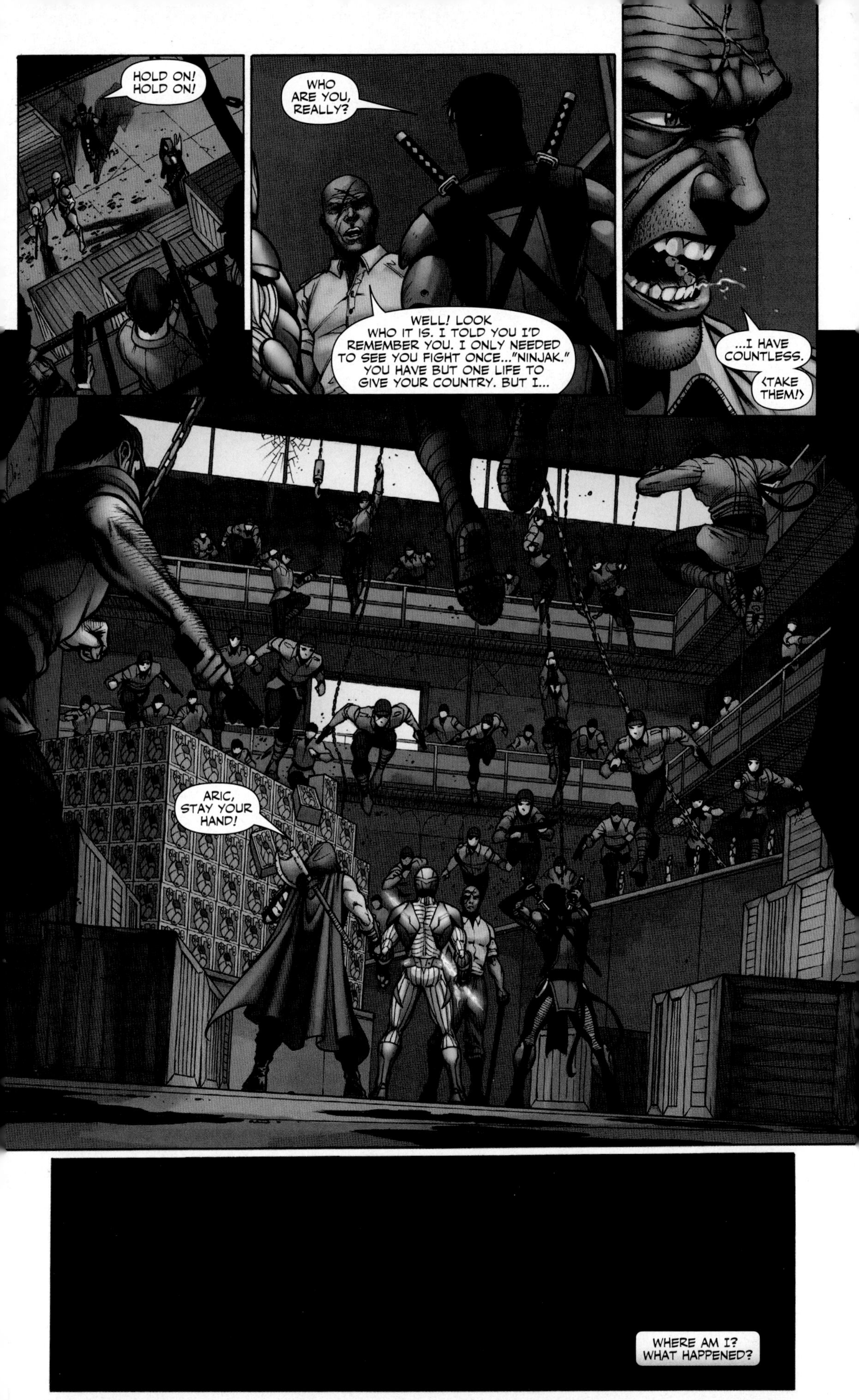
HOLD ON! HOLD ON!
WHO ARE YOU, REALLY?
WELL! LOOK WHO IT IS. I TOLD YOU I'D REMEMBER YOU. I ONLY NEEDED TO SEE YOU FIGHT ONCE..."NINJAK." YOU HAVE BUT ONE LIFE TO GIVE YOUR COUNTRY. BUT I...
...I HAVE COUNTLESS.
‹TAKE THEM!›
ARIC, STAY YOUR HAND!
WHERE AM I? WHAT HAPPENED?

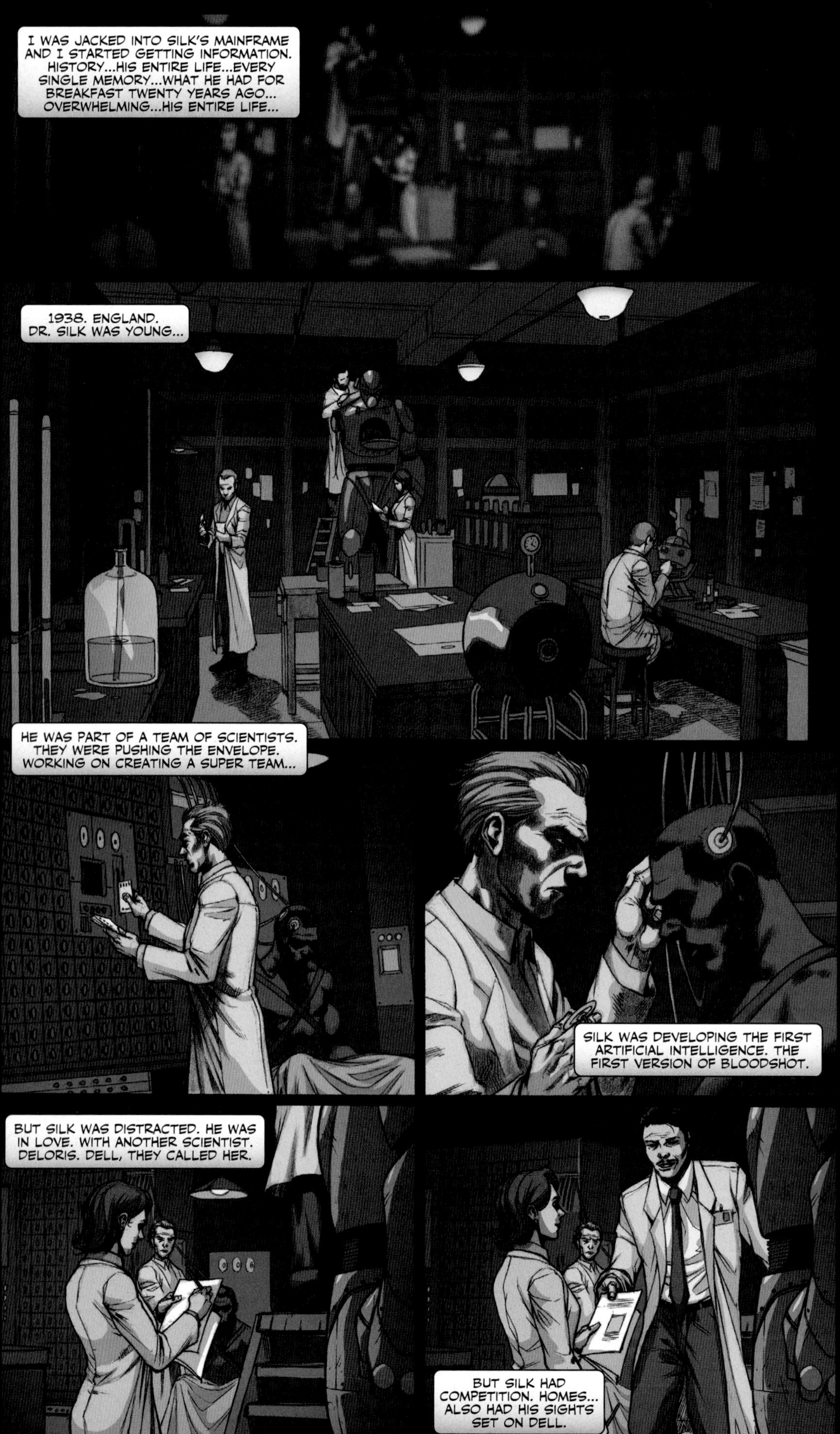
I WAS JACKED INTO SILK'S MAINFRAME AND I STARTED GETTING INFORMATION. HISTORY...HIS ENTIRE LIFE...EVERY SINGLE MEMORY...WHAT HE HAD FOR BREAKFAST TWENTY YEARS AGO... OVERWHELMING...HIS ENTIRE LIFE...
1938. ENGLAND. DR. SILK WAS YOUNG...
HE WAS PART OF A TEAM OF SCIENTISTS. THEY WERE PUSHING THE ENVELOPE. WORKING ON CREATING A SUPER TEAM...
SILK WAS DEVELOPING THE FIRST ARTIFICIAL INTELLIGENCE. THE FIRST VERSION OF BLOODSHOT.
BUT SILK WAS DISTRACTED. HE WAS IN LOVE. WITH ANOTHER SCIENTIST. DELORIS. DELL, THEY CALLED HER.
BUT SILK HAD COMPETITION. HOMES... ALSO HAD HIS SIGHTS SET ON DELL.

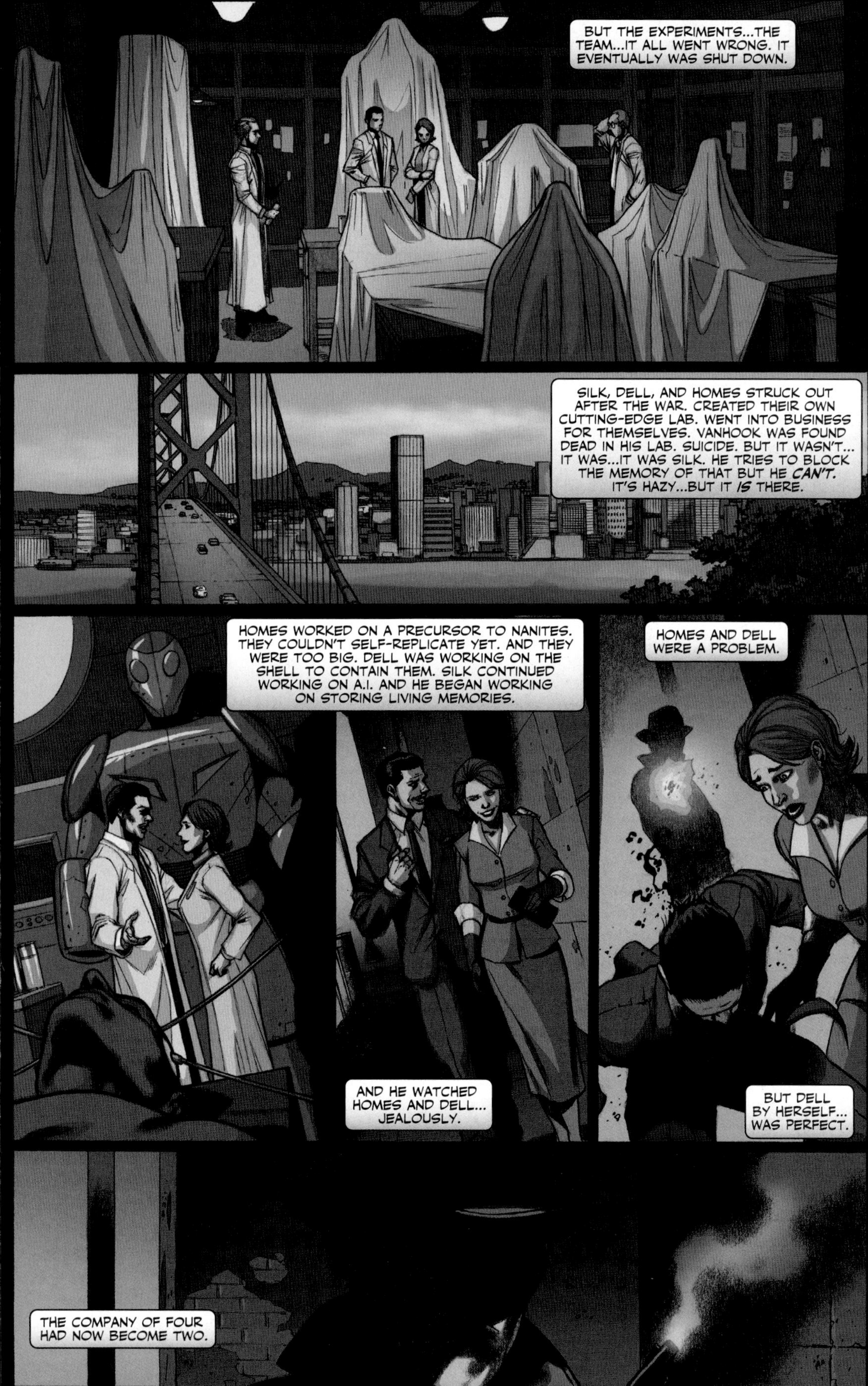
BUT THE EXPERIMENTS...THE TEAM...IT ALL WENT WRONG. IT EVENTUALLY WAS SHUT DOWN.
SILK, DELL, AND HOMES STRUCK OUT AFTER THE WAR. CREATED THEIR OWN CUTTING-EDGE LAB. WENT INTO BUSINESS FOR THEMSELVES. VANHOOK WAS FOUND DEAD IN HIS LAB. SUICIDE. BUT IT WASN'T... IT WAS...IT WAS SILK. HE TRIES TO BLOCK THE MEMORY OF THAT BUT HE *CAN'T.* IT'S HAZY...BUT IT *IS* THERE.
HOMES WORKED ON A PRECURSOR TO NANITES. THEY COULDN'T SELF-REPLICATE YET. AND THEY WERE TOO BIG. DELL WAS WORKING ON THE SHELL TO CONTAIN THEM. SILK CONTINUED WORKING ON A.I. AND HE BEGAN WORKING ON STORING LIVING MEMORIES.
AND HE WATCHED HOMES AND DELL... JEALOUSLY.
HOMES AND DELL WERE A PROBLEM.
BUT DELL BY HERSELF... WAS PERFECT.
THE COMPANY OF FOUR HAD NOW BECOME TWO.

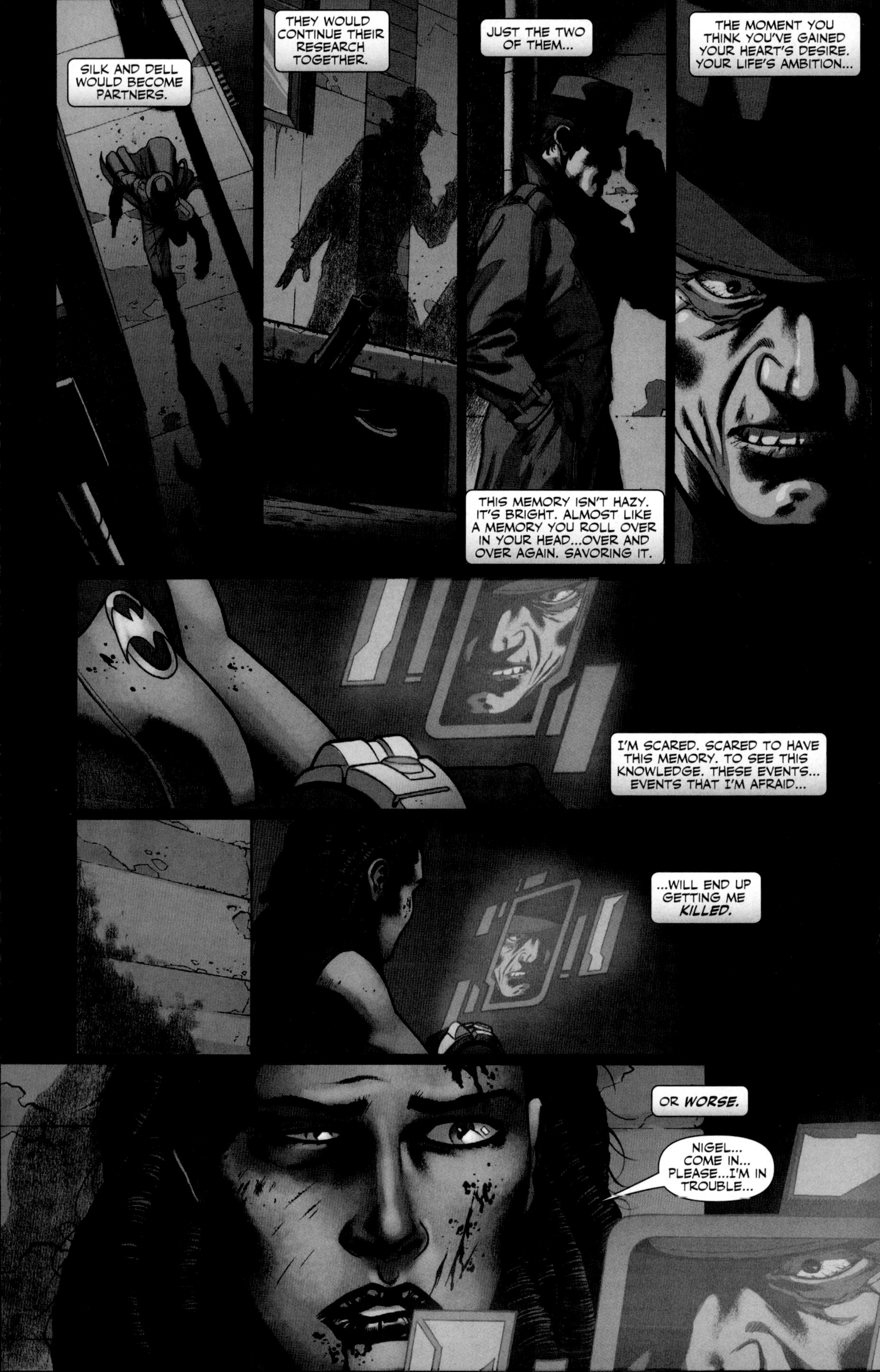
SILK AND DELL WOULD BECOME PARTNERS.
THEY WOULD CONTINUE THEIR RESEARCH TOGETHER.
JUST THE TWO OF THEM...
THE MOMENT YOU THINK YOU'VE GAINED YOUR HEART'S DESIRE. YOUR LIFE'S AMBITION...
THIS MEMORY ISN'T HAZY. IT'S BRIGHT. ALMOST LIKE A MEMORY YOU ROLL OVER IN YOUR HEAD...OVER AND OVER AGAIN. SAVORING IT.
I'M SCARED. SCARED TO HAVE THIS MEMORY. TO SEE THIS KNOWLEDGE. THESE EVENTS... EVENTS THAT I'M AFRAID...
...WILL END UP GETTING ME *KILLED.*
OR *WORSE.*
NIGEL... COME IN... PLEASE...I'M IN TROUBLE...

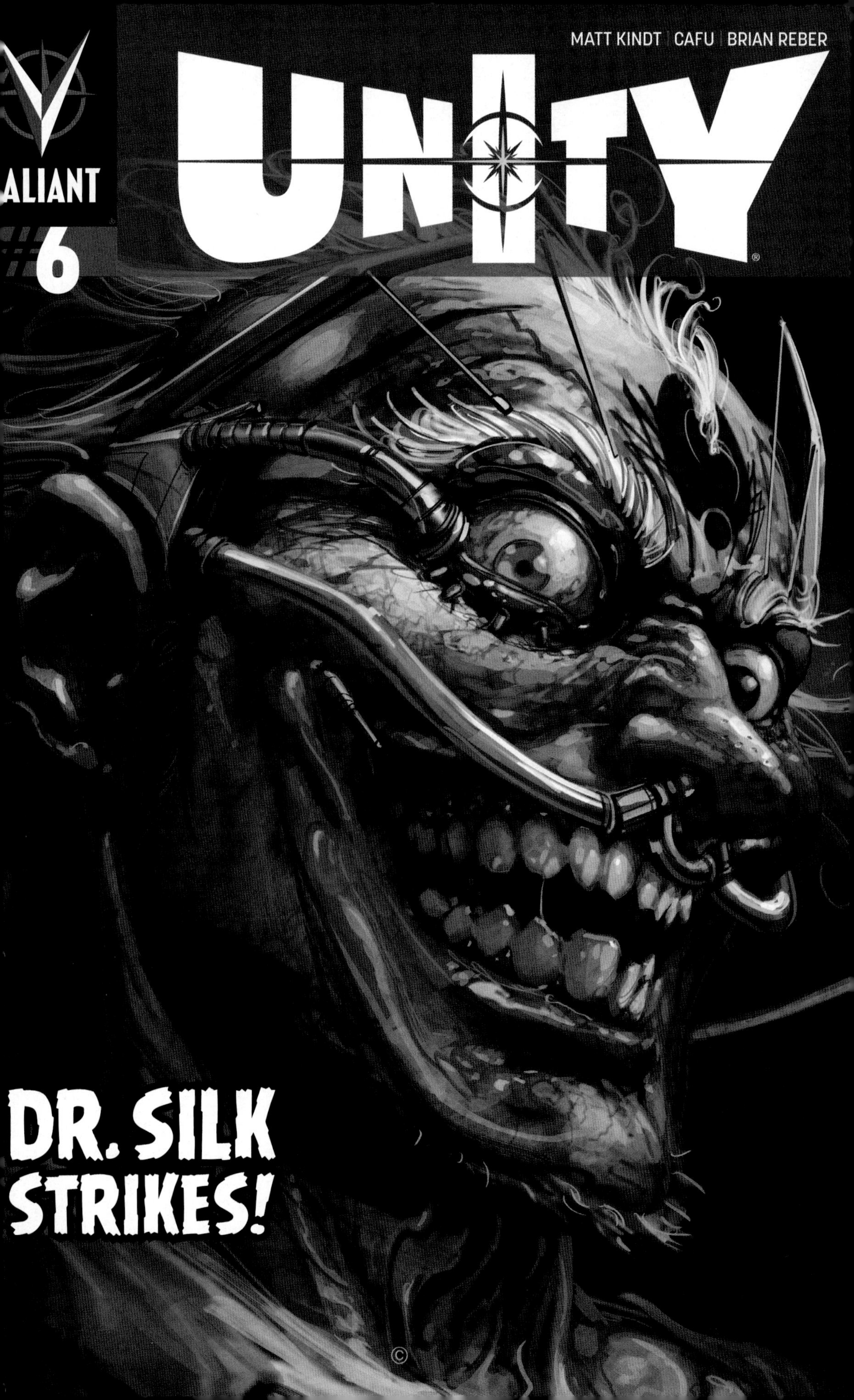
MATT KINDT | CAFU | BRIAN REBER
UNITY
VALIANT
#6
DR. SILK STRIKES!

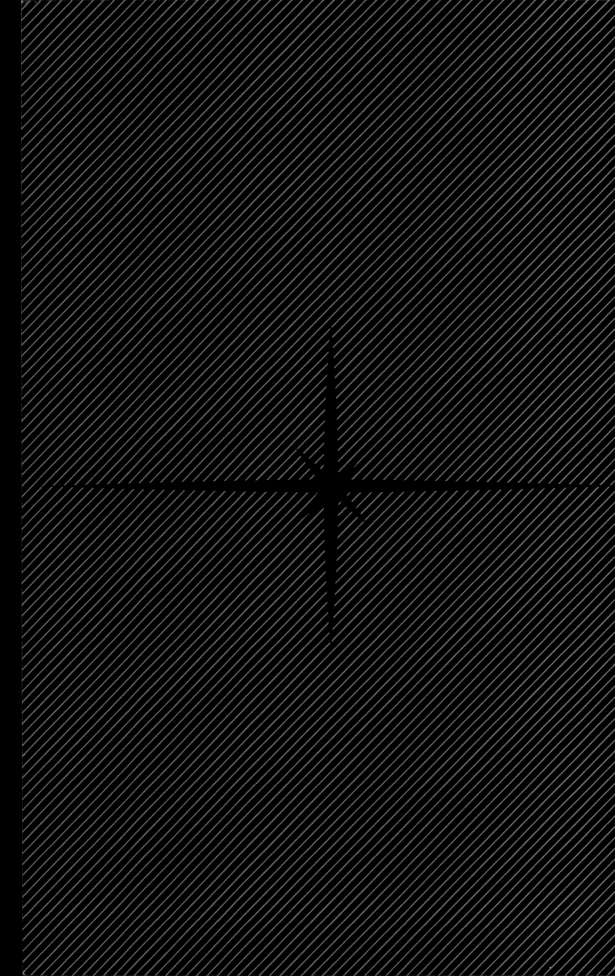

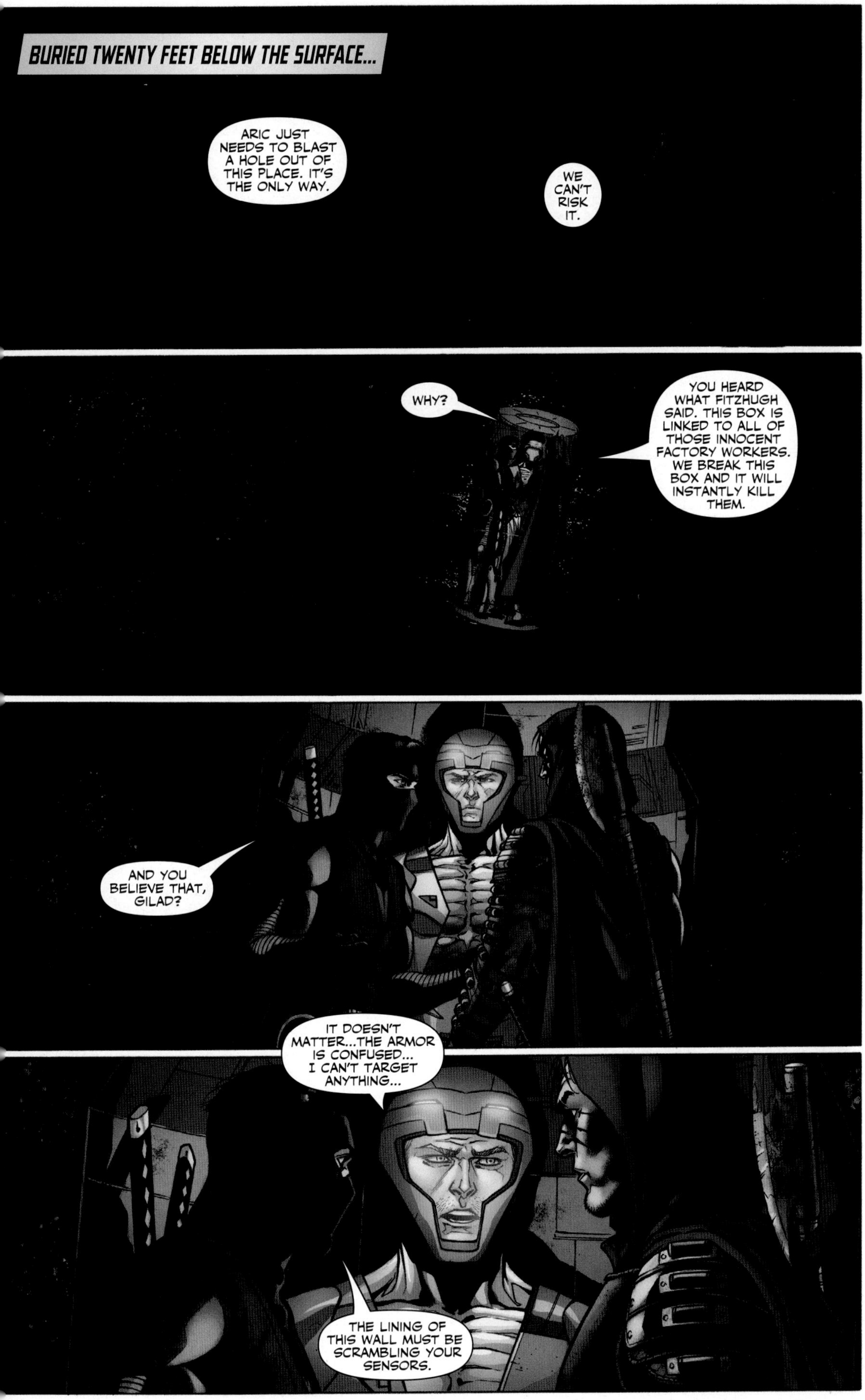
BURIED TWENTY FEET BELOW THE SURFACE...
ARIC JUST NEEDS TO BLAST A HOLE OUT OF THIS PLACE. IT'S THE ONLY WAY.
WE CAN'T RISK IT.
WHY?
YOU HEARD WHAT FITZHUGH SAID. THIS BOX IS LINKED TO ALL OF THOSE INNOCENT FACTORY WORKERS. WE BREAK THIS BOX AND IT WILL INSTANTLY KILL THEM.
AND YOU BELIEVE THAT, GILAD?
IT DOESN'T MATTER...THE ARMOR IS CONFUSED... I CAN'T TARGET ANYTHING...
THE LINING OF THIS WALL MUST BE SCRAMBLING YOUR SENSORS.

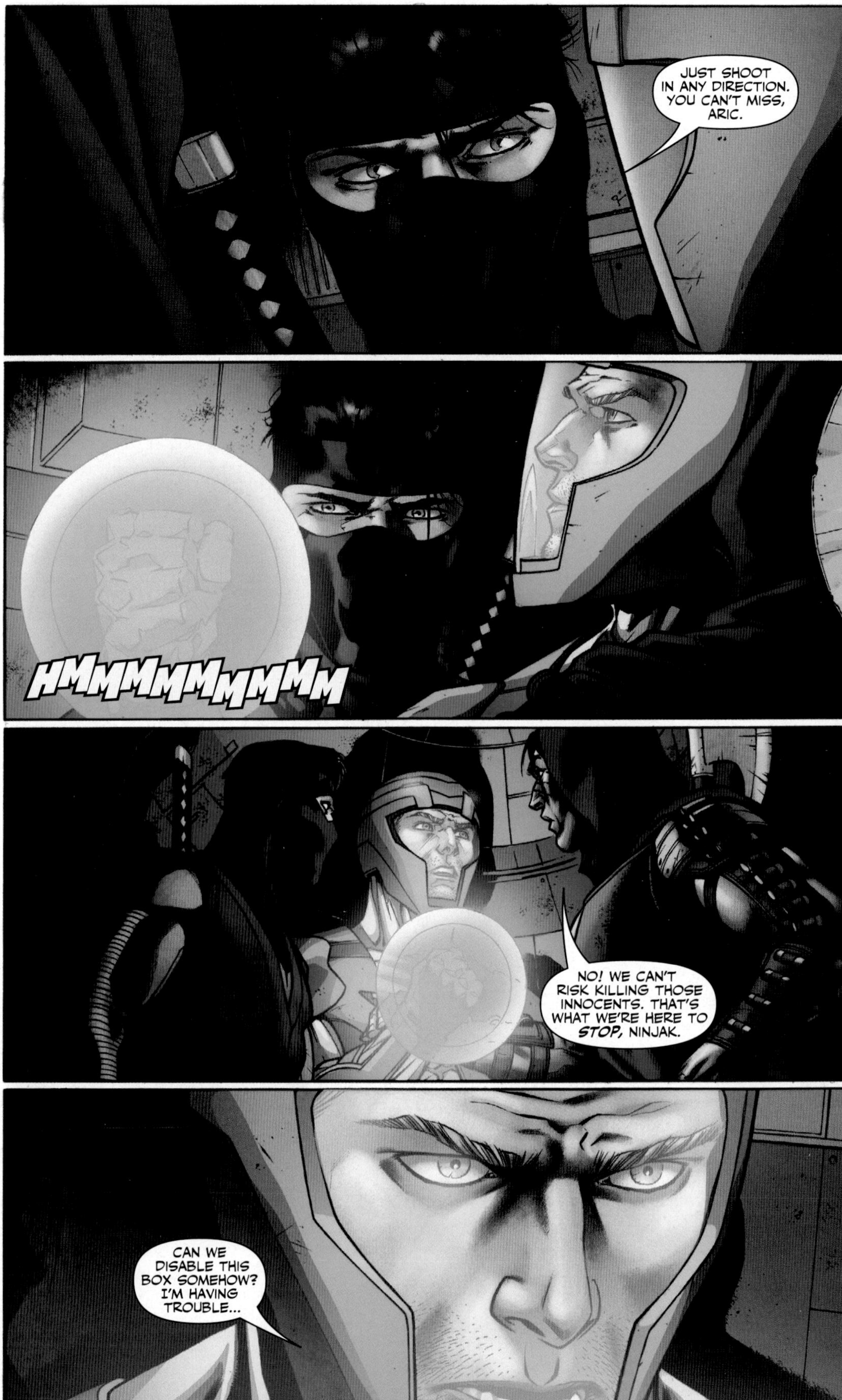
JUST SHOOT IN ANY DIRECTION. YOU CAN'T MISS, ARIC.
HMMMMMMMMMMM
NO! WE CAN'T RISK KILLING THOSE INNOCENTS. THAT'S WHAT WE'RE HERE TO STOP, NINJAK.
CAN WE DISABLE THIS BOX SOMEHOW? I'M HAVING TROUBLE...

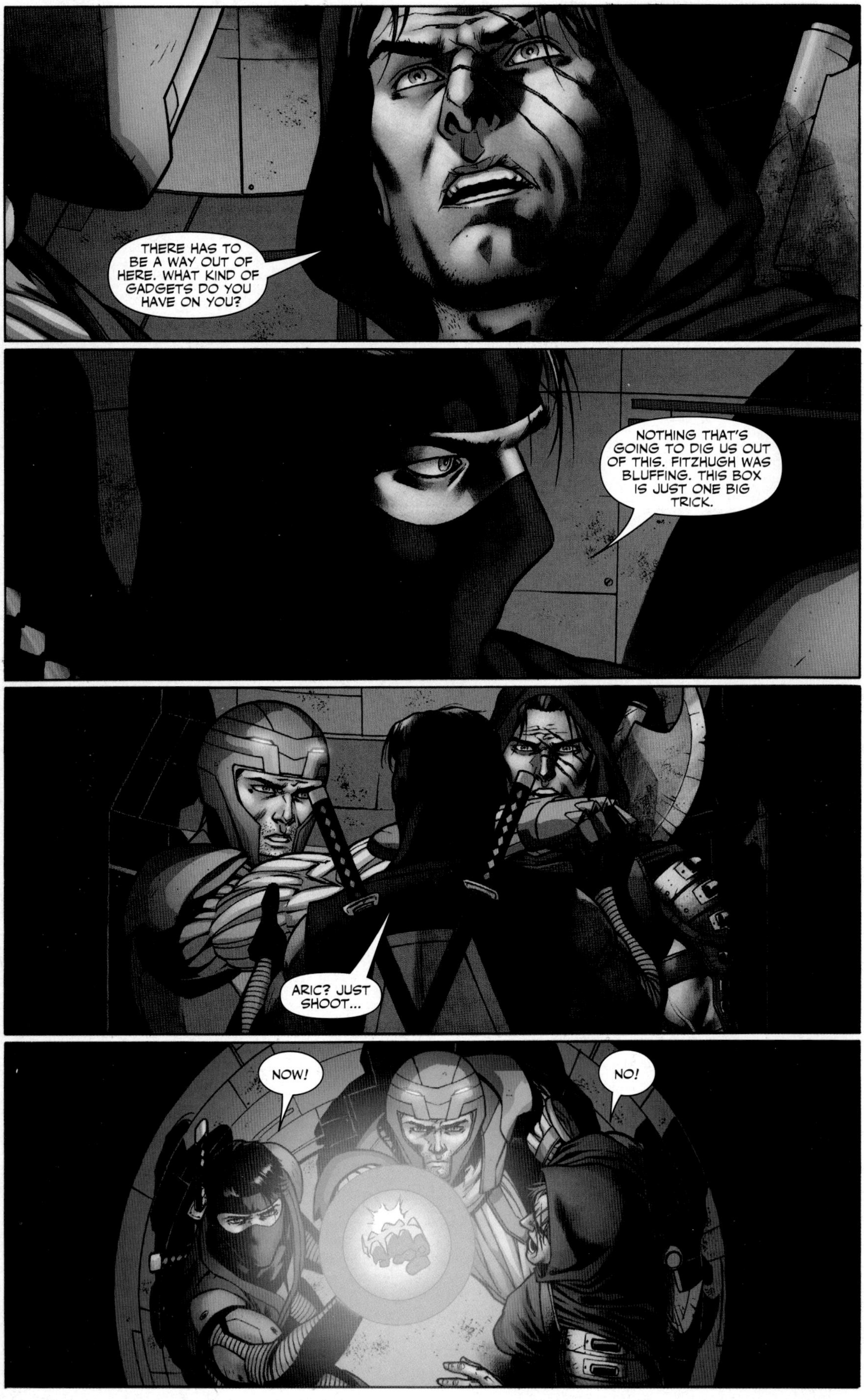
THERE HAS TO BE A WAY OUT OF HERE. WHAT KIND OF GADGETS DO YOU HAVE ON YOU?
NOTHING THAT'S GOING TO DIG US OUT OF THIS. FITZHUGH WAS BLUFFING. THIS BOX IS JUST ONE BIG TRICK.
ARIC? JUST SHOOT...
NOW!
NO!

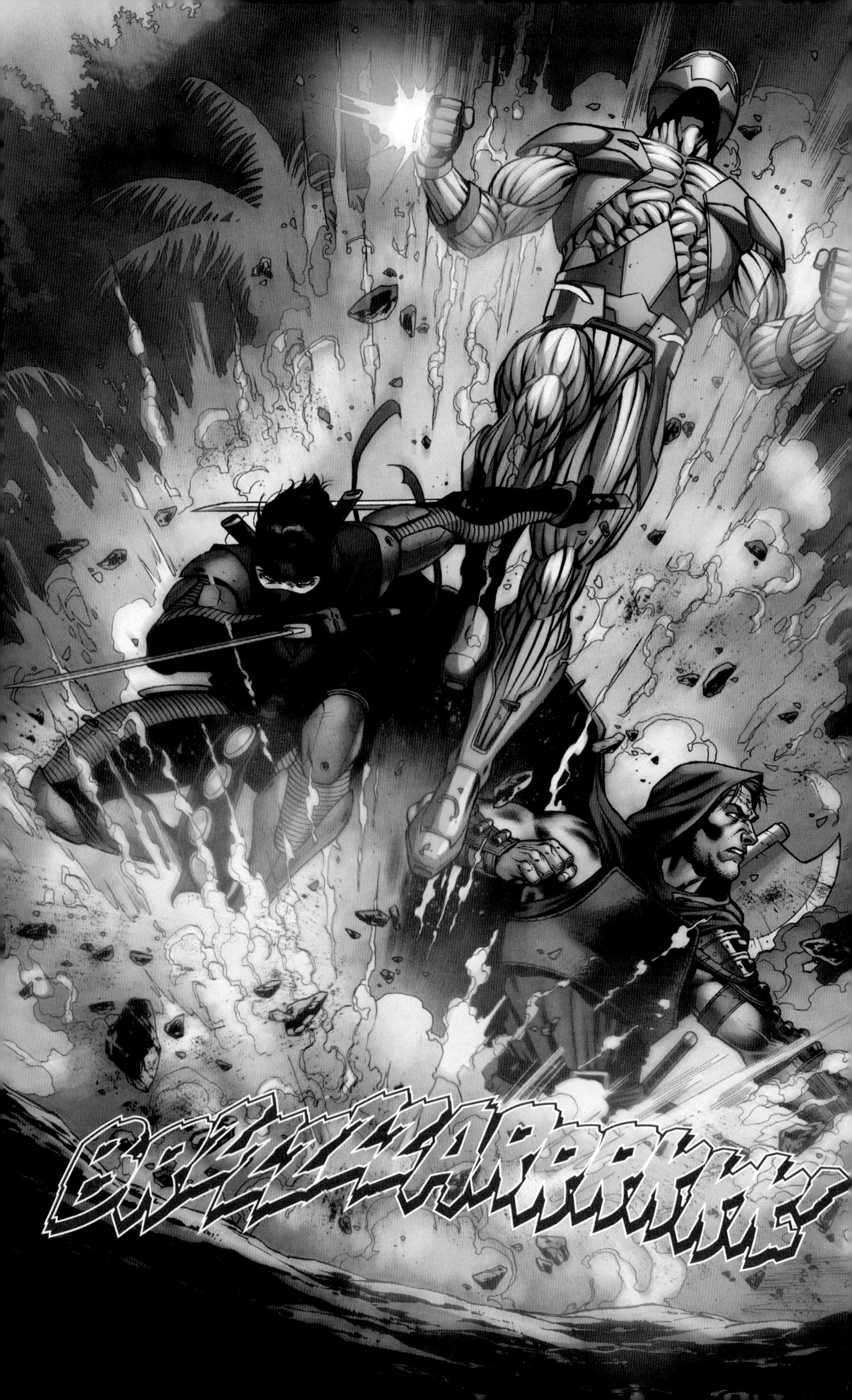
BBZZZARRRKK!

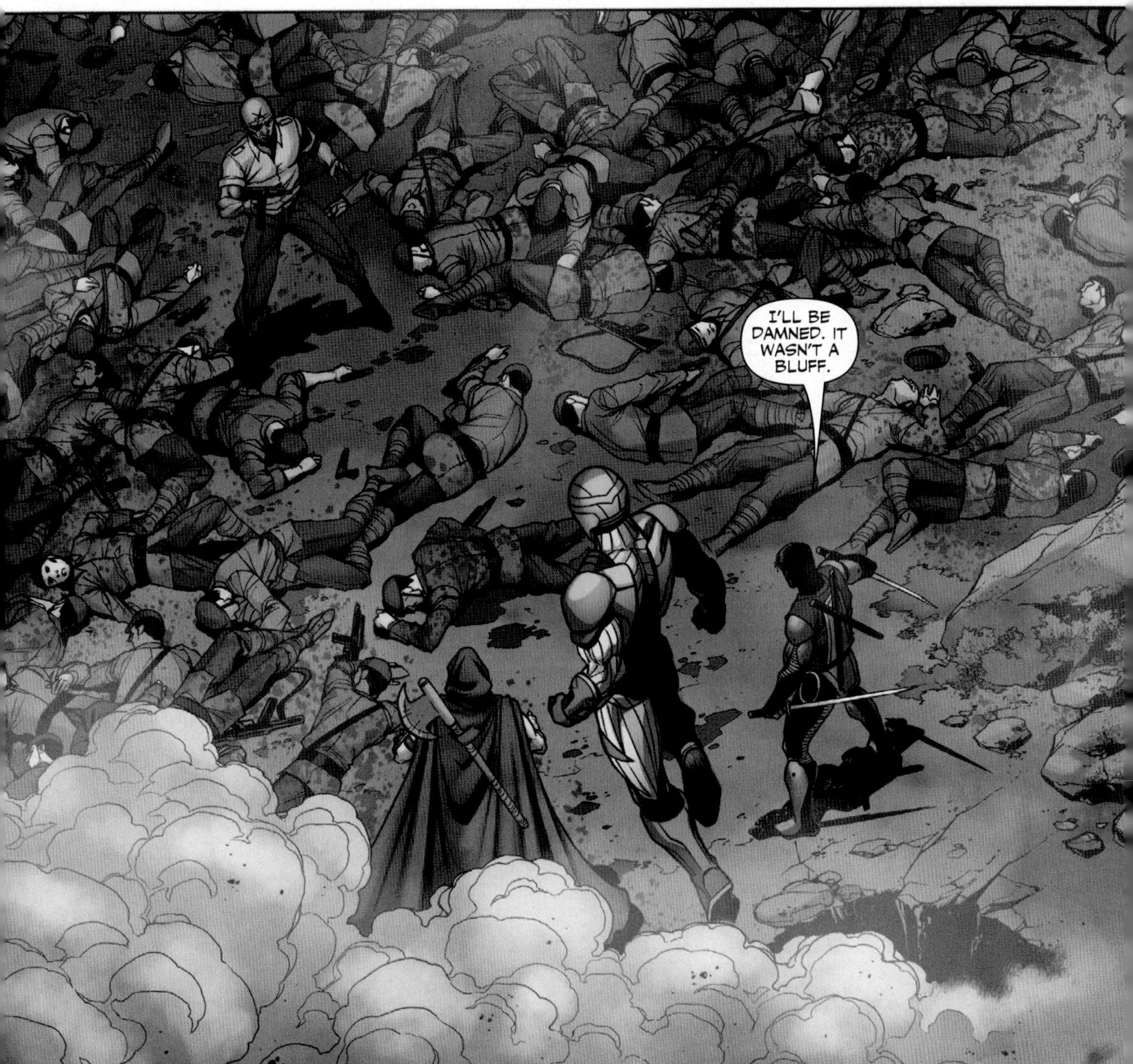
I'LL BE DAMNED. IT WASN'T A BLUFF.

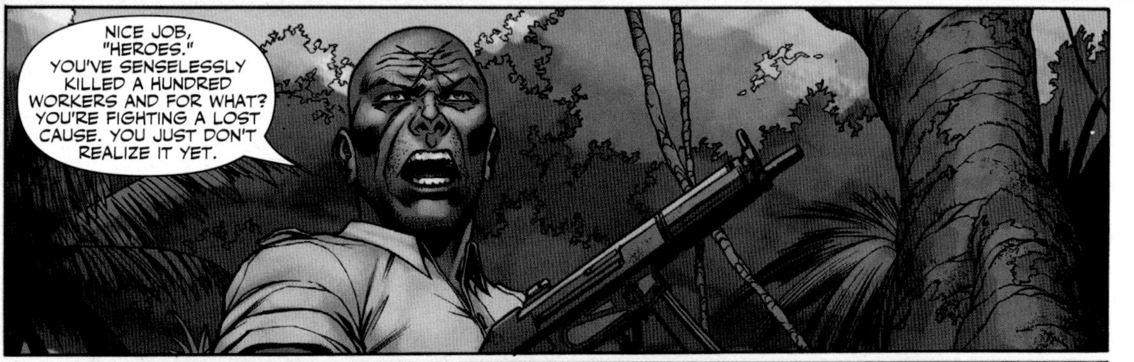
NICE JOB, "HEROES." YOU'VE SENSELESSLY KILLED A HUNDRED WORKERS AND FOR WHAT? YOU'RE FIGHTING A LOST CAUSE. YOU JUST DON'T REALIZE IT YET.

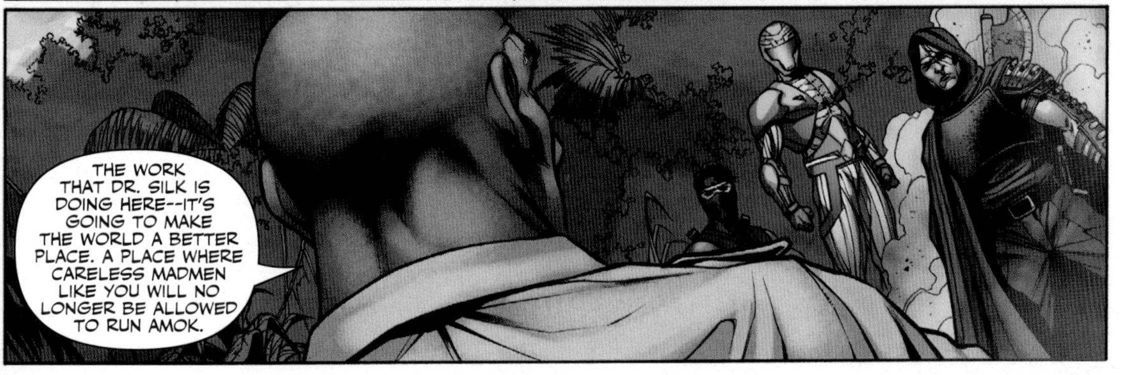
THE WORK THAT DR. SILK IS DOING HERE--IT'S GOING TO MAKE THE WORLD A BETTER PLACE. A PLACE WHERE CARELESS MADMEN LIKE YOU WILL NO LONGER BE ALLOWED TO RUN AMOK.

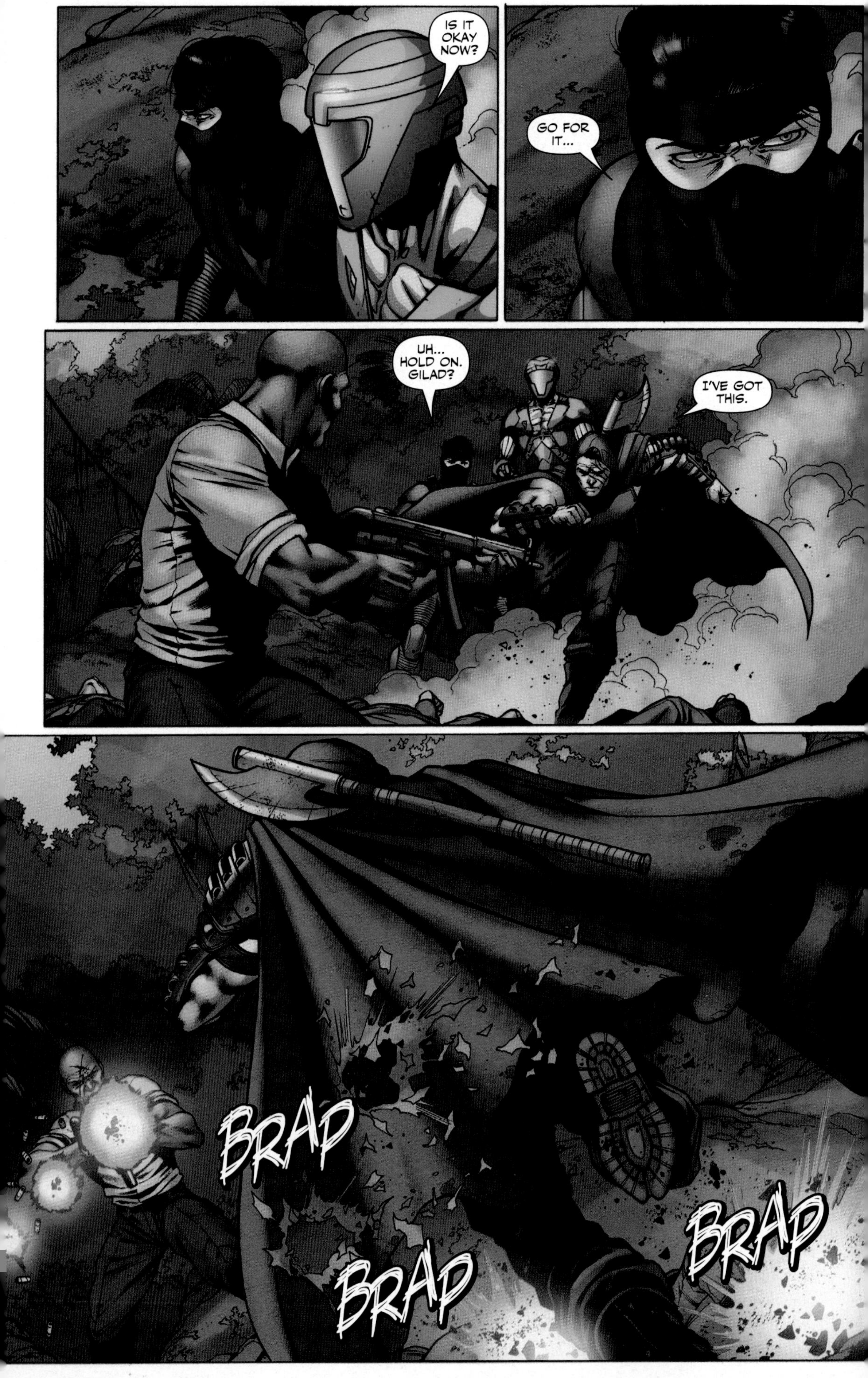
IS IT OKAY NOW?
GO FOR IT...
UH... HOLD ON. GILAD?
I'VE GOT THIS.
BRAP
BRAP
BRAP

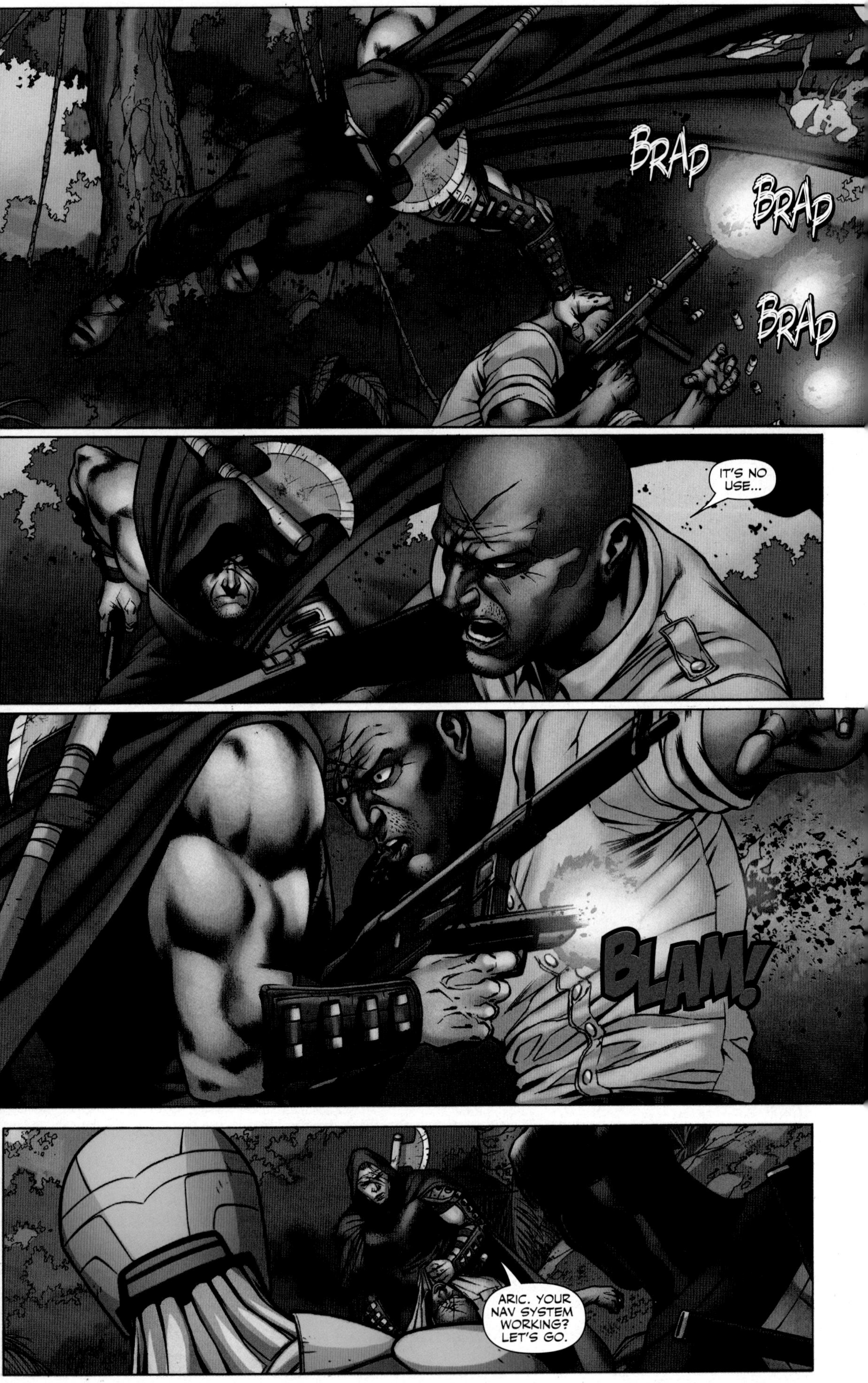
BRAP
BRAP
BRAP
IT'S NO USE...
BLAM!
ARIC. YOUR NAV SYSTEM WORKING? LET'S GO.

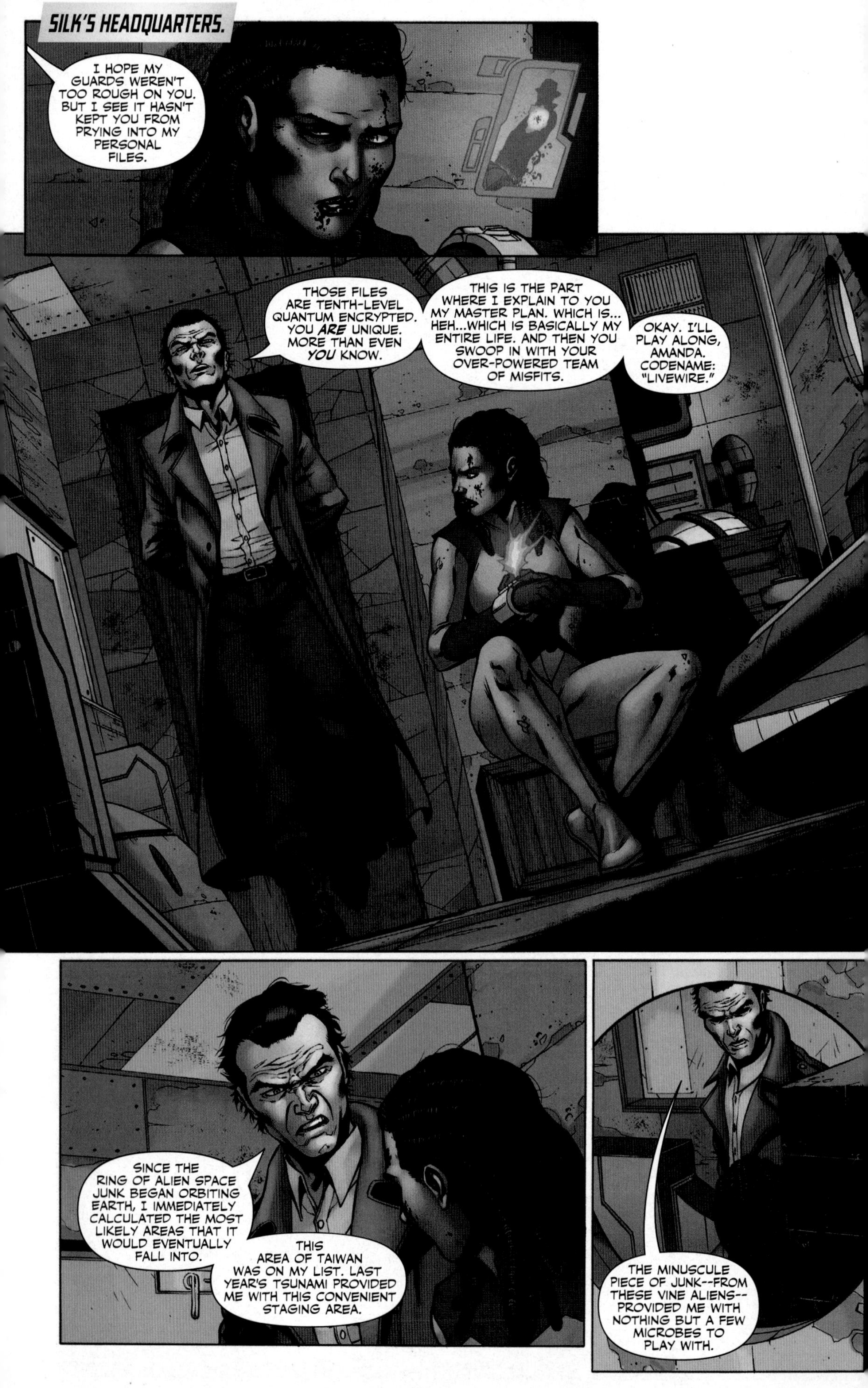
SILK'S HEADQUARTERS.
I HOPE MY GUARDS WEREN'T TOO ROUGH ON YOU. BUT I SEE IT HASN'T KEPT YOU FROM PRYING INTO MY PERSONAL FILES.
THOSE FILES ARE TENTH-LEVEL QUANTUM ENCRYPTED. YOU ARE UNIQUE. MORE THAN EVEN YOU KNOW.
THIS IS THE PART WHERE I EXPLAIN TO YOU MY MASTER PLAN. WHICH IS... HEH...WHICH IS BASICALLY MY ENTIRE LIFE. AND THEN YOU SWOOP IN WITH YOUR OVER-POWERED TEAM OF MISFITS.
OKAY. I'LL PLAY ALONG, AMANDA. CODENAME: "LIVEWIRE."
SINCE THE RING OF ALIEN SPACE JUNK BEGAN ORBITING EARTH, I IMMEDIATELY CALCULATED THE MOST LIKELY AREAS THAT IT WOULD EVENTUALLY FALL INTO.
THIS AREA OF TAIWAN WAS ON MY LIST. LAST YEAR'S TSUNAMI PROVIDED ME WITH THIS CONVENIENT STAGING AREA.
THE MINUSCULE PIECE OF JUNK--FROM THESE VINE ALIENS--PROVIDED ME WITH NOTHING BUT A FEW MICROBES TO PLAY WITH.

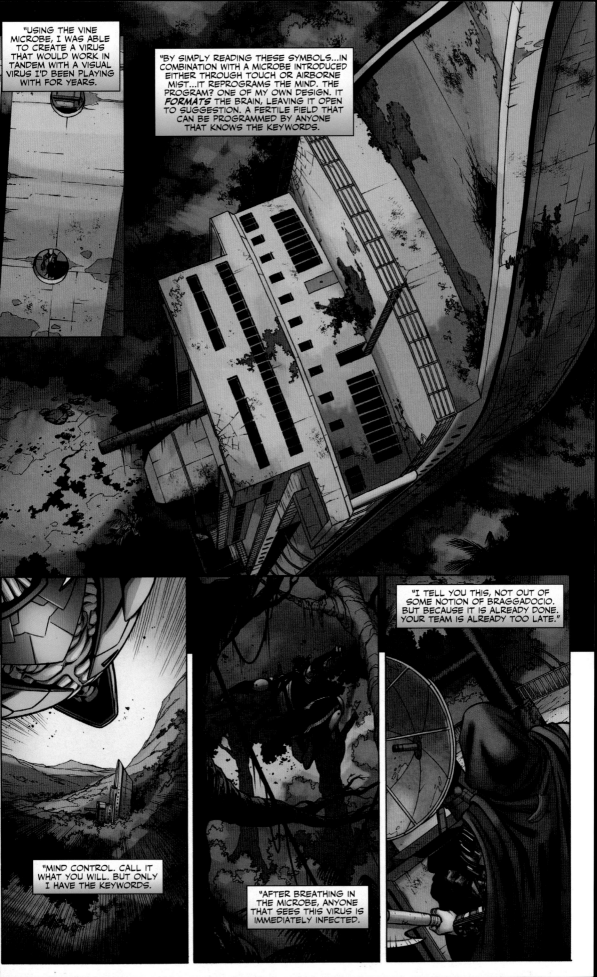

"USING THE VINE MICROBE, I WAS ABLE TO CREATE A VIRUS THAT WOULD WORK IN TANDEM WITH A VISUAL VIRUS I'D BEEN PLAYING WITH FOR YEARS.

"BY SIMPLY READING THESE SYMBOLS...IN COMBINATION WITH A MICROBE INTRODUCED EITHER THROUGH TOUCH OR AIRBORNE MIST...IT REPROGRAMS THE MIND. THE PROGRAM? ONE OF MY OWN DESIGN. IT *FORMATS* THE BRAIN, LEAVING IT OPEN TO SUGGESTION. A FERTILE FIELD THAT CAN BE PROGRAMMED BY ANYONE THAT KNOWS THE KEYWORDS.

"I TELL YOU THIS, NOT OUT OF SOME NOTION OF BRAGGADOCIO. BUT BECAUSE IT IS ALREADY DONE. YOUR TEAM IS ALREADY TOO LATE."

"MIND CONTROL. CALL IT WHAT YOU WILL. BUT ONLY I HAVE THE KEYWORDS.

"AFTER BREATHING IN THE MICROBE, ANYONE THAT SEES THIS VIRUS IS IMMEDIATELY INFECTED.

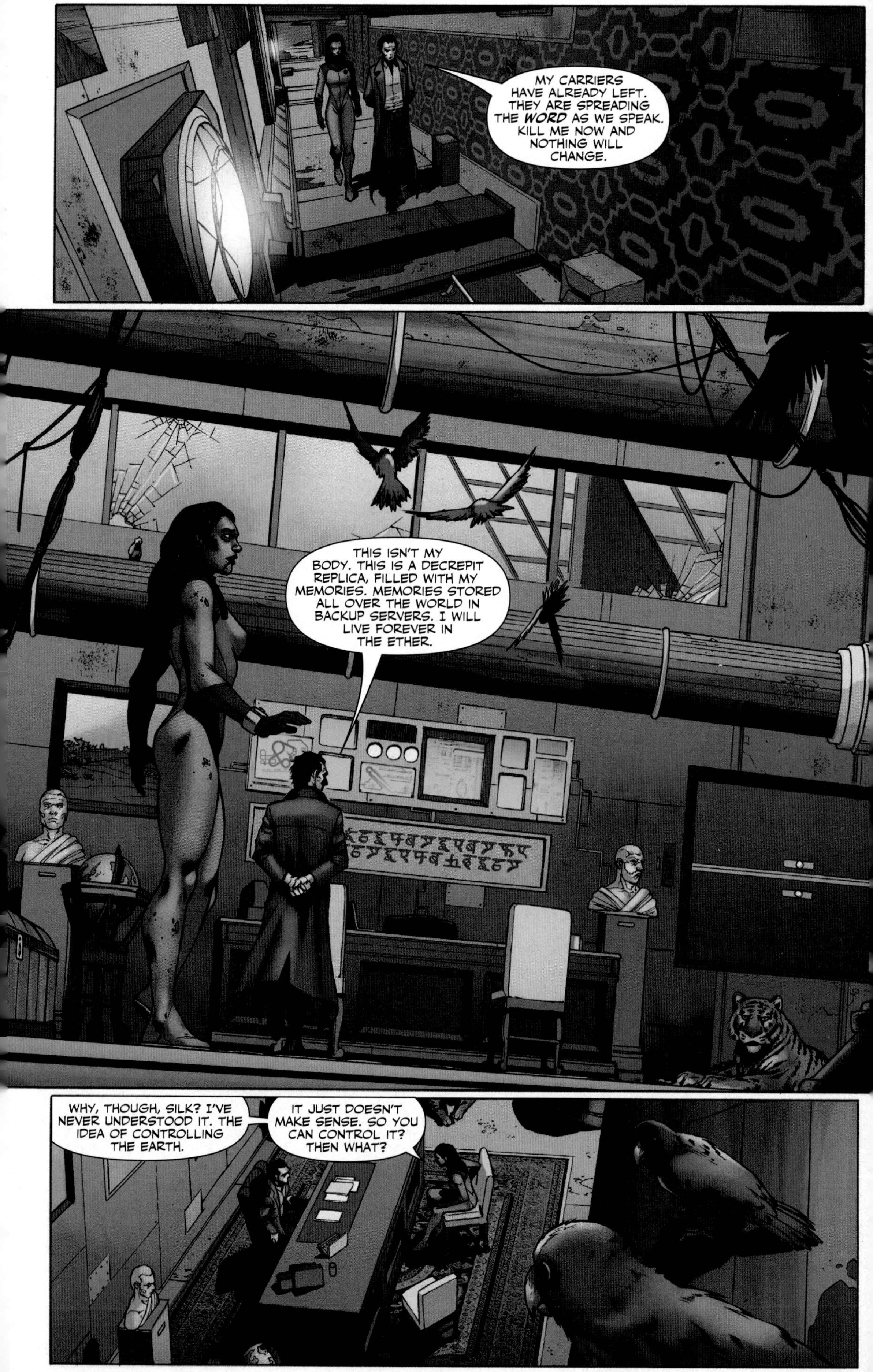
MY CARRIERS HAVE ALREADY LEFT. THEY ARE SPREADING THE *WORD* AS WE SPEAK. KILL ME NOW AND NOTHING WILL CHANGE.
THIS ISN'T MY BODY. THIS IS A DECREPIT REPLICA, FILLED WITH MY MEMORIES. MEMORIES STORED ALL OVER THE WORLD IN BACKUP SERVERS. I WILL LIVE FOREVER IN THE ETHER.
WHY, THOUGH, SILK? I'VE NEVER UNDERSTOOD IT. THE IDEA OF CONTROLLING THE EARTH.
IT JUST DOESN'T MAKE SENSE. SO YOU CAN CONTROL IT? THEN WHAT?

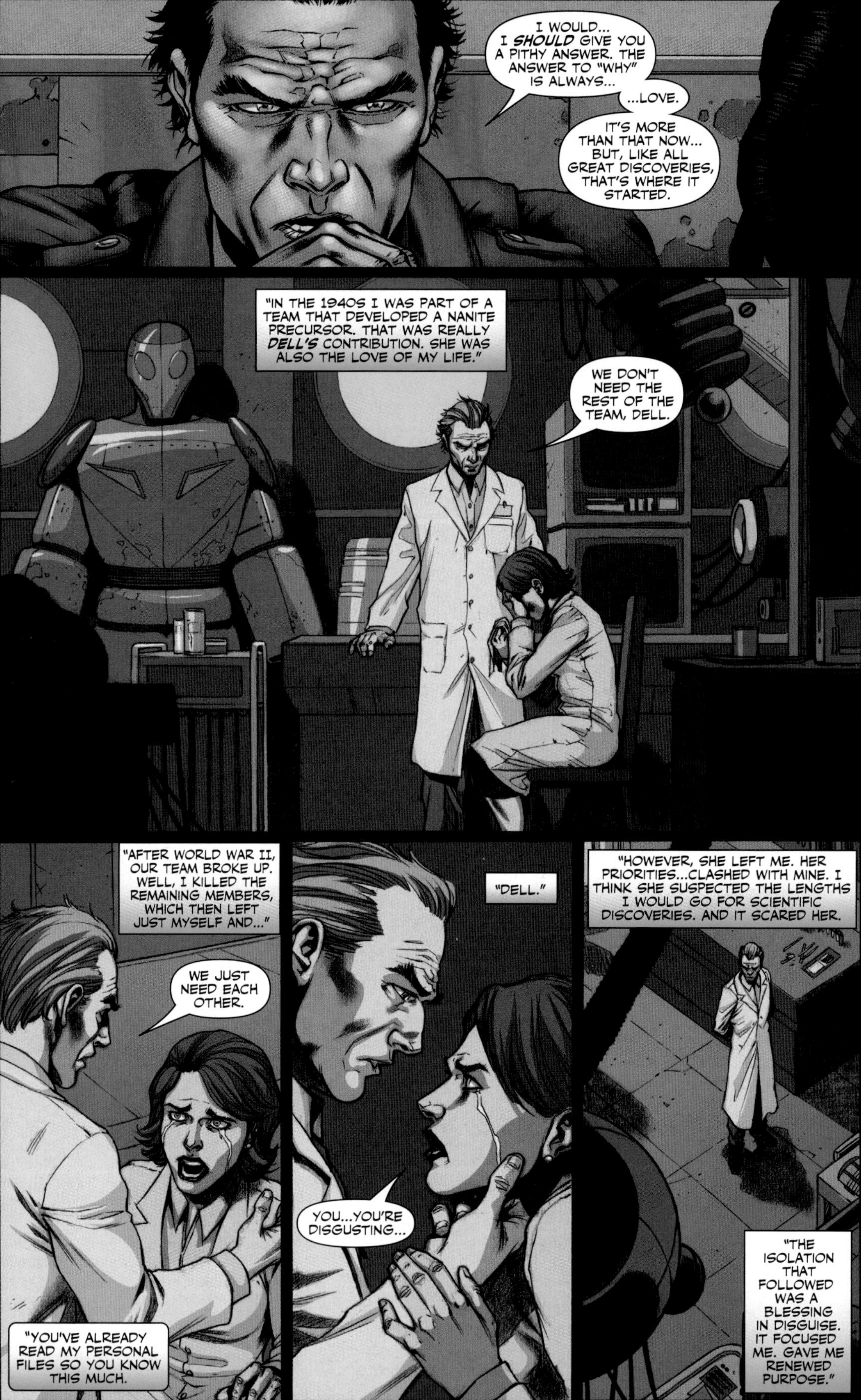
I WOULD... I SHOULD GIVE YOU A PITHY ANSWER. THE ANSWER TO "WHY" IS ALWAYS...
...LOVE.
IT'S MORE THAN THAT NOW... BUT, LIKE ALL GREAT DISCOVERIES, THAT'S WHERE IT STARTED.
"IN THE 1940S I WAS PART OF A TEAM THAT DEVELOPED A NANITE PRECURSOR. THAT WAS REALLY DELL'S CONTRIBUTION. SHE WAS ALSO THE LOVE OF MY LIFE."
WE DON'T NEED THE REST OF THE TEAM, DELL.
"AFTER WORLD WAR II, OUR TEAM BROKE UP. WELL, I KILLED THE REMAINING MEMBERS, WHICH THEN LEFT JUST MYSELF AND..."
WE JUST NEED EACH OTHER.
"YOU'VE ALREADY READ MY PERSONAL FILES SO YOU KNOW THIS MUCH.
"DELL."
YOU...YOU'RE DISGUSTING...
"HOWEVER, SHE LEFT ME. HER PRIORITIES...CLASHED WITH MINE. I THINK SHE SUSPECTED THE LENGTHS I WOULD GO FOR SCIENTIFIC DISCOVERIES. AND IT SCARED HER.
"THE ISOLATION THAT FOLLOWED WAS A BLESSING IN DISGUISE. IT FOCUSED ME. GAVE ME RENEWED PURPOSE."

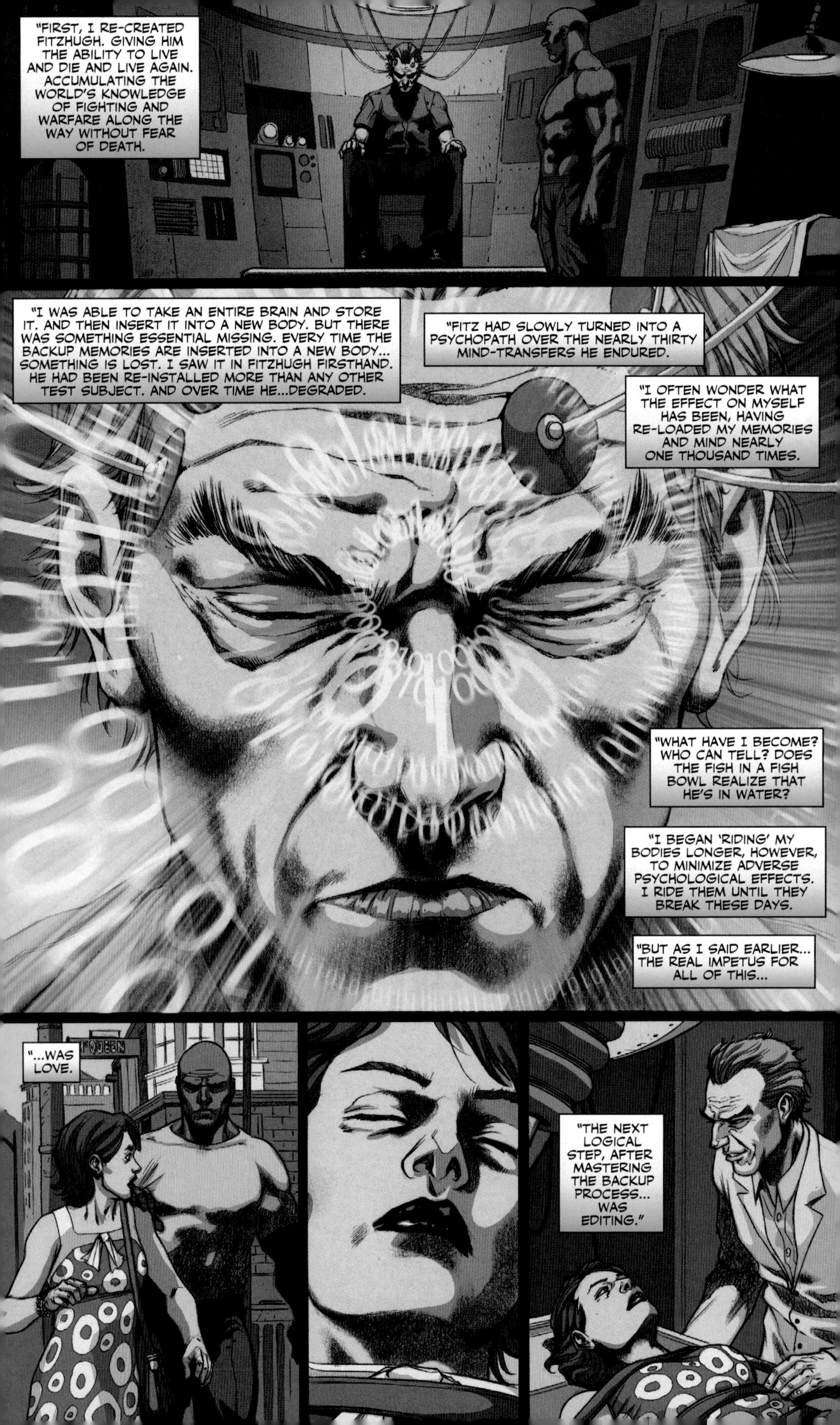
"FIRST, I RE-CREATED FITZHUGH. GIVING HIM THE ABILITY TO LIVE AND DIE AND LIVE AGAIN. ACCUMULATING THE WORLD'S KNOWLEDGE OF FIGHTING AND WARFARE ALONG THE WAY WITHOUT FEAR OF DEATH.
"I WAS ABLE TO TAKE AN ENTIRE BRAIN AND STORE IT. AND THEN INSERT IT INTO A NEW BODY. BUT THERE WAS SOMETHING ESSENTIAL MISSING. EVERY TIME THE BACKUP MEMORIES ARE INSERTED INTO A NEW BODY... SOMETHING IS LOST. I SAW IT IN FITZHUGH FIRSTHAND. HE HAD BEEN RE-INSTALLED MORE THAN ANY OTHER TEST SUBJECT. AND OVER TIME HE...DEGRADED.
"FITZ HAD SLOWLY TURNED INTO A PSYCHOPATH OVER THE NEARLY THIRTY MIND-TRANSFERS HE ENDURED.
"I OFTEN WONDER WHAT THE EFFECT ON MYSELF HAS BEEN, HAVING RE-LOADED MY MEMORIES AND MIND NEARLY ONE THOUSAND TIMES.
"WHAT HAVE I BECOME? WHO CAN TELL? DOES THE FISH IN A FISH BOWL REALIZE THAT HE'S IN WATER?
"I BEGAN 'RIDING' MY BODIES LONGER, HOWEVER, TO MINIMIZE ADVERSE PSYCHOLOGICAL EFFECTS. I RIDE THEM UNTIL THEY BREAK THESE DAYS.
"BUT AS I SAID EARLIER... THE REAL IMPETUS FOR ALL OF THIS...
"...WAS LOVE.
McQUEEN
"THE NEXT LOGICAL STEP, AFTER MASTERING THE BACKUP PROCESS... WAS EDITING."

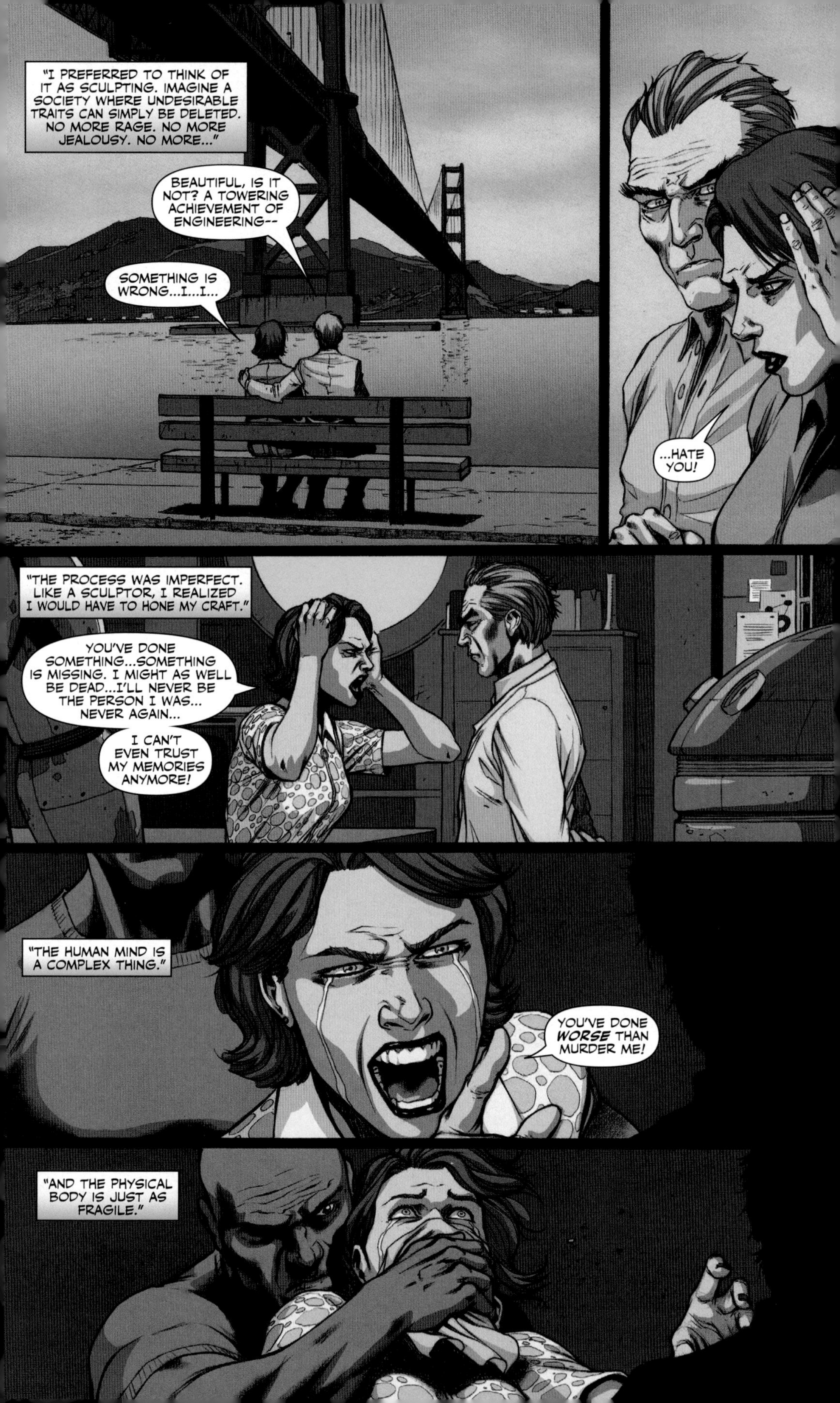
"I PREFERRED TO THINK OF IT AS SCULPTING. IMAGINE A SOCIETY WHERE UNDESIRABLE TRAITS CAN SIMPLY BE DELETED. NO MORE RAGE. NO MORE JEALOUSY. NO MORE..."
BEAUTIFUL, IS IT NOT? A TOWERING ACHIEVEMENT OF ENGINEERING--
SOMETHING IS WRONG...I...I...
...HATE YOU!
"THE PROCESS WAS IMPERFECT. LIKE A SCULPTOR, I REALIZED I WOULD HAVE TO HONE MY CRAFT."
YOU'VE DONE SOMETHING...SOMETHING IS MISSING. I MIGHT AS WELL BE DEAD...I'LL NEVER BE THE PERSON I WAS... NEVER AGAIN...
I CAN'T EVEN TRUST MY MEMORIES ANYMORE!
"THE HUMAN MIND IS A COMPLEX THING."
YOU'VE DONE *WORSE* THAN MURDER ME!
"AND THE PHYSICAL BODY IS JUST AS FRAGILE."

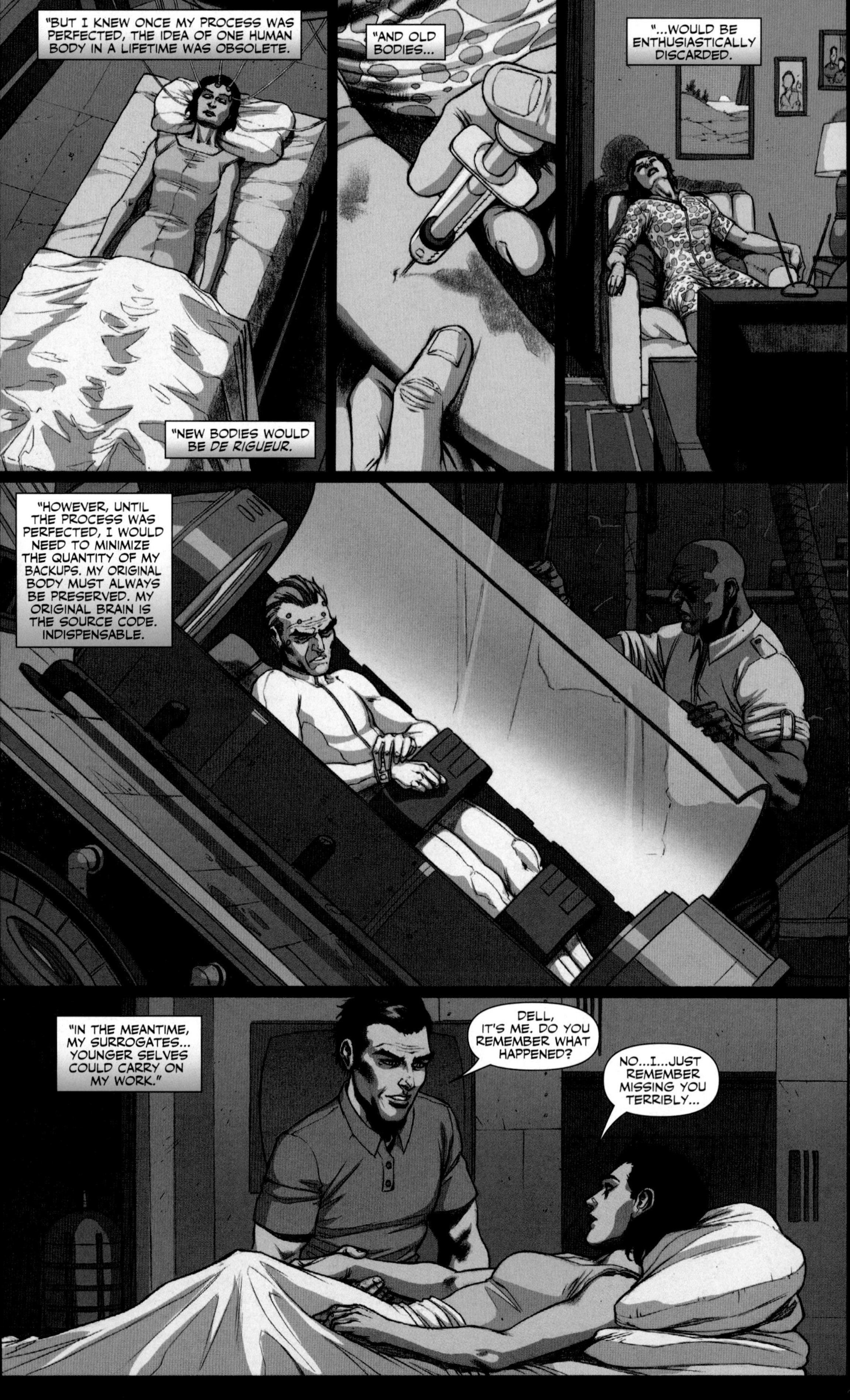
"BUT I KNEW ONCE MY PROCESS WAS PERFECTED, THE IDEA OF ONE HUMAN BODY IN A LIFETIME WAS OBSOLETE.
"NEW BODIES WOULD BE *DE RIGUEUR*.
"AND OLD BODIES...
"...WOULD BE ENTHUSIASTICALLY DISCARDED.
"HOWEVER, UNTIL THE PROCESS WAS PERFECTED, I WOULD NEED TO MINIMIZE THE QUANTITY OF MY BACKUPS. MY ORIGINAL BODY MUST ALWAYS BE PRESERVED. MY ORIGINAL BRAIN IS THE SOURCE CODE. INDISPENSABLE.
"IN THE MEANTIME, MY SURROGATES... YOUNGER SELVES COULD CARRY ON MY WORK."
DELL, IT'S ME. DO YOU REMEMBER WHAT HAPPENED?
NO...I...JUST REMEMBER MISSING YOU TERRIBLY...

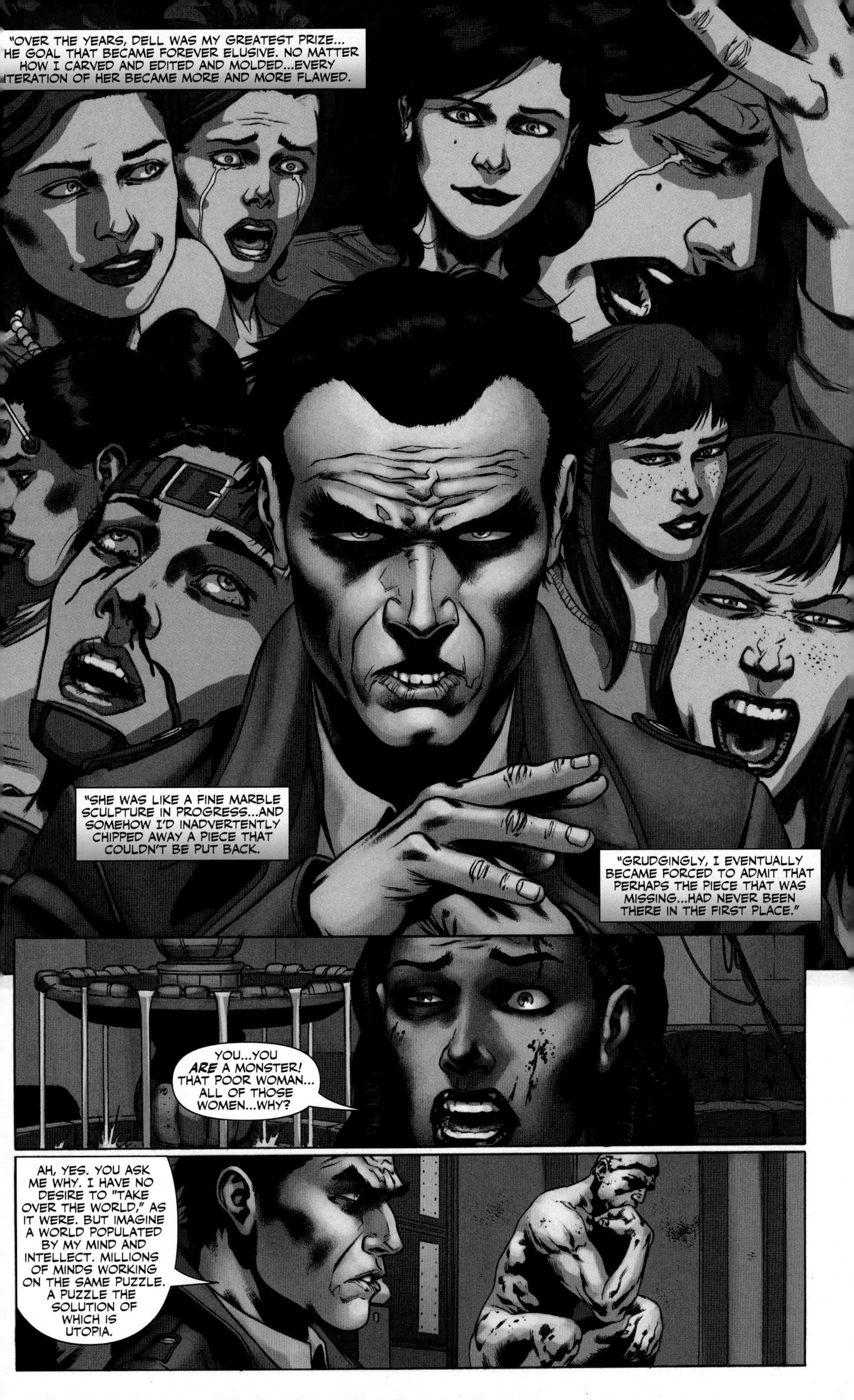
"OVER THE YEARS, DELL WAS MY GREATEST PRIZE... HE GOAL THAT BECAME FOREVER ELUSIVE. NO MATTER HOW I CARVED AND EDITED AND MOLDED...EVERY ITERATION OF HER BECAME MORE AND MORE FLAWED.
"SHE WAS LIKE A FINE MARBLE SCULPTURE IN PROGRESS...AND SOMEHOW I'D INADVERTENTLY CHIPPED AWAY A PIECE THAT COULDN'T BE PUT BACK.
"GRUDGINGLY, I EVENTUALLY BECAME FORCED TO ADMIT THAT PERHAPS THE PIECE THAT WAS MISSING...HAD NEVER BEEN THERE IN THE FIRST PLACE."
YOU...YOU *ARE* A MONSTER! THAT POOR WOMAN... ALL OF THOSE WOMEN...WHY?
AH, YES. YOU ASK ME WHY. I HAVE NO DESIRE TO "TAKE OVER THE WORLD," AS IT WERE. BUT IMAGINE A WORLD POPULATED BY MY MIND AND INTELLECT. MILLIONS OF MINDS WORKING ON THE SAME PUZZLE. A PUZZLE THE SOLUTION OF WHICH IS UTOPIA.

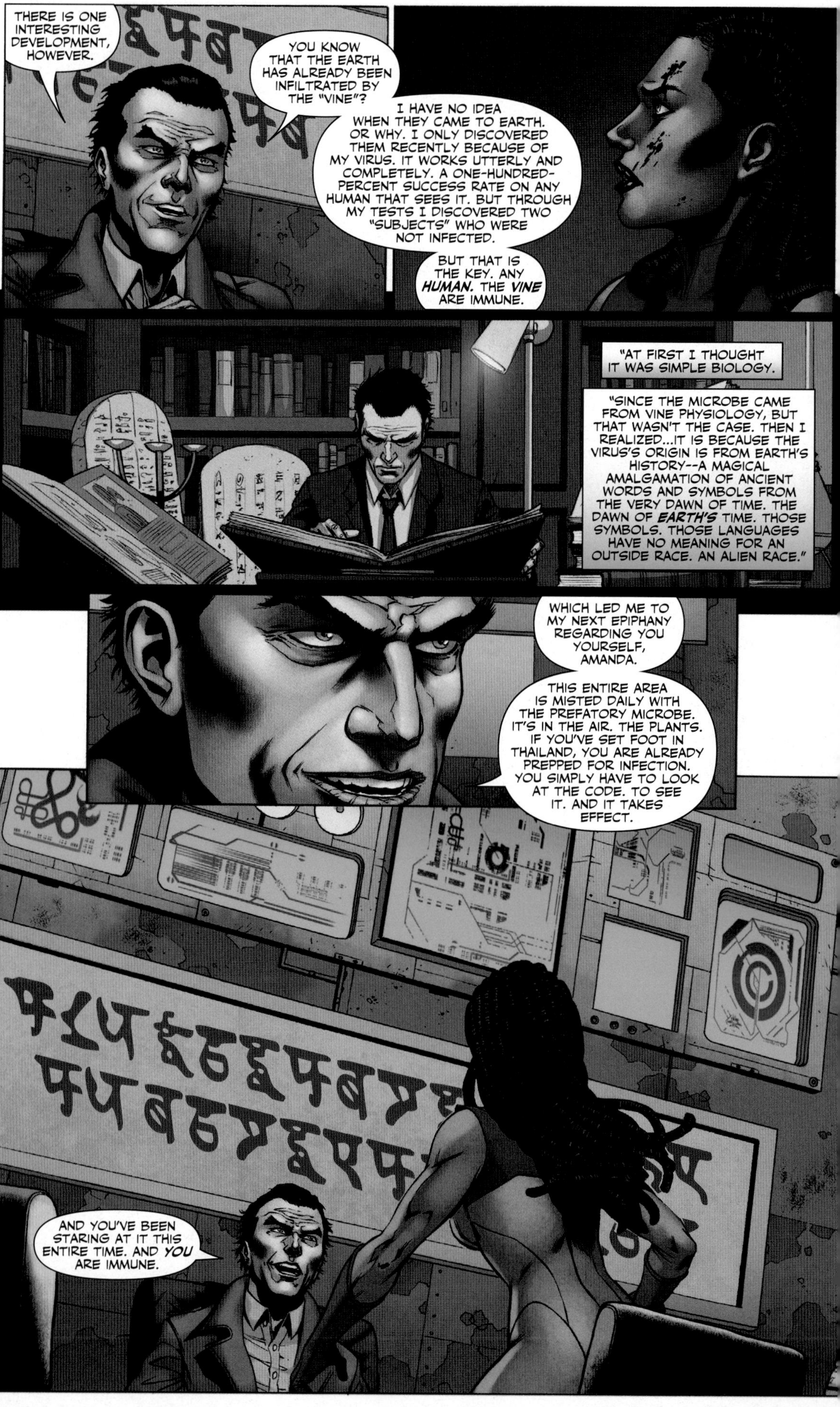
THERE IS ONE INTERESTING DEVELOPMENT, HOWEVER.
YOU KNOW THAT THE EARTH HAS ALREADY BEEN INFILTRATED BY THE "VINE"?
I HAVE NO IDEA WHEN THEY CAME TO EARTH. OR WHY. I ONLY DISCOVERED THEM RECENTLY BECAUSE OF MY VIRUS. IT WORKS UTTERLY AND COMPLETELY. A ONE-HUNDRED-PERCENT SUCCESS RATE ON ANY HUMAN THAT SEES IT. BUT THROUGH MY TESTS I DISCOVERED TWO "SUBJECTS" WHO WERE NOT INFECTED.
BUT THAT IS THE KEY. ANY ***HUMAN.*** THE ***VINE*** ARE IMMUNE.
"AT FIRST I THOUGHT IT WAS SIMPLE BIOLOGY.
"SINCE THE MICROBE CAME FROM VINE PHYSIOLOGY, BUT THAT WASN'T THE CASE. THEN I REALIZED...IT IS BECAUSE THE VIRUS'S ORIGIN IS FROM EARTH'S HISTORY--A MAGICAL AMALGAMATION OF ANCIENT WORDS AND SYMBOLS FROM THE VERY DAWN OF TIME. THE DAWN OF ***EARTH'S*** TIME. THOSE SYMBOLS. THOSE LANGUAGES HAVE NO MEANING FOR AN OUTSIDE RACE. AN ALIEN RACE."
WHICH LED ME TO MY NEXT EPIPHANY REGARDING YOU YOURSELF, AMANDA.
THIS ENTIRE AREA IS MISTED DAILY WITH THE PREFATORY MICROBE. IT'S IN THE AIR. THE PLANTS. IF YOU'VE SET FOOT IN THAILAND, YOU ARE ALREADY PREPPED FOR INFECTION. YOU SIMPLY HAVE TO LOOK AT THE CODE. TO SEE IT. AND IT TAKES EFFECT.
AND YOU'VE BEEN STARING AT IT THIS ENTIRE TIME. AND ***YOU*** ARE IMMUNE.

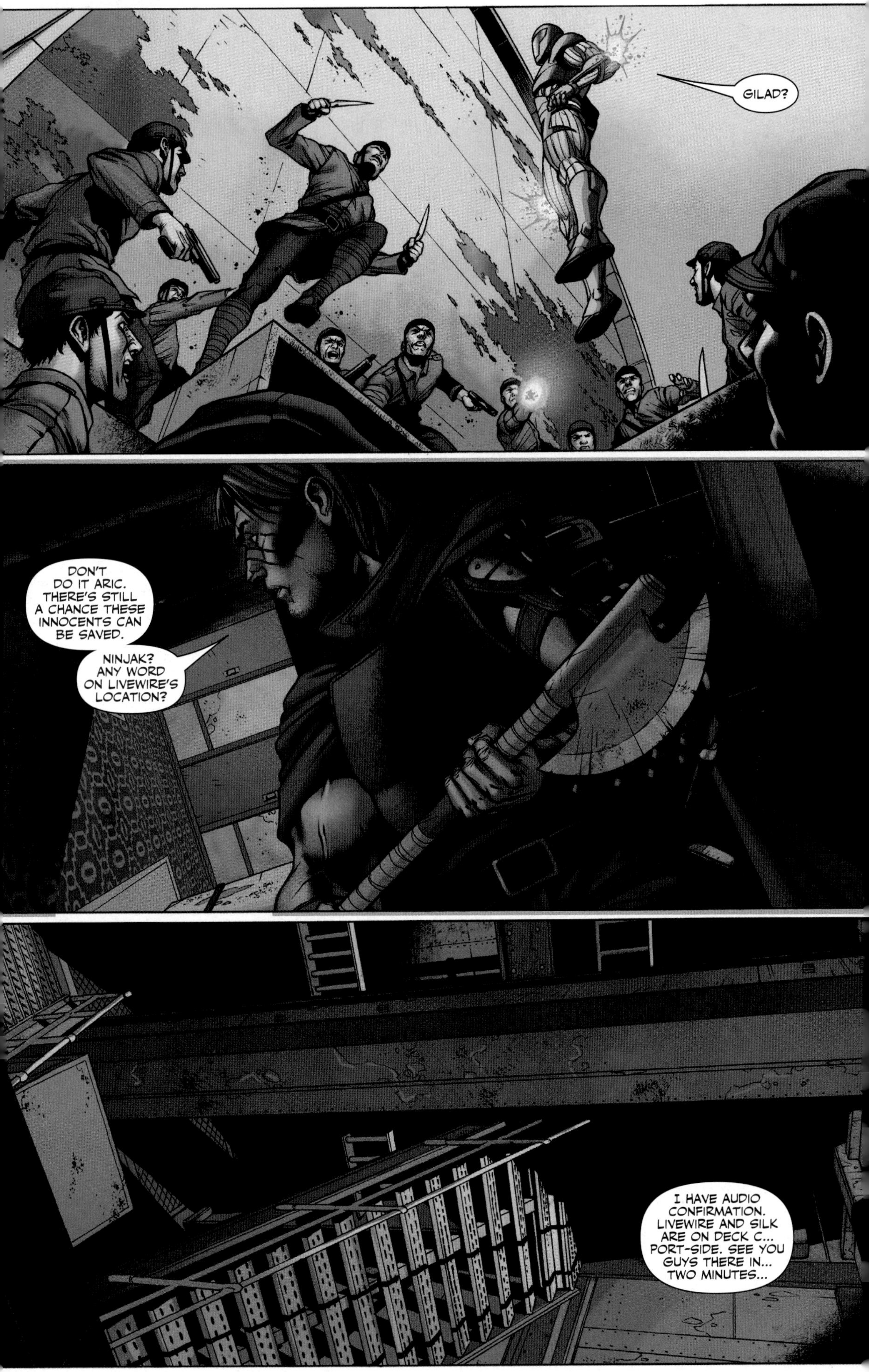
GILAD?
DON'T DO IT ARIC. THERE'S STILL A CHANCE THESE INNOCENTS CAN BE SAVED.
NINJAK? ANY WORD ON LIVEWIRE'S LOCATION?
I HAVE AUDIO CONFIRMATION. LIVEWIRE AND SILK ARE ON DECK C... PORT-SIDE. SEE YOU GUYS THERE IN... TWO MINUTES...

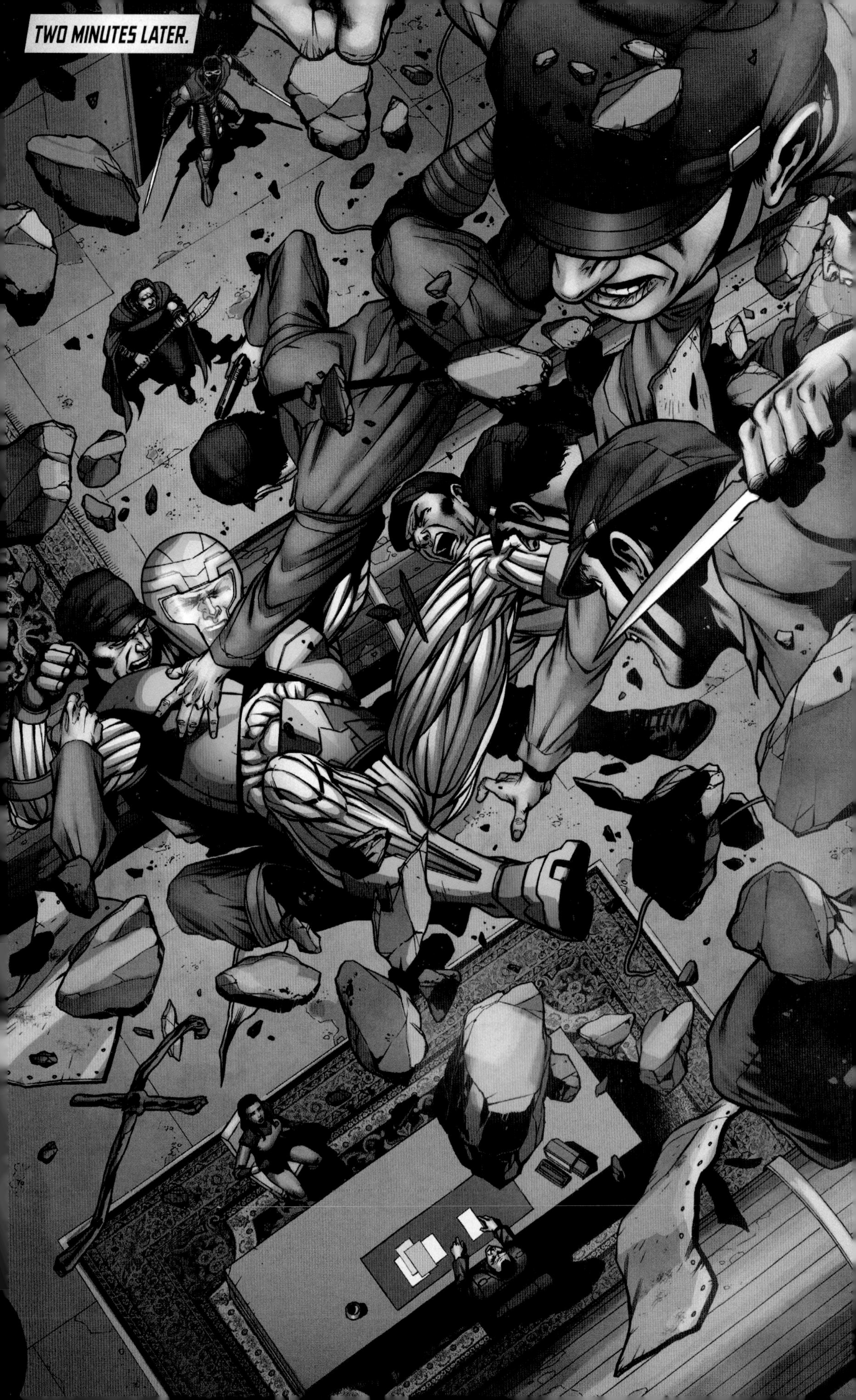
TWO MINUTES LATER.

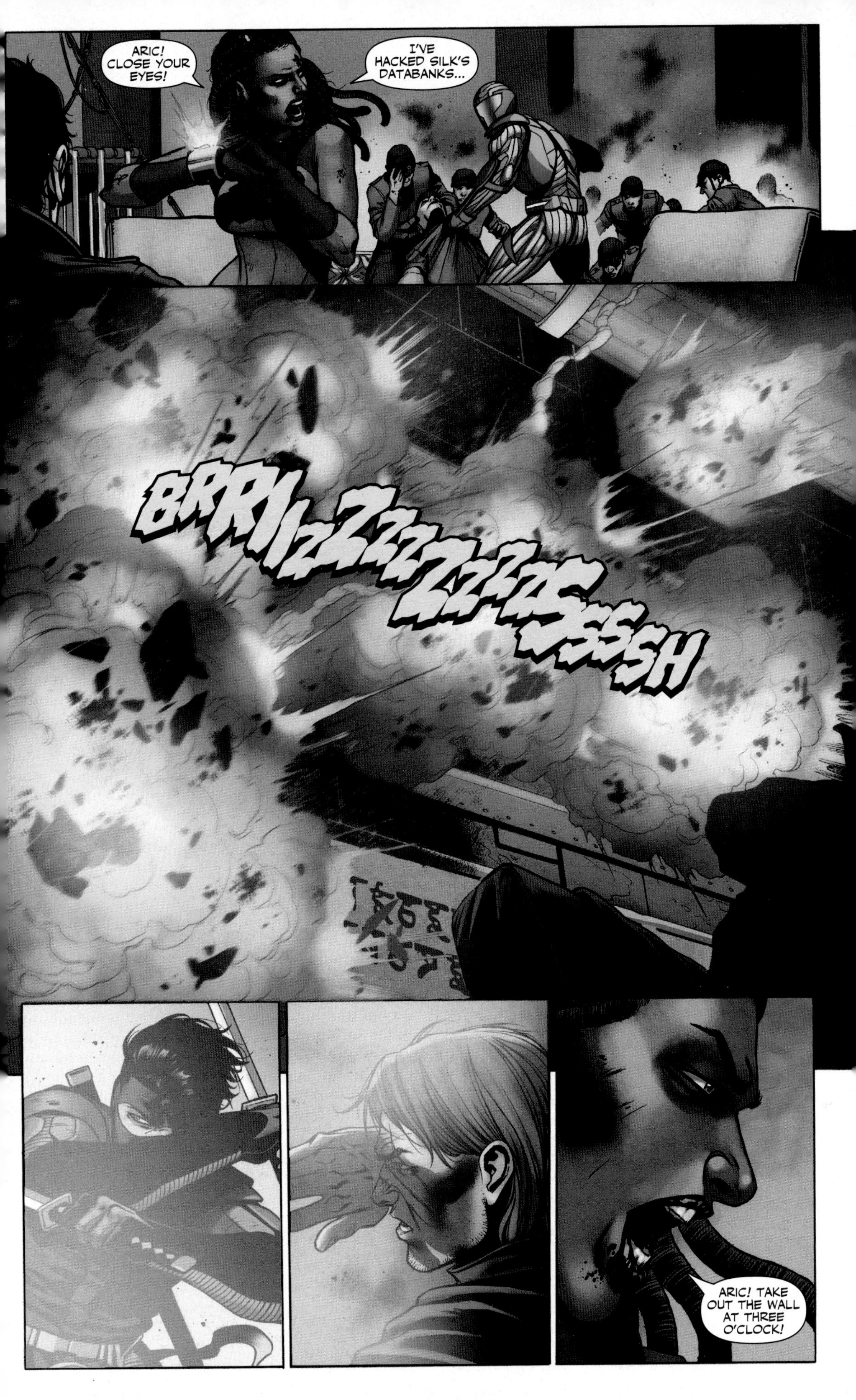
ARIC! CLOSE YOUR EYES!
I'VE HACKED SILK'S DATABANKS...
BRRIIZZZZZZZZSSSSH
ARIC! TAKE OUT THE WALL AT THREE O'CLOCK!

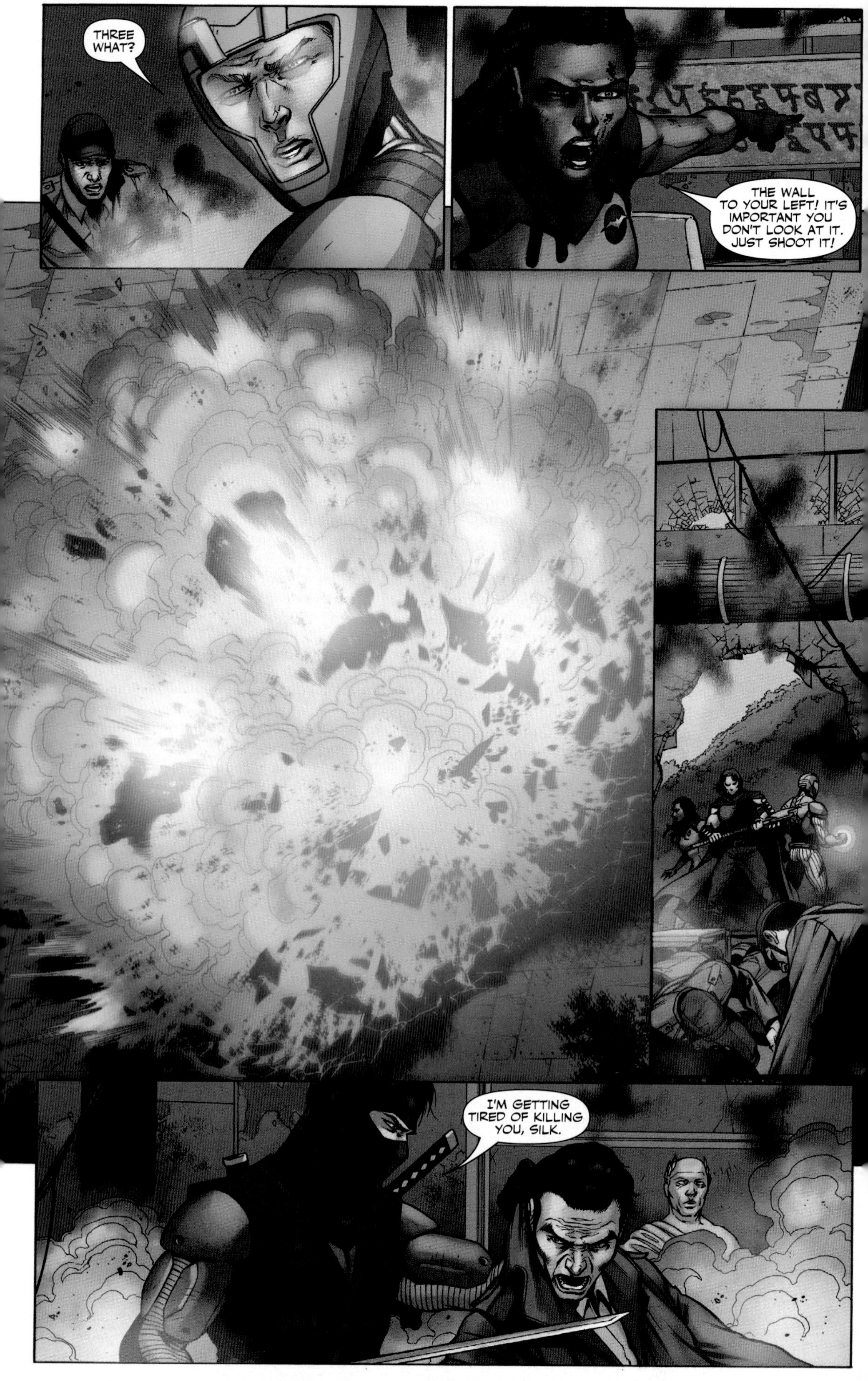
THREE WHAT?
THE WALL TO YOUR LEFT! IT'S IMPORTANT YOU DON'T LOOK AT IT. JUST SHOOT IT!
I'M GETTING TIRED OF KILLING YOU, SILK.

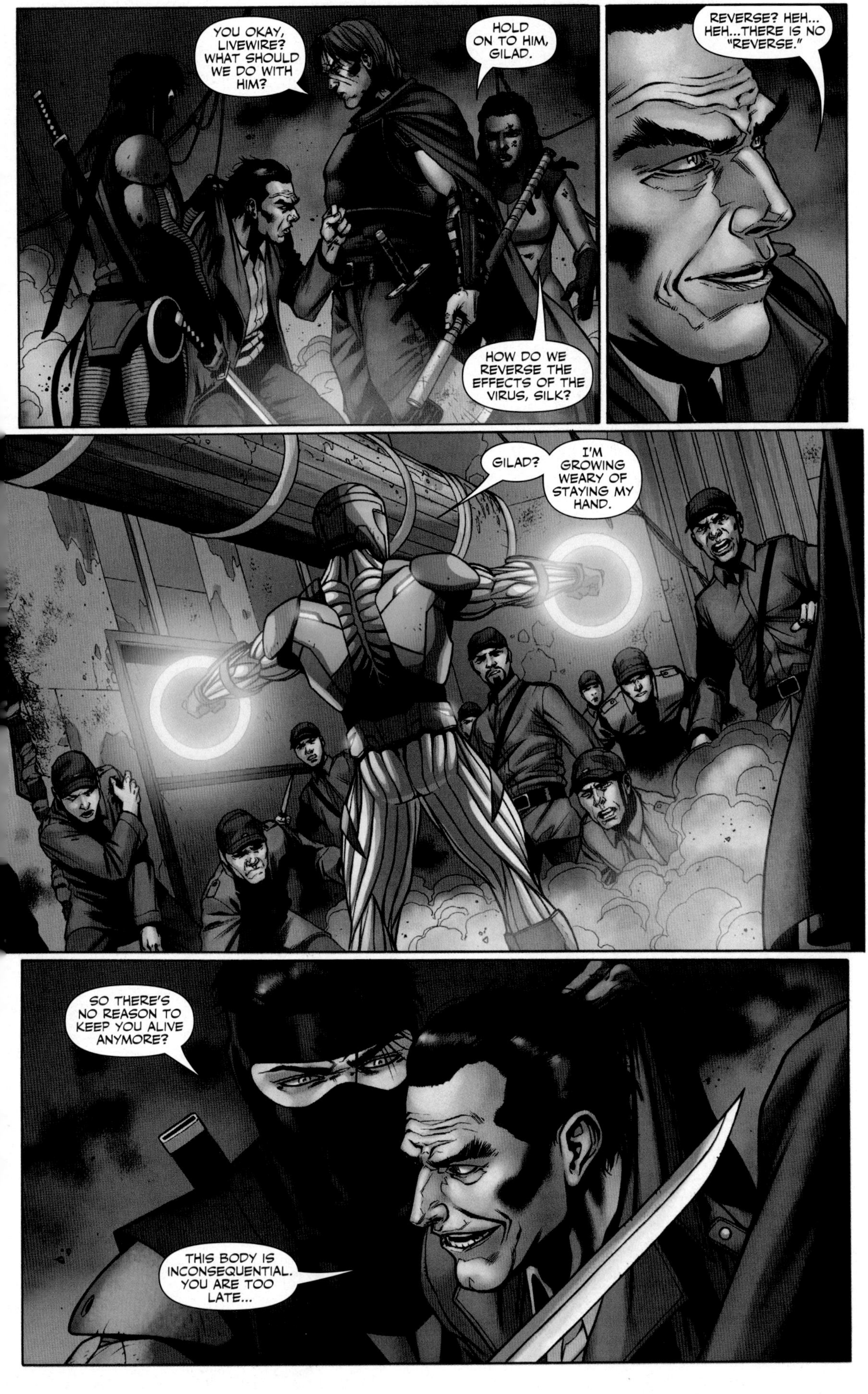
YOU OKAY, LIVEWIRE? WHAT SHOULD WE DO WITH HIM?
HOLD ON TO HIM, GILAD.
HOW DO WE REVERSE THE EFFECTS OF THE VIRUS, SILK?
REVERSE? HEH... HEH...THERE IS NO "REVERSE."
GILAD?
I'M GROWING WEARY OF STAYING MY HAND.
SO THERE'S NO REASON TO KEEP YOU ALIVE ANYMORE?
THIS BODY IS INCONSEQUENTIAL. YOU ARE TOO LATE...

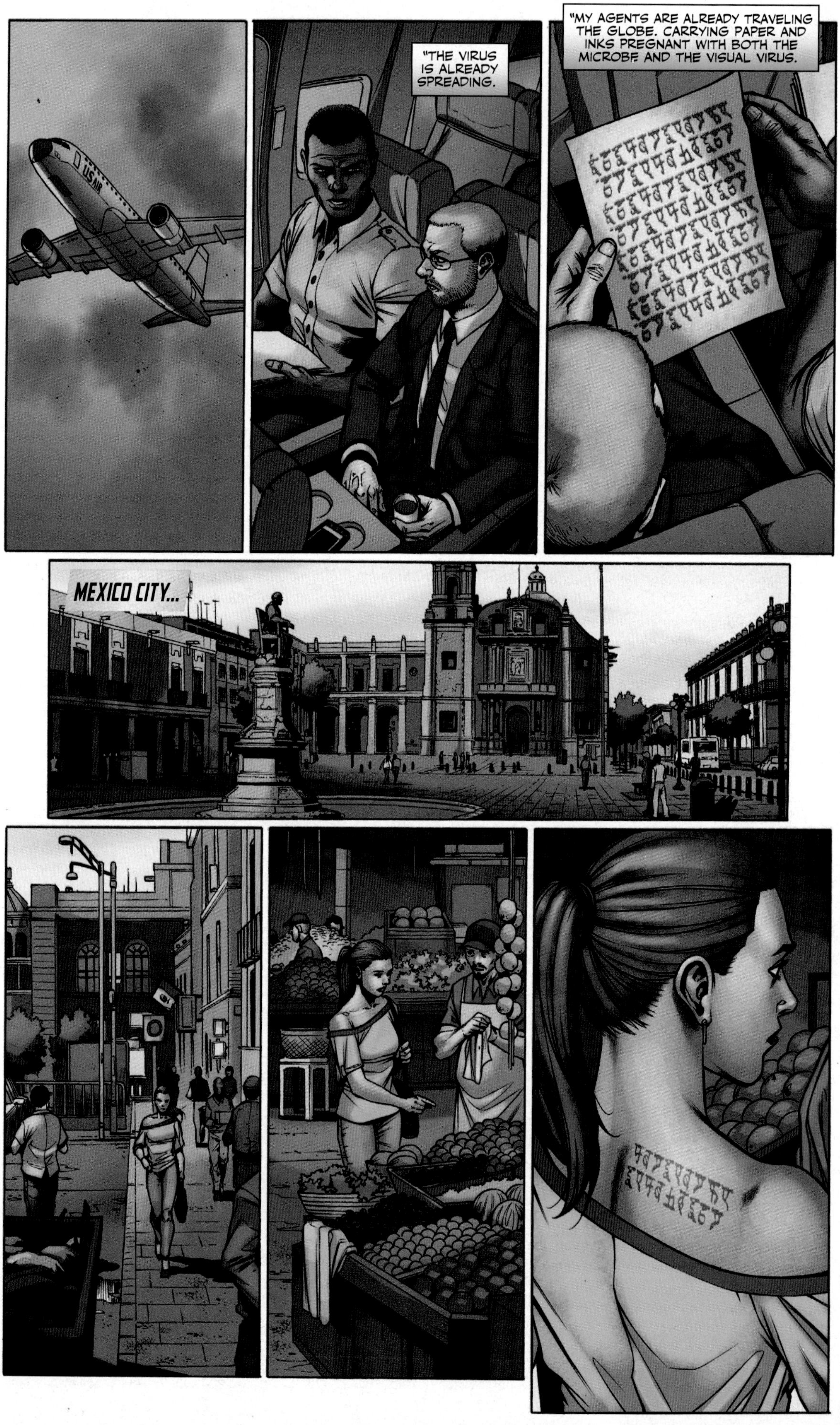
"THE VIRUS IS ALREADY SPREADING.
"MY AGENTS ARE ALREADY TRAVELING THE GLOBE. CARRYING PAPER AND INKS PREGNANT WITH BOTH THE MICROBE AND THE VISUAL VIRUS.
MEXICO CITY...
US AIR

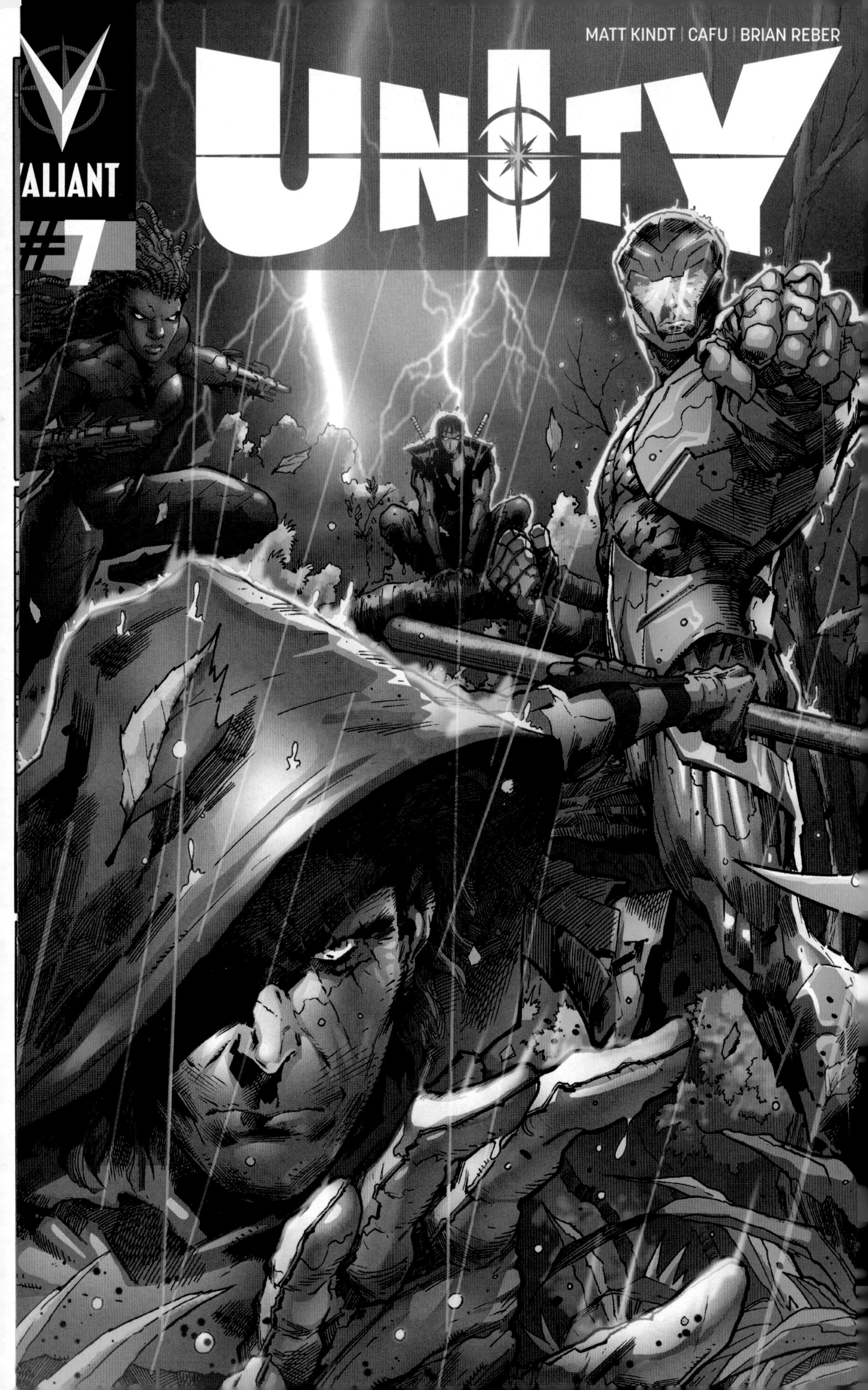

VALIANT
#7
UNITY
MATT KINDT | CAFU | BRIAN REBER

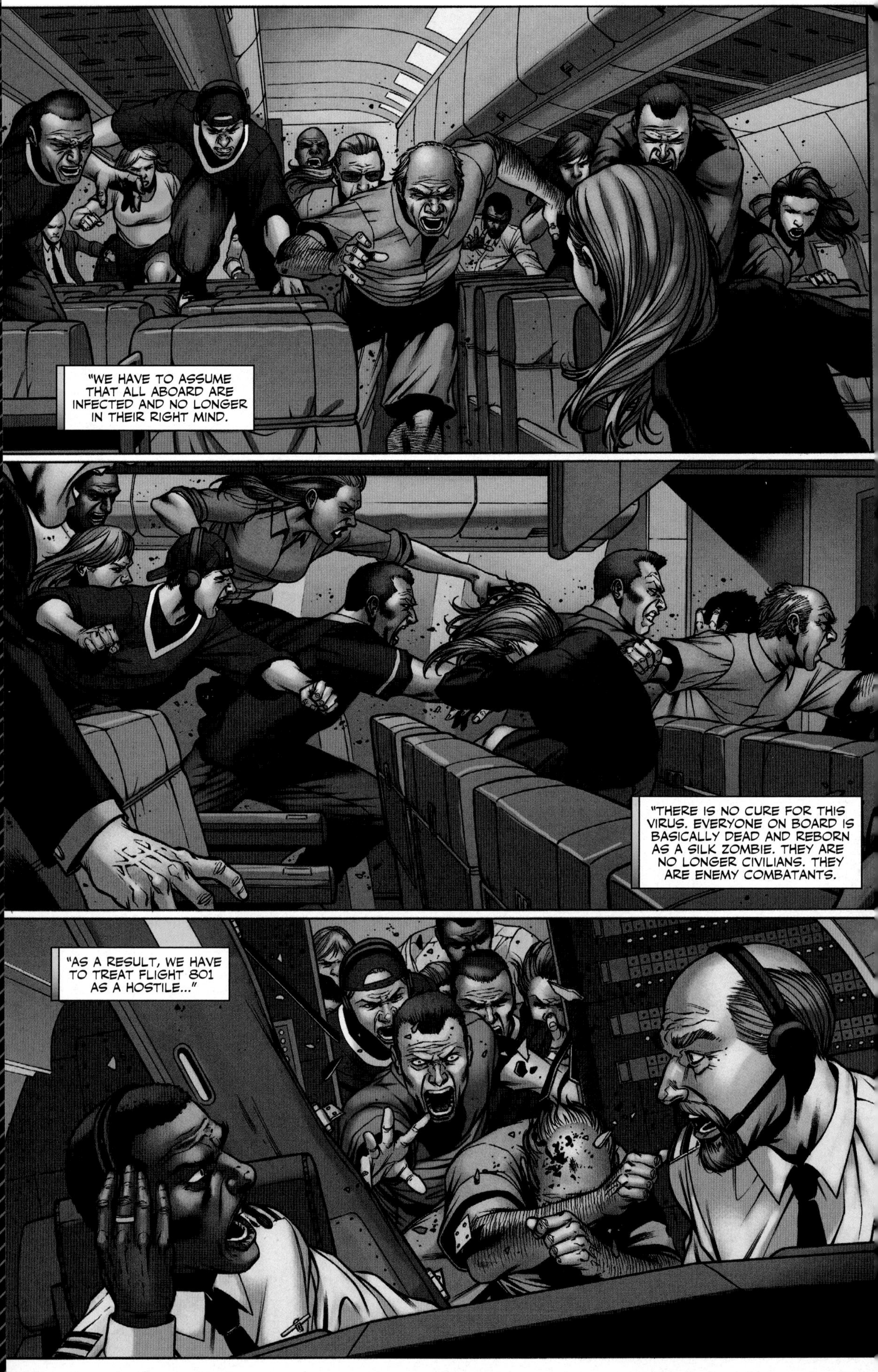
"WE HAVE TO ASSUME THAT ALL ABOARD ARE INFECTED AND NO LONGER IN THEIR RIGHT MIND.
"THERE IS NO CURE FOR THIS VIRUS. EVERYONE ON BOARD IS BASICALLY DEAD AND REBORN AS A SILK ZOMBIE. THEY ARE NO LONGER CIVILIANS. THEY ARE ENEMY COMBATANTS.
"AS A RESULT, WE HAVE TO TREAT FLIGHT 801 AS A HOSTILE..."

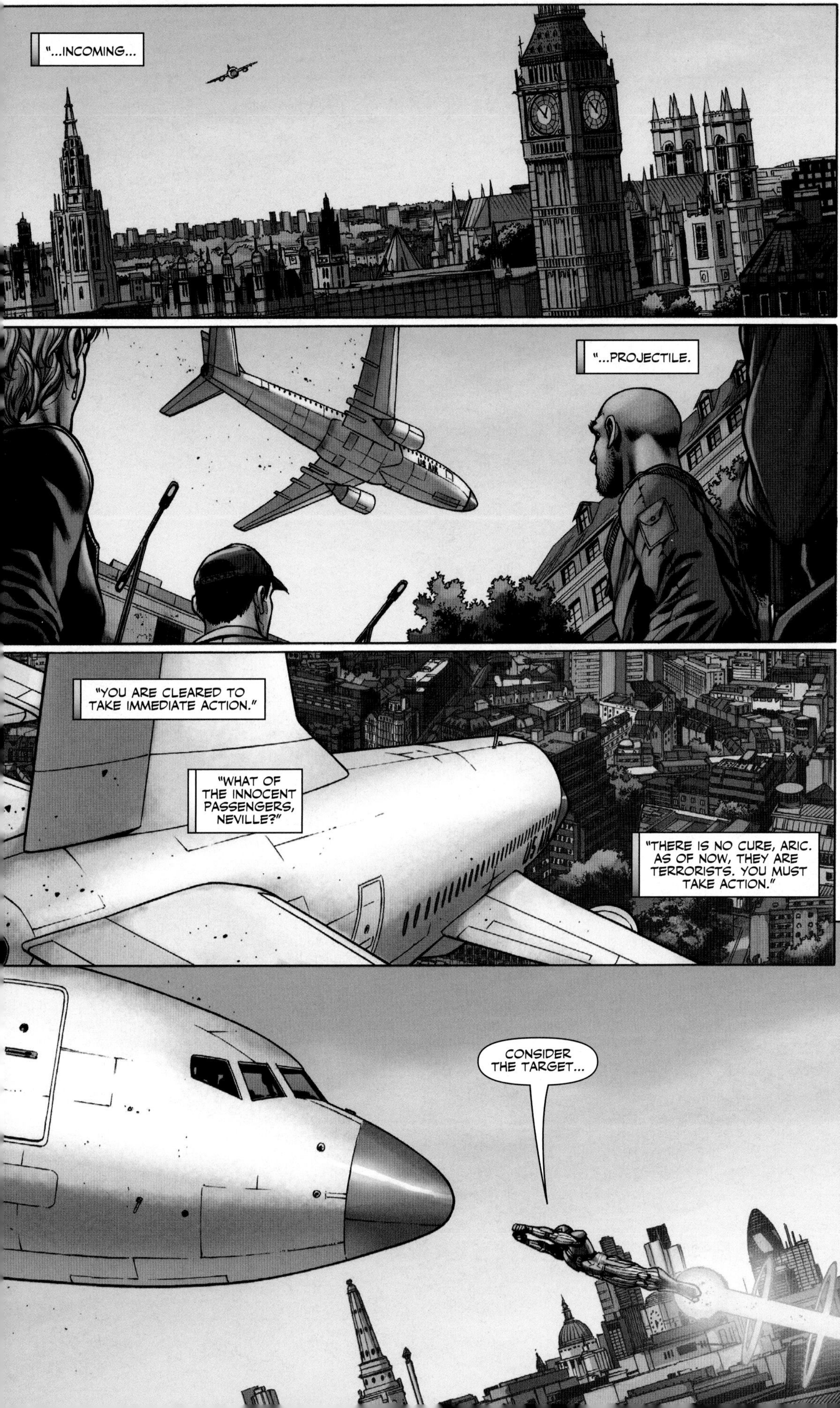
"...INCOMING...
"...PROJECTILE.
"YOU ARE CLEARED TO TAKE IMMEDIATE ACTION."
"WHAT OF THE INNOCENT PASSENGERS, NEVILLE?"
"THERE IS NO CURE, ARIC. AS OF NOW, THEY ARE TERRORISTS. YOU MUST TAKE ACTION."
CONSIDER THE TARGET...

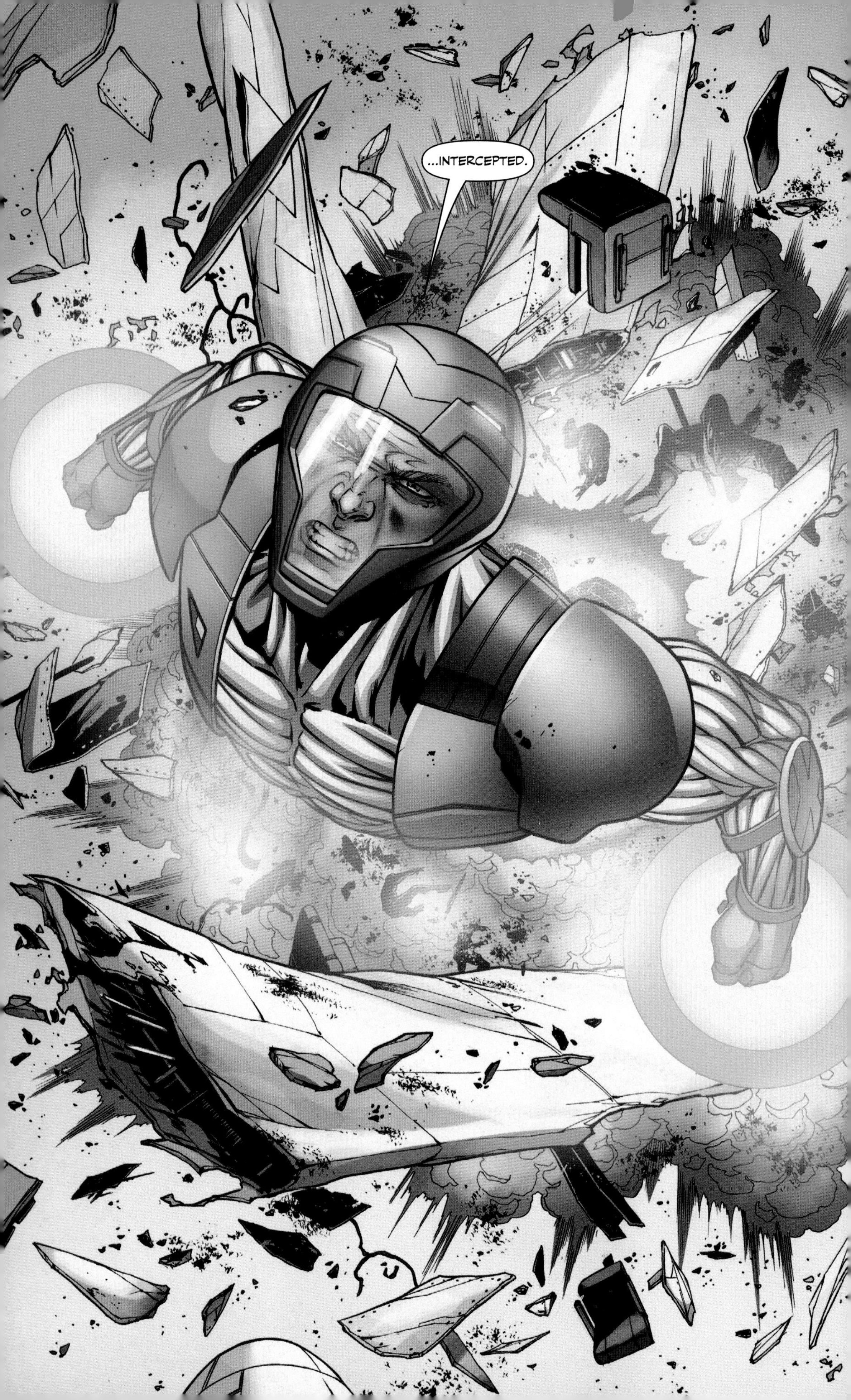
...INTERCEPTED.

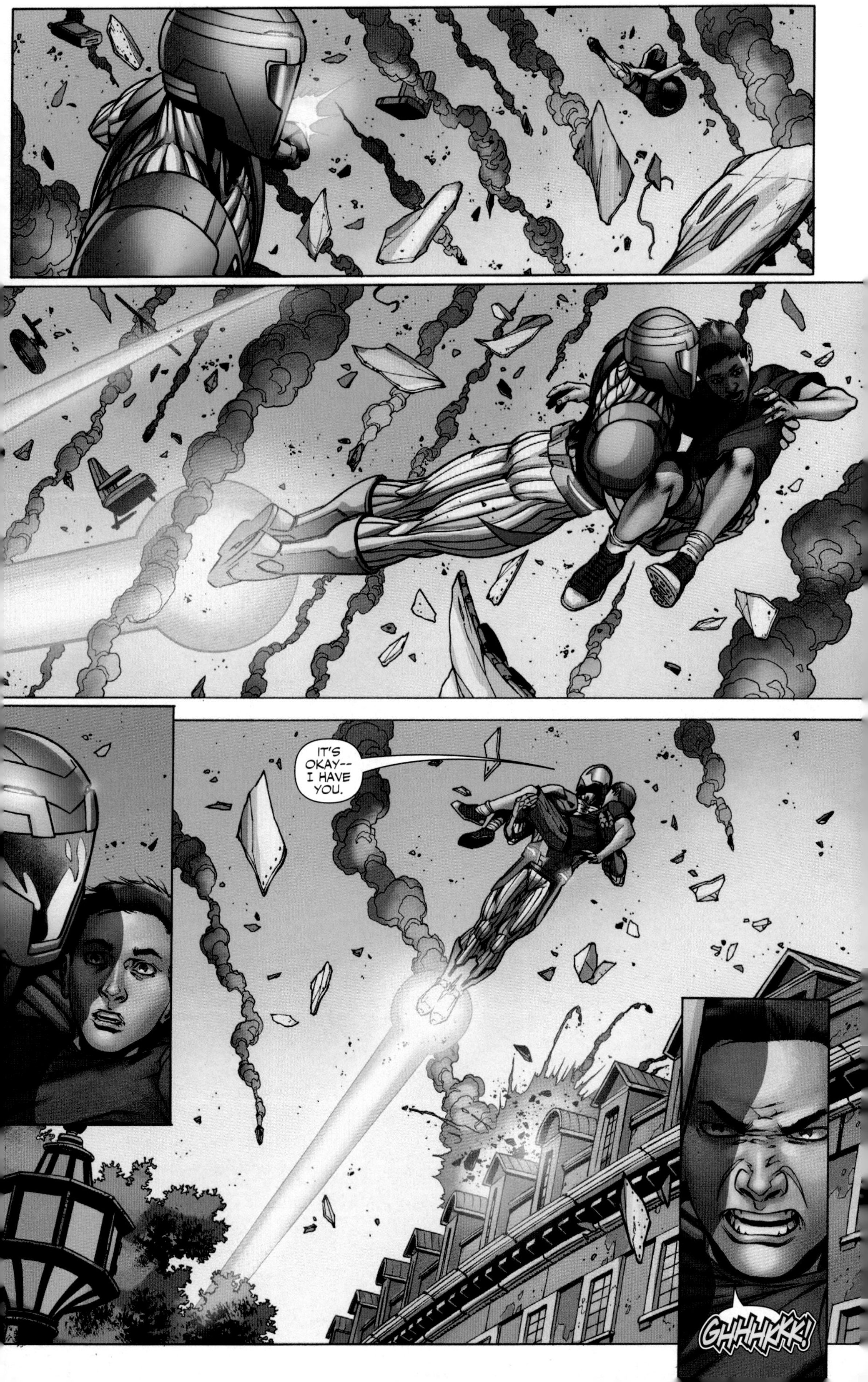
IT'S OKAY-- I HAVE YOU.
GHHHKKK!

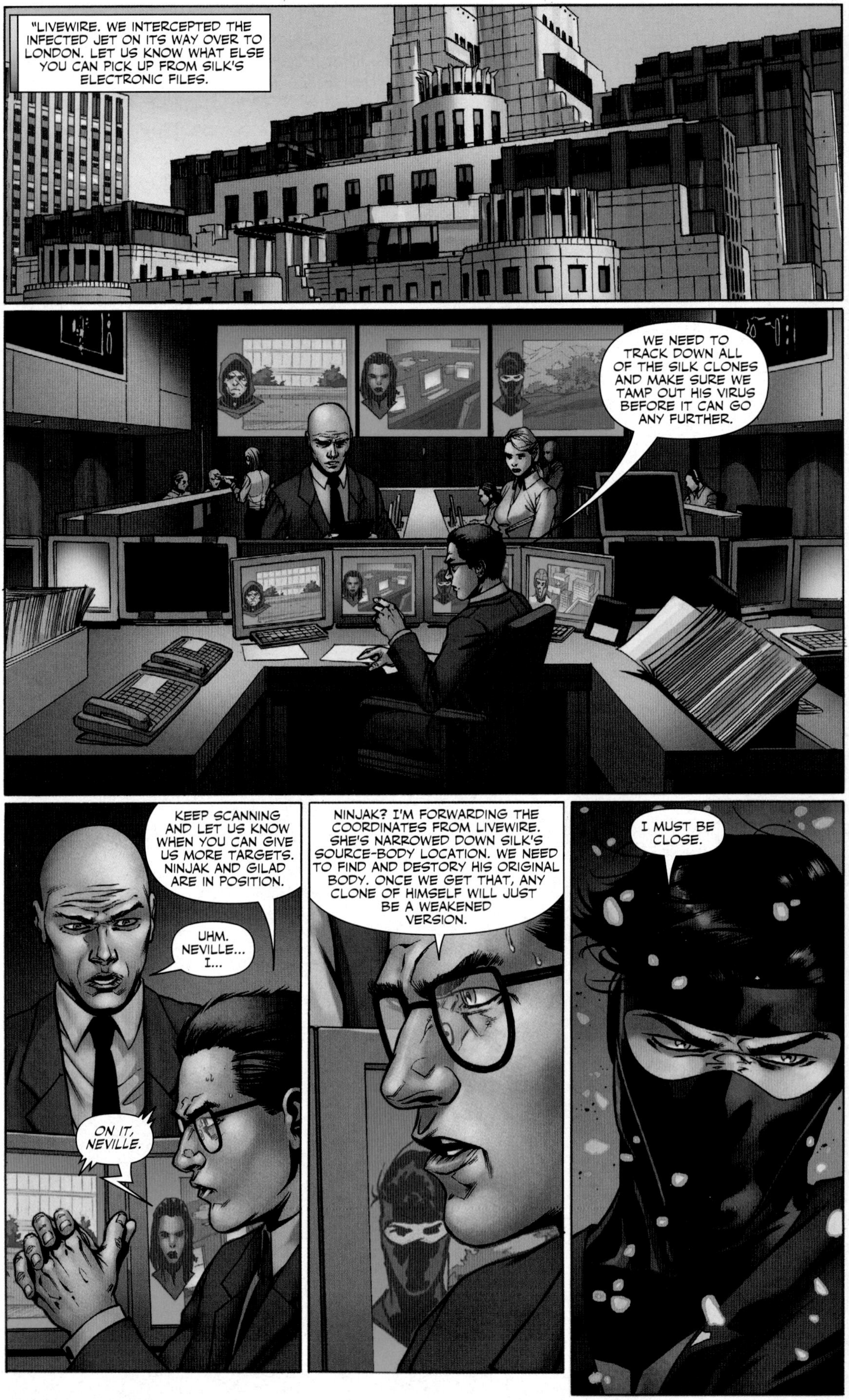
"LIVEWIRE. WE INTERCEPTED THE INFECTED JET ON ITS WAY OVER TO LONDON. LET US KNOW WHAT ELSE YOU CAN PICK UP FROM SILK'S ELECTRONIC FILES.
WE NEED TO TRACK DOWN ALL OF THE SILK CLONES AND MAKE SURE WE TAMP OUT HIS VIRUS BEFORE IT CAN GO ANY FURTHER.
KEEP SCANNING AND LET US KNOW WHEN YOU CAN GIVE US MORE TARGETS. NINJAK AND GILAD ARE IN POSITION.
UHM. NEVILLE... I...
ON IT, NEVILLE.
NINJAK? I'M FORWARDING THE COORDINATES FROM LIVEWIRE. SHE'S NARROWED DOWN SILK'S SOURCE-BODY LOCATION. WE NEED TO FIND AND DESTORY HIS ORIGINAL BODY. ONCE WE GET THAT, ANY CLONE OF HIMSELF WILL JUST BE A WEAKENED VERSION.
I MUST BE CLOSE.

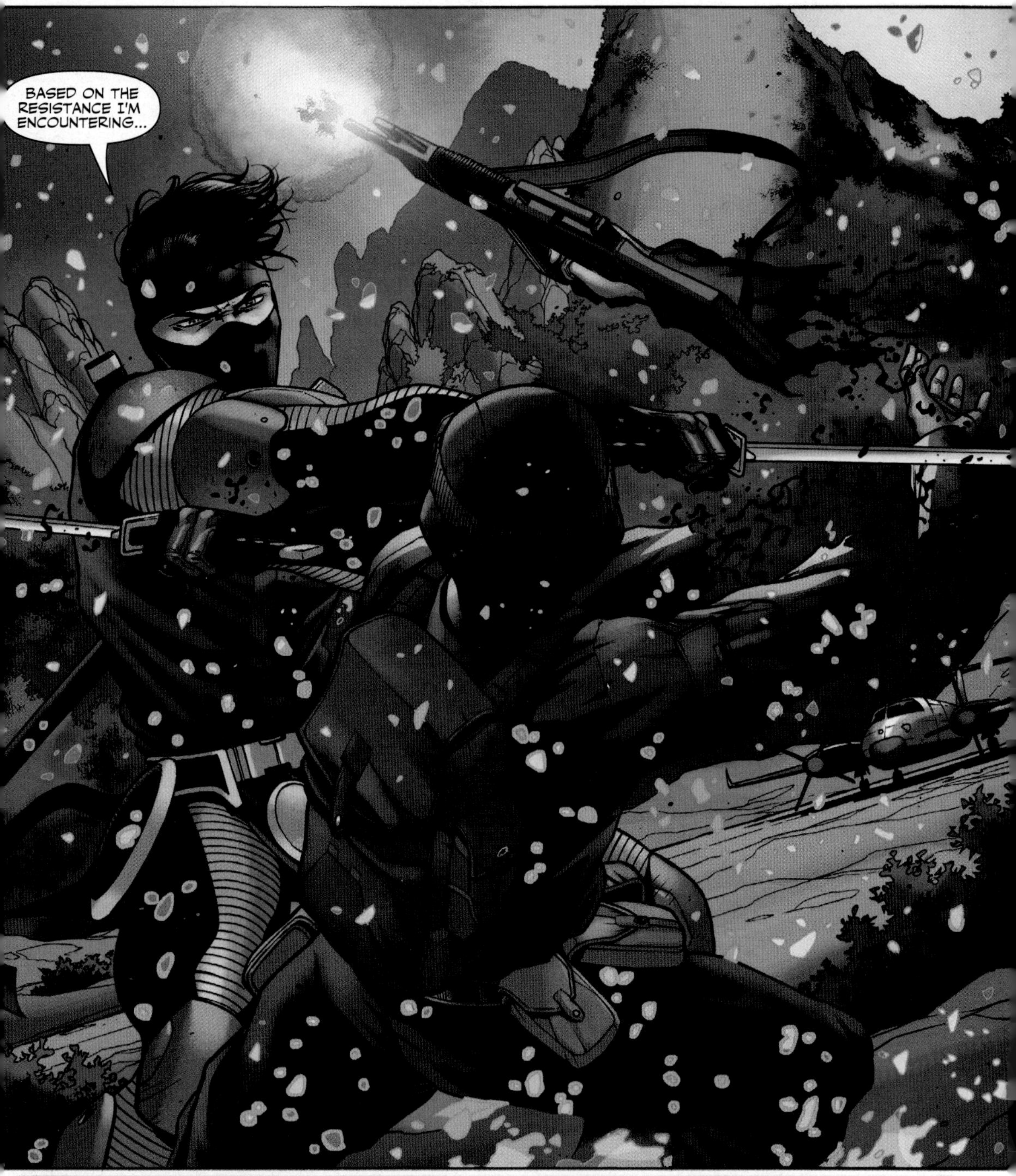
BASED ON THE RESISTANCE I'M ENCOUNTERING...

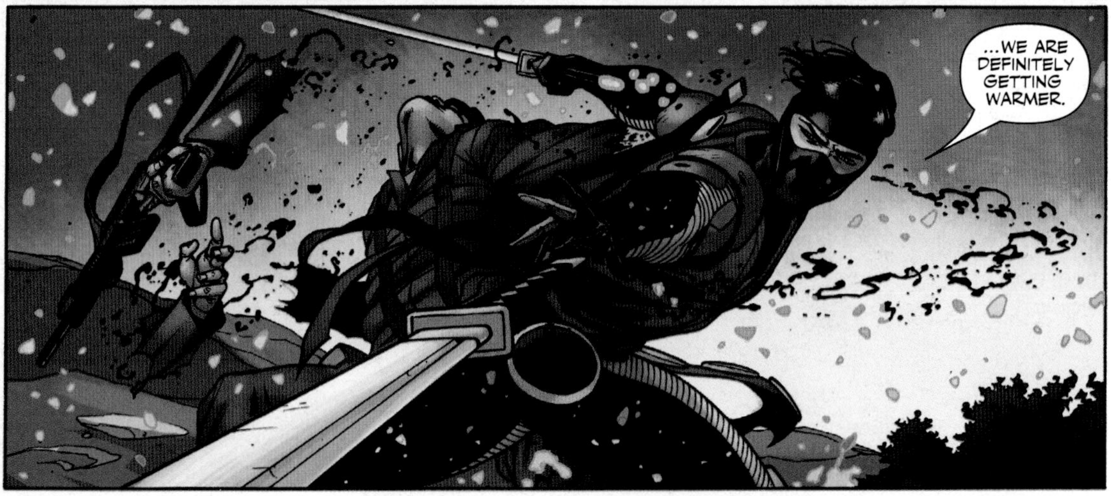
...WE ARE DEFINITELY GETTING WARMER.

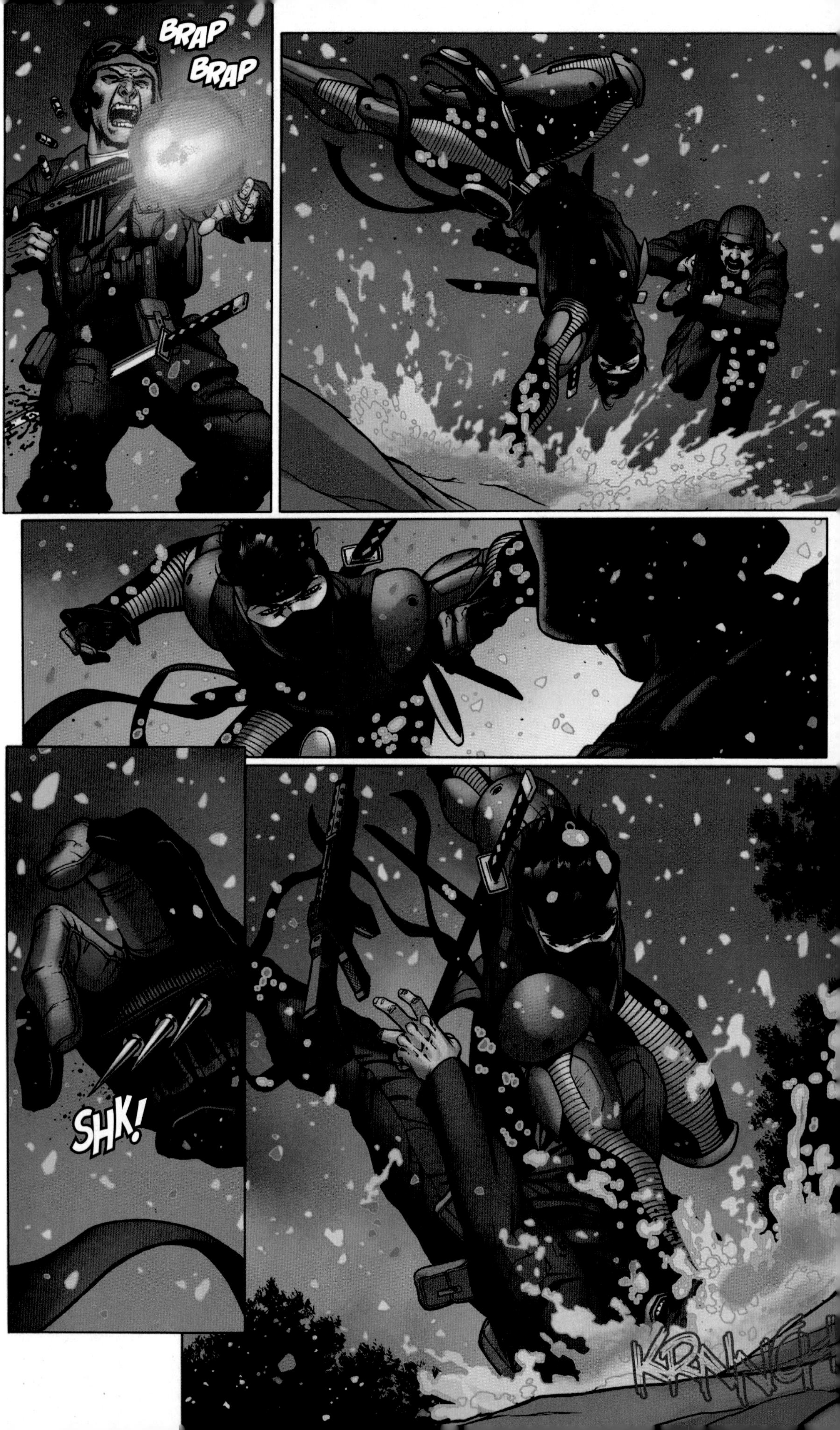
BRAP
BRAP
SHK!
KRNCH

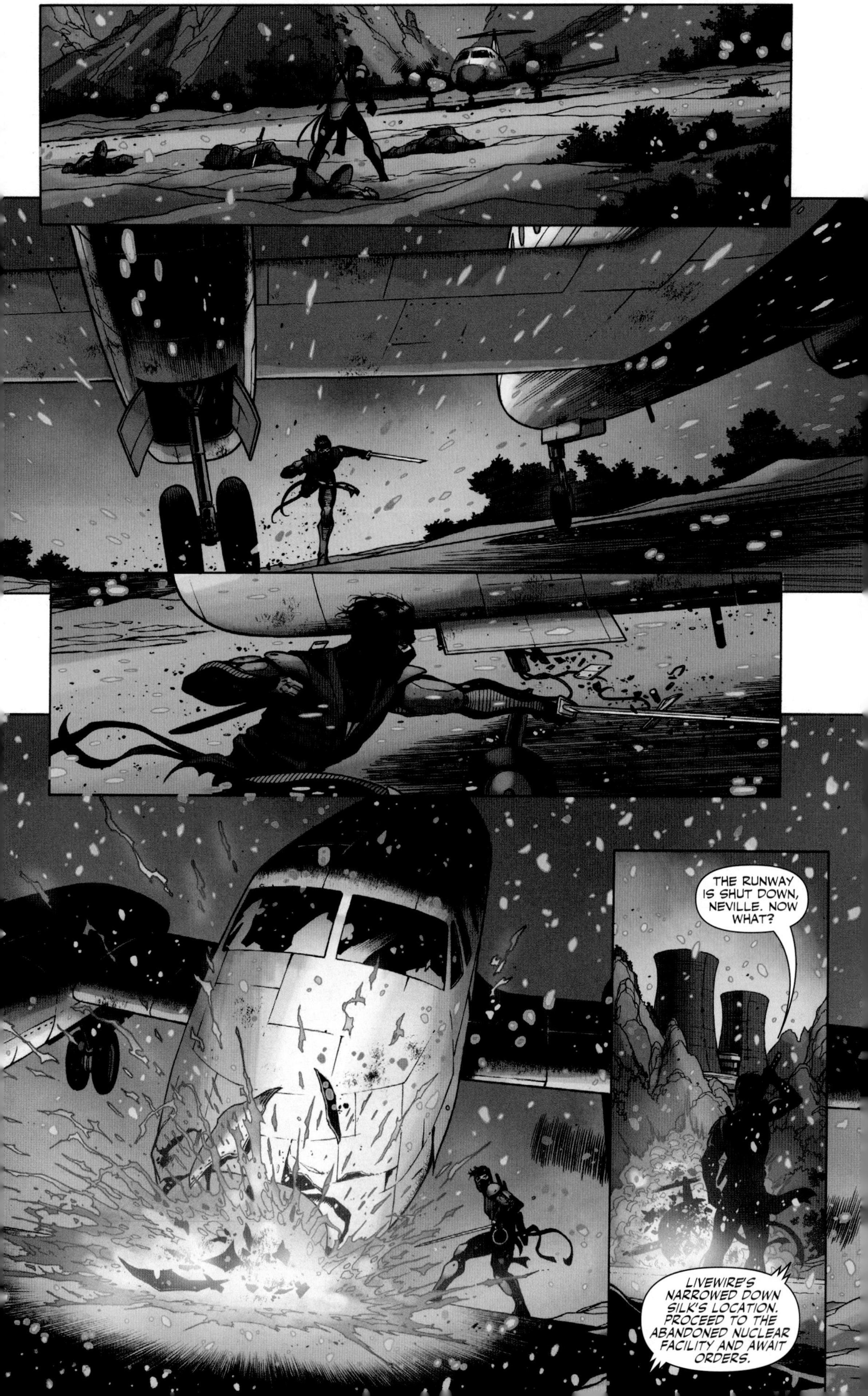
THE RUNWAY IS SHUT DOWN, NEVILLE. NOW WHAT?
LIVEWIRE'S NARROWED DOWN SILK'S LOCATION. PROCEED TO THE ABANDONED NUCLEAR FACILITY AND AWAIT ORDERS.

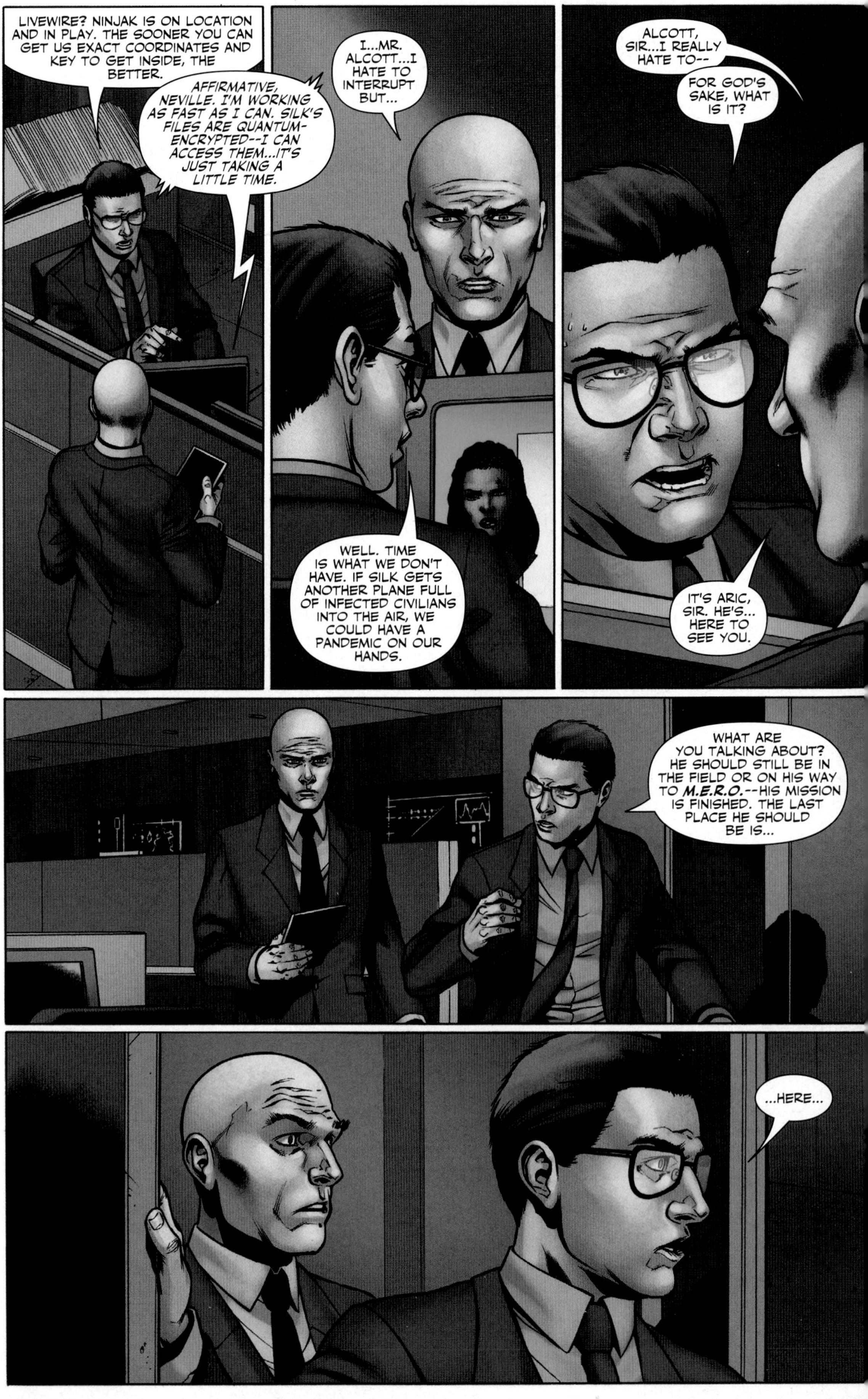
LIVEWIRE? NINJAK IS ON LOCATION AND IN PLAY. THE SOONER YOU CAN GET US EXACT COORDINATES AND KEY TO GET INSIDE, THE BETTER.
AFFIRMATIVE, NEVILLE. I'M WORKING AS FAST AS I CAN. SILK'S FILES ARE QUANTUM-ENCRYPTED--I CAN ACCESS THEM...IT'S JUST TAKING A LITTLE TIME.
I...MR. ALCOTT...I HATE TO INTERRUPT BUT...
WELL. TIME IS WHAT WE DON'T HAVE. IF SILK GETS ANOTHER PLANE FULL OF INFECTED CIVILIANS INTO THE AIR, WE COULD HAVE A PANDEMIC ON OUR HANDS.
ALCOTT, SIR...I REALLY HATE TO--
FOR GOD'S SAKE, WHAT IS IT?
IT'S ARIC, SIR. HE'S... HERE TO SEE YOU.
WHAT ARE YOU TALKING ABOUT? HE SHOULD STILL BE IN THE FIELD OR ON HIS WAY TO M.E.R.O.--HIS MISSION IS FINISHED. THE LAST PLACE HE SHOULD BE IS...
...HERE...

I UNDERSTAND THAT WHAT I DID WAS NECESSARY.

BUT IF THERE IS A CHANCE THAT SILK'S VIRUS CAN BE REVERSED, THEN I INSIST YOU TRY. I WON'T BE RESPONSIBLE FOR THE DEATH OF INNOCENTS.

GET THIS KID INTO QUARANTINE IMMEDIATELY! AND LOCK DOWN THE OFFICE AND CONFIRM THAT HE HASN'T INFECTED THE ENTIRE SECTION.

WE'RE RACING THE CLOCK HERE, ARIC. IF THERE WAS ANOTHER WAY I WOULDN'T HAVE GIVEN YOU THE ORDER. THE VIRUS DESTROYS THE BRAIN OF ITS VICTIM AND REPLACES IT WITH WHATEVER SILK PUTS THERE. THAT CHILD WAS DEAD BEFORE YOU WERE IN THE AIR.

I CAN APPRECIATE THE SENTIMENT. YOU'RE NEEDED BACK AT M.E.R.O., YOUR NEW BOSS OVER THERE, CAPSHAW, HAS BEEN ON MY ASS TO GET YOU BACK. SO GO. WE CAN TAKE IT FROM HERE.

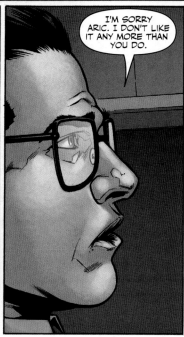

I'M SORRY ARIC. I DON'T LIKE IT ANY MORE THAN YOU DO.

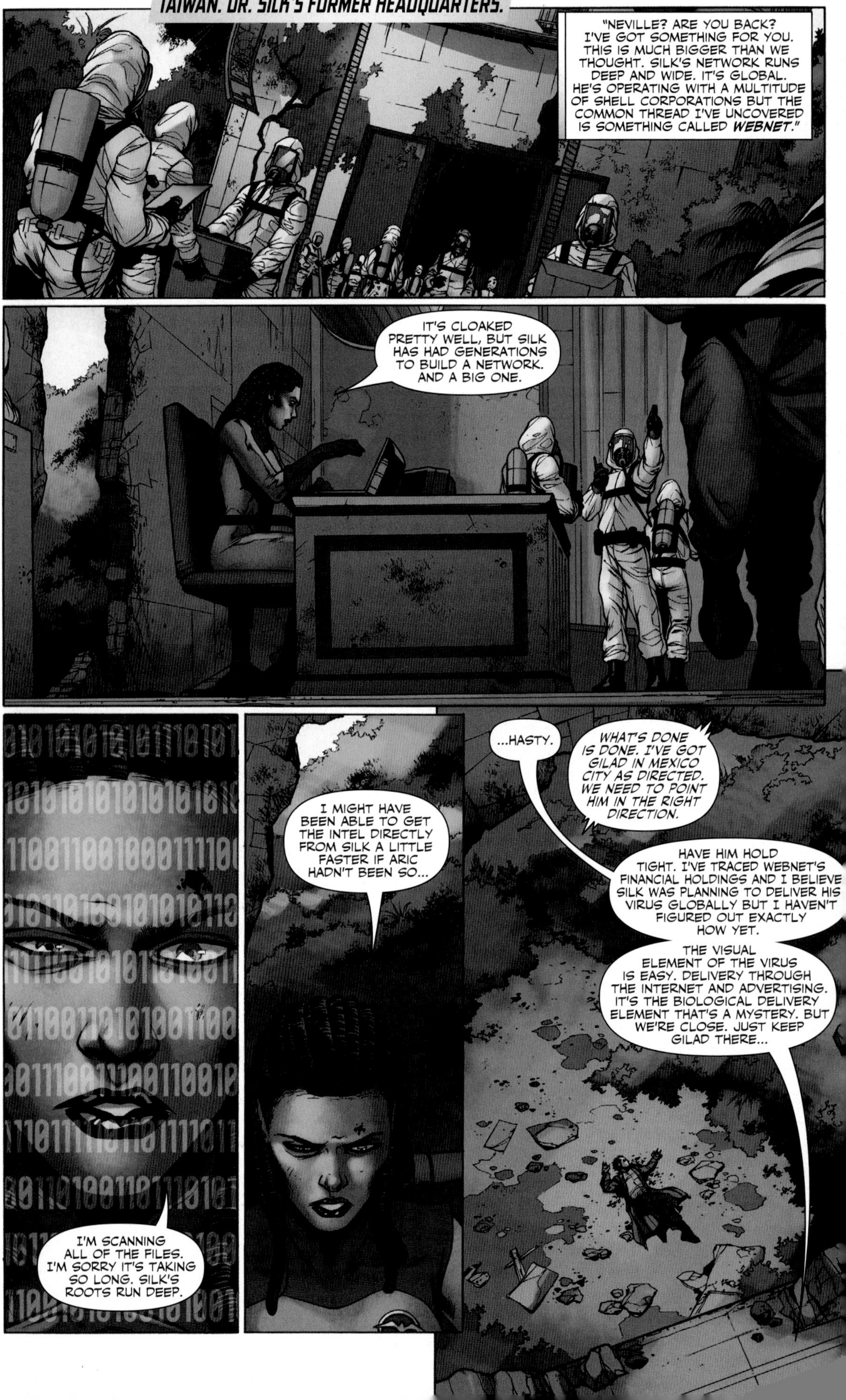
TAIWAN. DR. SILK'S FORMER HEADQUARTERS.
"NEVILLE? ARE YOU BACK? I'VE GOT SOMETHING FOR YOU. THIS IS MUCH BIGGER THAN WE THOUGHT. SILK'S NETWORK RUNS DEEP AND WIDE. IT'S GLOBAL. HE'S OPERATING WITH A MULTITUDE OF SHELL CORPORATIONS BUT THE COMMON THREAD I'VE UNCOVERED IS SOMETHING CALLED WEBNET."
IT'S CLOAKED PRETTY WELL, BUT SILK HAS HAD GENERATIONS TO BUILD A NETWORK. AND A BIG ONE.
I'M SCANNING ALL OF THE FILES. I'M SORRY IT'S TAKING SO LONG. SILK'S ROOTS RUN DEEP.
I MIGHT HAVE BEEN ABLE TO GET THE INTEL DIRECTLY FROM SILK A LITTLE FASTER IF ARIC HADN'T BEEN SO...
...HASTY.
WHAT'S DONE IS DONE. I'VE GOT GILAD IN MEXICO CITY AS DIRECTED. WE NEED TO POINT HIM IN THE RIGHT DIRECTION.
HAVE HIM HOLD TIGHT. I'VE TRACED WEBNET'S FINANCIAL HOLDINGS AND I BELIEVE SILK WAS PLANNING TO DELIVER HIS VIRUS GLOBALLY BUT I HAVEN'T FIGURED OUT EXACTLY HOW YET.
THE VISUAL ELEMENT OF THE VIRUS IS EASY. DELIVERY THROUGH THE INTERNET AND ADVERTISING. IT'S THE BIOLOGICAL DELIVERY ELEMENT THAT'S A MYSTERY. BUT WE'RE CLOSE. JUST KEEP GILAD THERE...

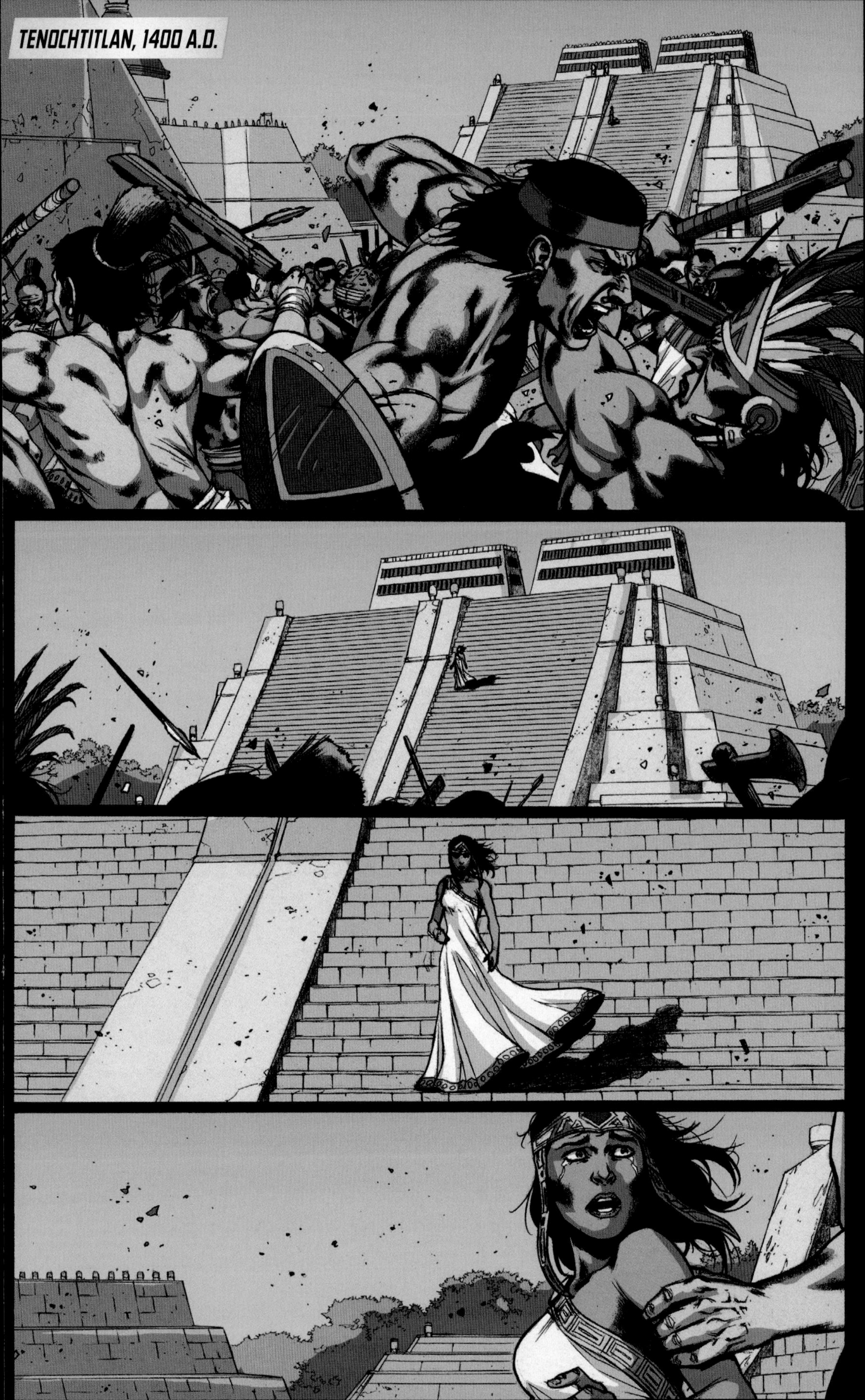
TENOCHTITLAN, 1400 A.D.

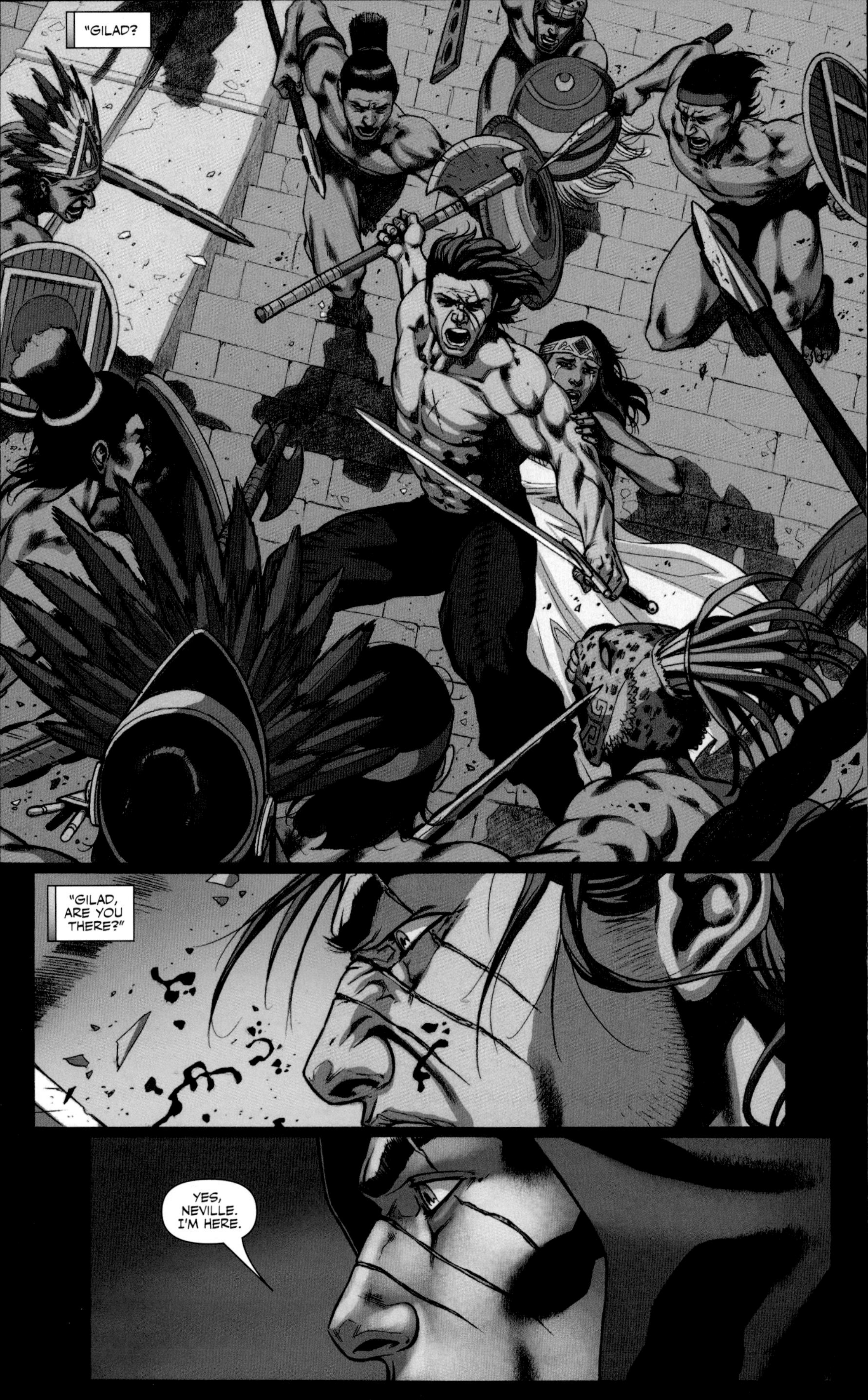
"GILAD?
"GILAD, ARE YOU THERE?"
YES, NEVILLE. I'M HERE.

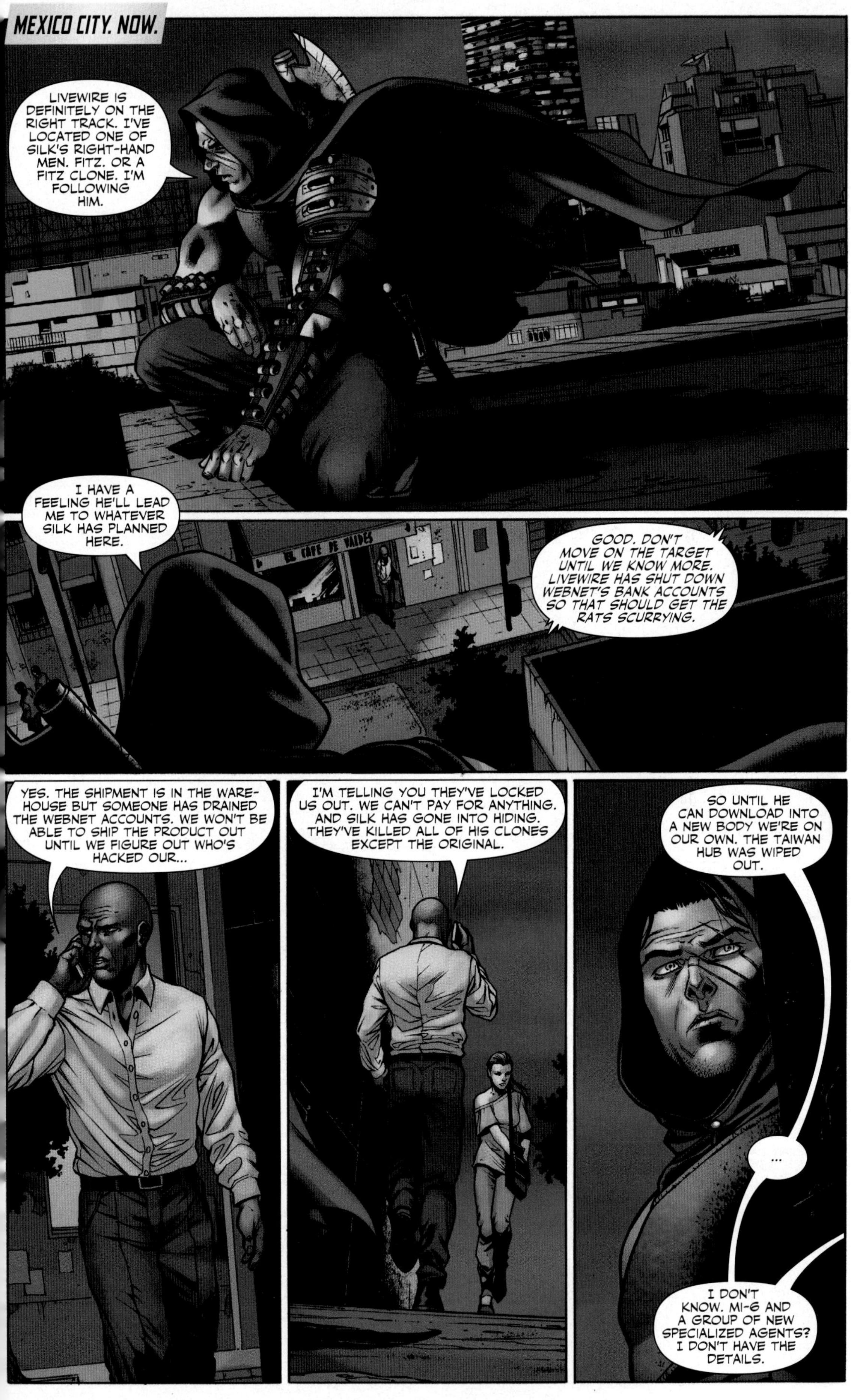
MEXICO CITY. NOW.
LIVEWIRE IS DEFINITELY ON THE RIGHT TRACK. I'VE LOCATED ONE OF SILK'S RIGHT-HAND MEN. FITZ. OR A FITZ CLONE. I'M FOLLOWING HIM.
I HAVE A FEELING HE'LL LEAD ME TO WHATEVER SILK HAS PLANNED HERE.
GOOD. DON'T MOVE ON THE TARGET UNTIL WE KNOW MORE. LIVEWIRE HAS SHUT DOWN WEBNET'S BANK ACCOUNTS SO THAT SHOULD GET THE RATS SCURRYING.
YES. THE SHIPMENT IS IN THE WARE-HOUSE BUT SOMEONE HAS DRAINED THE WEBNET ACCOUNTS. WE WON'T BE ABLE TO SHIP THE PRODUCT OUT UNTIL WE FIGURE OUT WHO'S HACKED OUR...
I'M TELLING YOU THEY'VE LOCKED US OUT. WE CAN'T PAY FOR ANYTHING. AND SILK HAS GONE INTO HIDING. THEY'VE KILLED ALL OF HIS CLONES EXCEPT THE ORIGINAL.
SO UNTIL HE CAN DOWNLOAD INTO A NEW BODY WE'RE ON OUR OWN. THE TAIWAN HUB WAS WIPED OUT.
...
I DON'T KNOW. MI-6 AND A GROUP OF NEW SPECIALIZED AGENTS? I DON'T HAVE THE DETAILS.

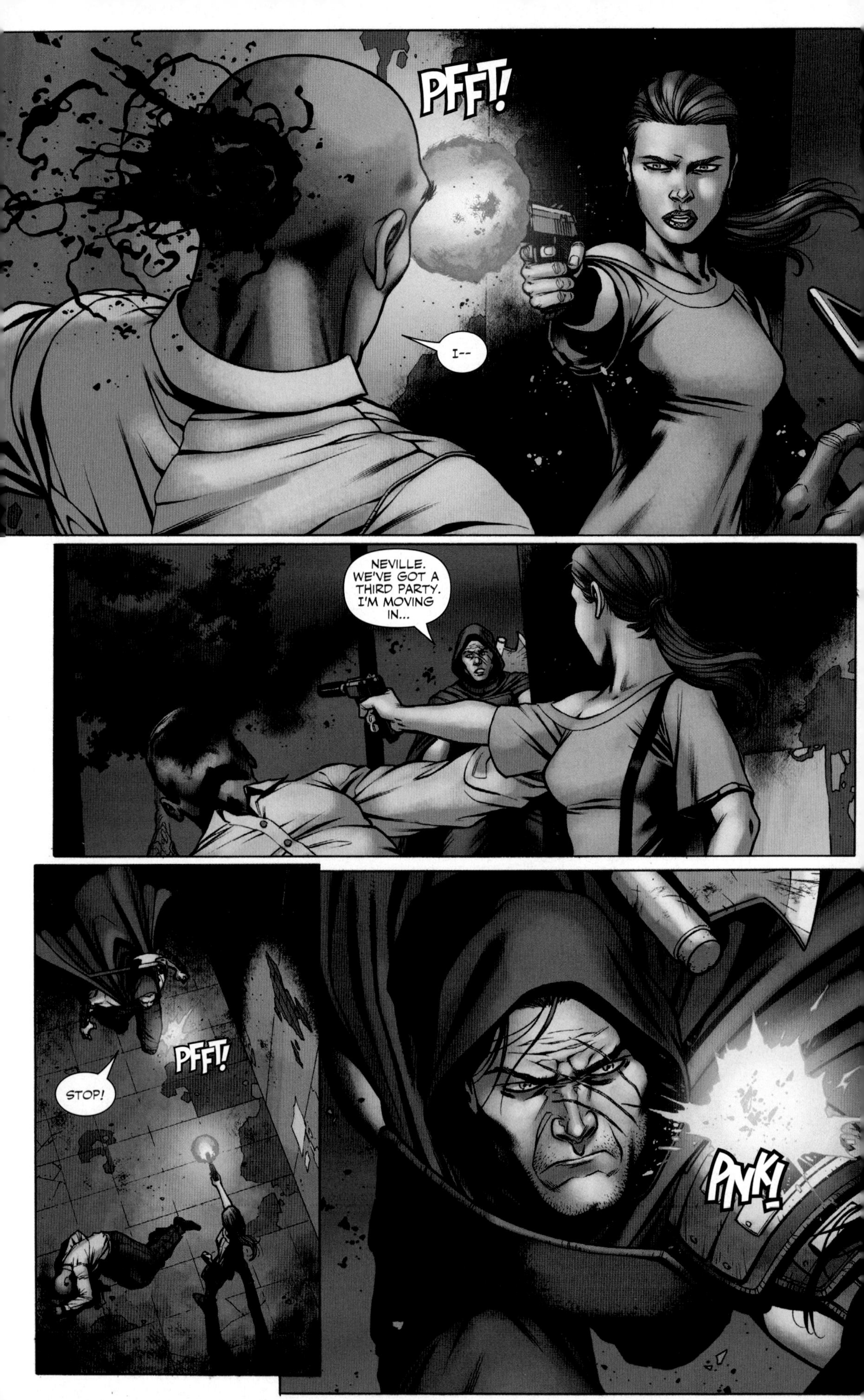
PFFT!
I--
NEVILLE. WE'VE GOT A THIRD PARTY. I'M MOVING IN...
PFFT!
STOP!
PNK!

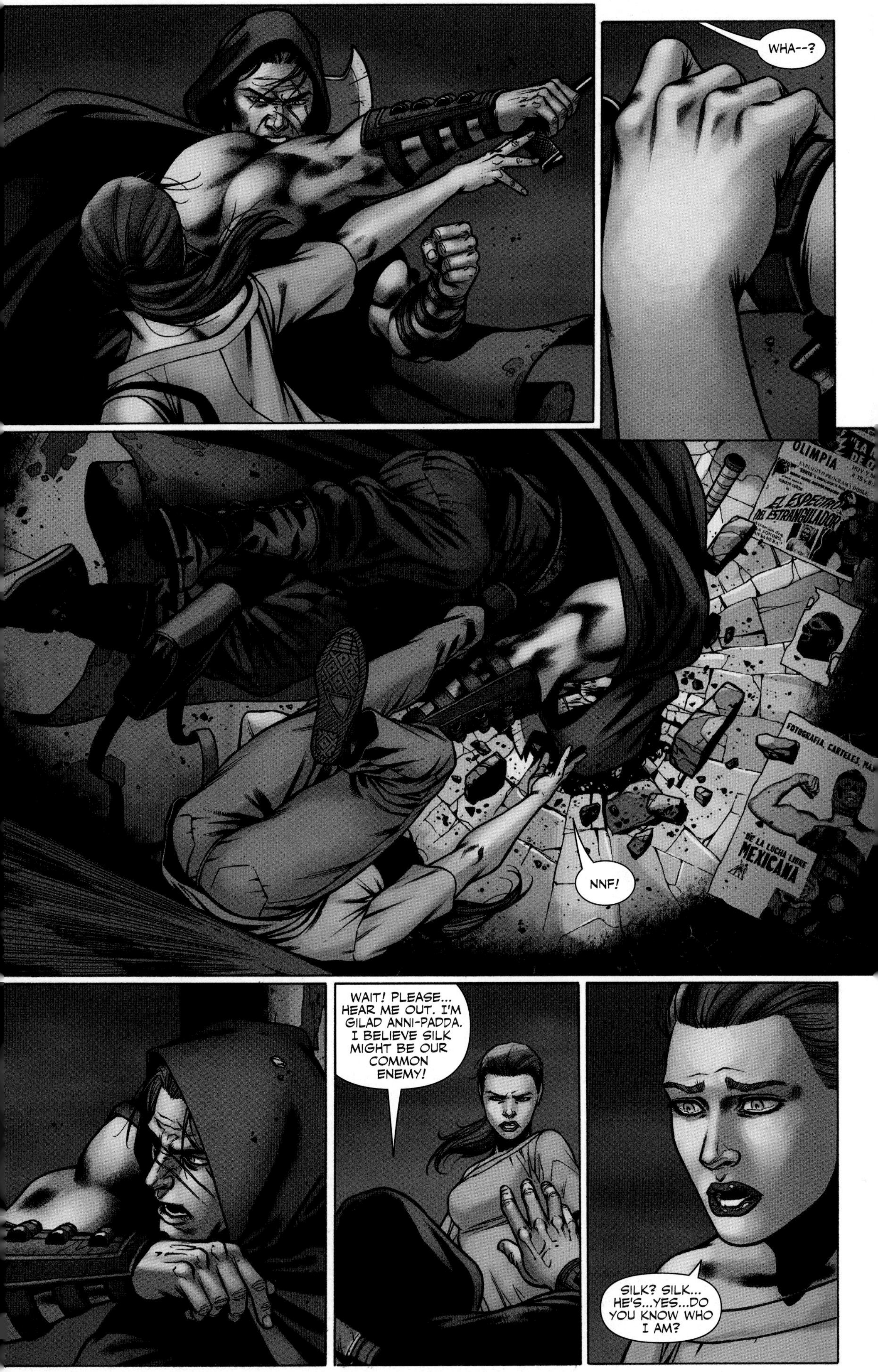
WHA--?
OLIMPIA
EL ESPECTRO DEL ESTRANGULADOR
FOTOGRAFIA, CARTELES,
DE LA LUCHA LIBRE MEXICANA
NNF!
WAIT! PLEASE... HEAR ME OUT. I'M GILAD ANNI-PADDA. I BELIEVE SILK MIGHT BE OUR COMMON ENEMY!
SILK? SILK... HE'S...YES...DO YOU KNOW WHO I AM?

MY NAME IS DELL. I WORKED WITH SILK LONG AGO. AND LONG AGO? HE BETRAYED ME. HE USED THE TECHNOLOGY WE'D CREATED TOGETHER. THE TECHNOLOGY TO TRANSFER A PERSON'S MIND. TO COPY THEM IN EFFECT.

HE DID THIS TO ME... TH-THOUSANDS OF TIMES. EDITING MY THOUGHTS. MY MIND.

HE TRIED TO MOLD ME INTO SOMETHING...AND LEFT ME LIKE THIS. A HOLLOW SHELL OF WHO I USED TO BE. BENT ON REVENGE.

HE BRANDED ME WITH HIS VIRUS. ON MY BACK. A SORT OF LIVING CARRIER OF THE INFECTION. BUT YOU KNOW IT'S A TWO-STAGE SYSTEM. YOU HAVE TO SEE THE SYMBOLS AND BE EXPOSED TO THE BIOLOGICAL PATHOGEN OR HIS BRAINWASHING WON'T TAKE EFFECT.

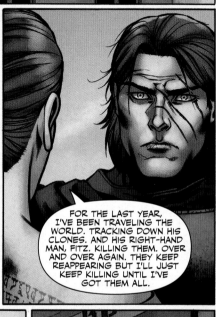

FOR THE LAST YEAR, I'VE BEEN TRAVELING THE WORLD. TRACKING DOWN HIS CLONES. AND HIS RIGHT-HAND MAN, FITZ. KILLING THEM. OVER AND OVER AGAIN. THEY KEEP REAPPEARING BUT I'LL JUST KEEP KILLING UNTIL I'VE GOT THEM ALL.

SOMETHING BIG IS GOING ON HERE. HE'S WORKING ON A WAY TO SPREAD HIS VIRUS WORLDWIDE. HE'S FIGURED OUT A WAY TO DISTRIBUTE GLOBALLY. WE THINK HE'S NEARLY READY, DELL. MY ALLIES HAVE TRACKED HIS ACTIVITIES HERE.

THE FITZ I JUST KILLED? HE'S BEEN COMING AND GOING FOR THE LAST WEEK. IN A PANIC. YOU GUYS MUST HAVE STIRRED SOMETHING UP. LET ME SHOW YOU SOMETHING.

THERE HAS BEEN A LOT OF ACTIVITY AROUND HERE...

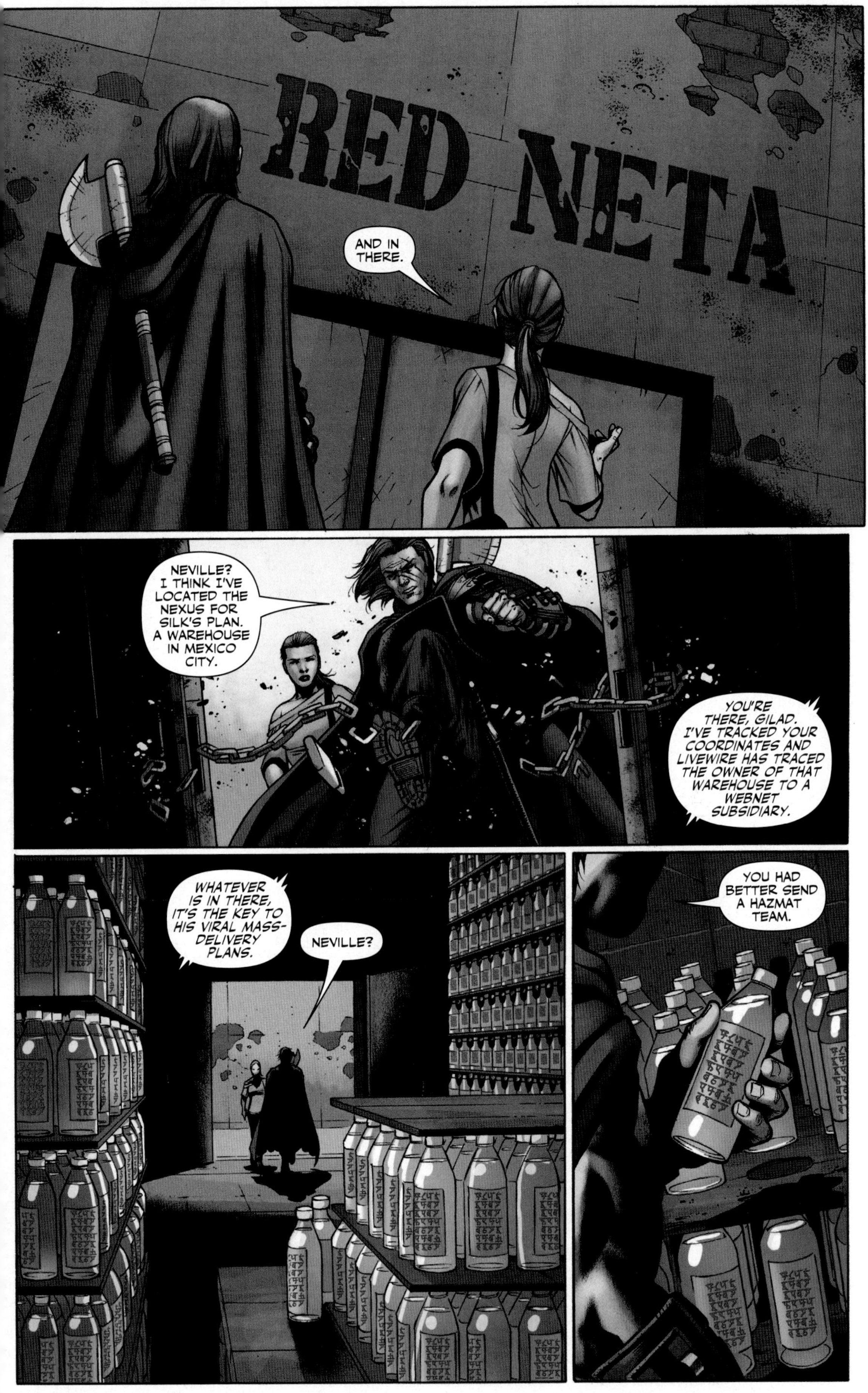
RED NETA
AND IN THERE.
NEVILLE? I THINK I'VE LOCATED THE NEXUS FOR SILK'S PLAN. A WAREHOUSE IN MEXICO CITY.
YOU'RE THERE, GILAD. I'VE TRACKED YOUR COORDINATES AND LIVEWIRE HAS TRACED THE OWNER OF THAT WAREHOUSE TO A WEBNET SUBSIDIARY.
WHATEVER IS IN THERE, IT'S THE KEY TO HIS VIRAL MASS-DELIVERY PLANS.
NEVILLE?
YOU HAD BETTER SEND A HAZMAT TEAM.

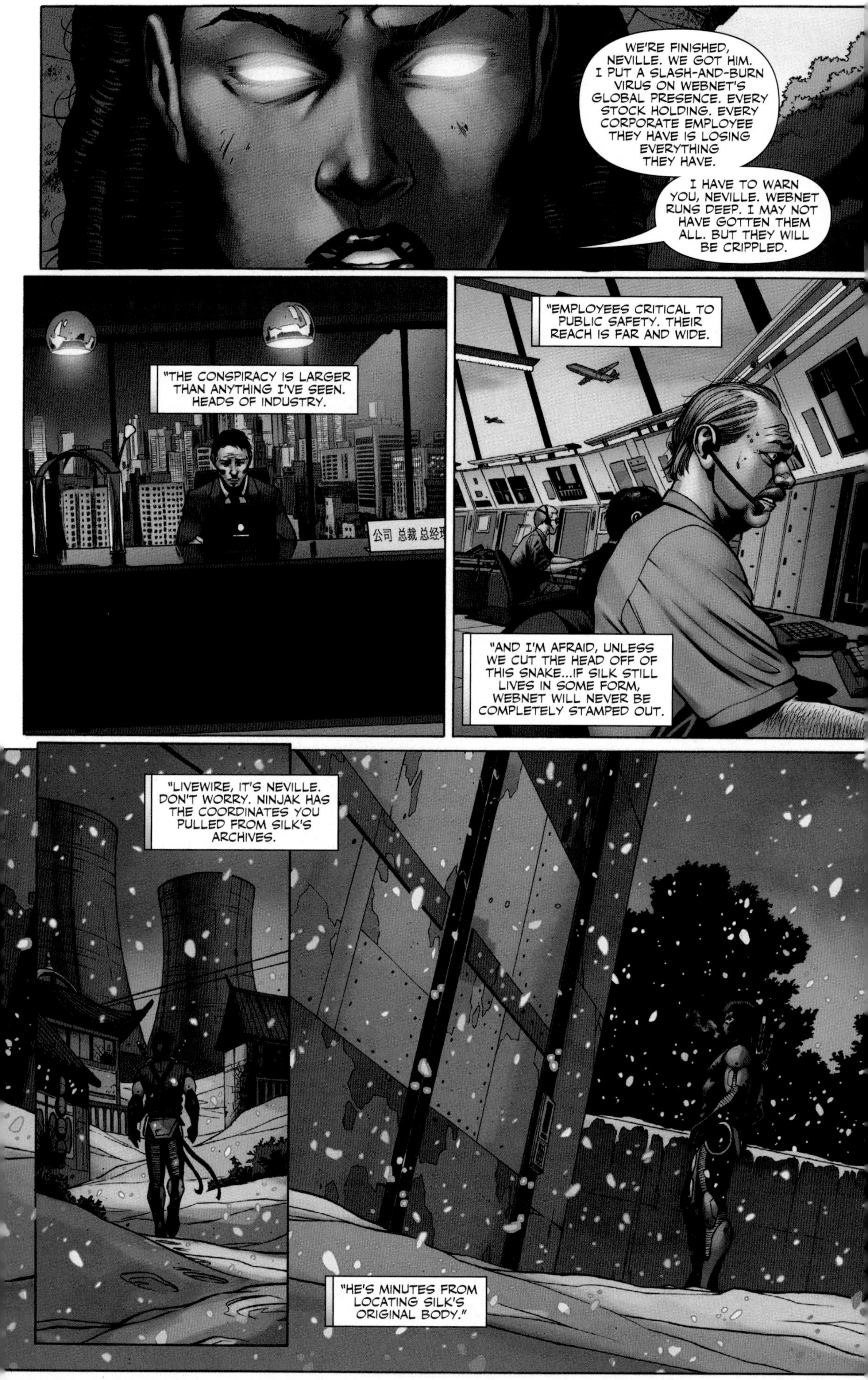
WE'RE FINISHED, NEVILLE. WE GOT HIM. I PUT A SLASH-AND-BURN VIRUS ON WEBNET'S GLOBAL PRESENCE. EVERY STOCK HOLDING. EVERY CORPORATE EMPLOYEE THEY HAVE IS LOSING EVERYTHING THEY HAVE.
I HAVE TO WARN YOU, NEVILLE. WEBNET RUNS DEEP. I MAY NOT HAVE GOTTEN THEM ALL. BUT THEY WILL BE CRIPPLED.
"THE CONSPIRACY IS LARGER THAN ANYTHING I'VE SEEN. HEADS OF INDUSTRY.
公司 总裁 总经理
"EMPLOYEES CRITICAL TO PUBLIC SAFETY. THEIR REACH IS FAR AND WIDE.
"AND I'M AFRAID, UNLESS WE CUT THE HEAD OFF OF THIS SNAKE...IF SILK STILL LIVES IN SOME FORM, WEBNET WILL NEVER BE COMPLETELY STAMPED OUT.
"LIVEWIRE, IT'S NEVILLE. DON'T WORRY. NINJAK HAS THE COORDINATES YOU PULLED FROM SILK'S ARCHIVES.
"HE'S MINUTES FROM LOCATING SILK'S ORIGINAL BODY."

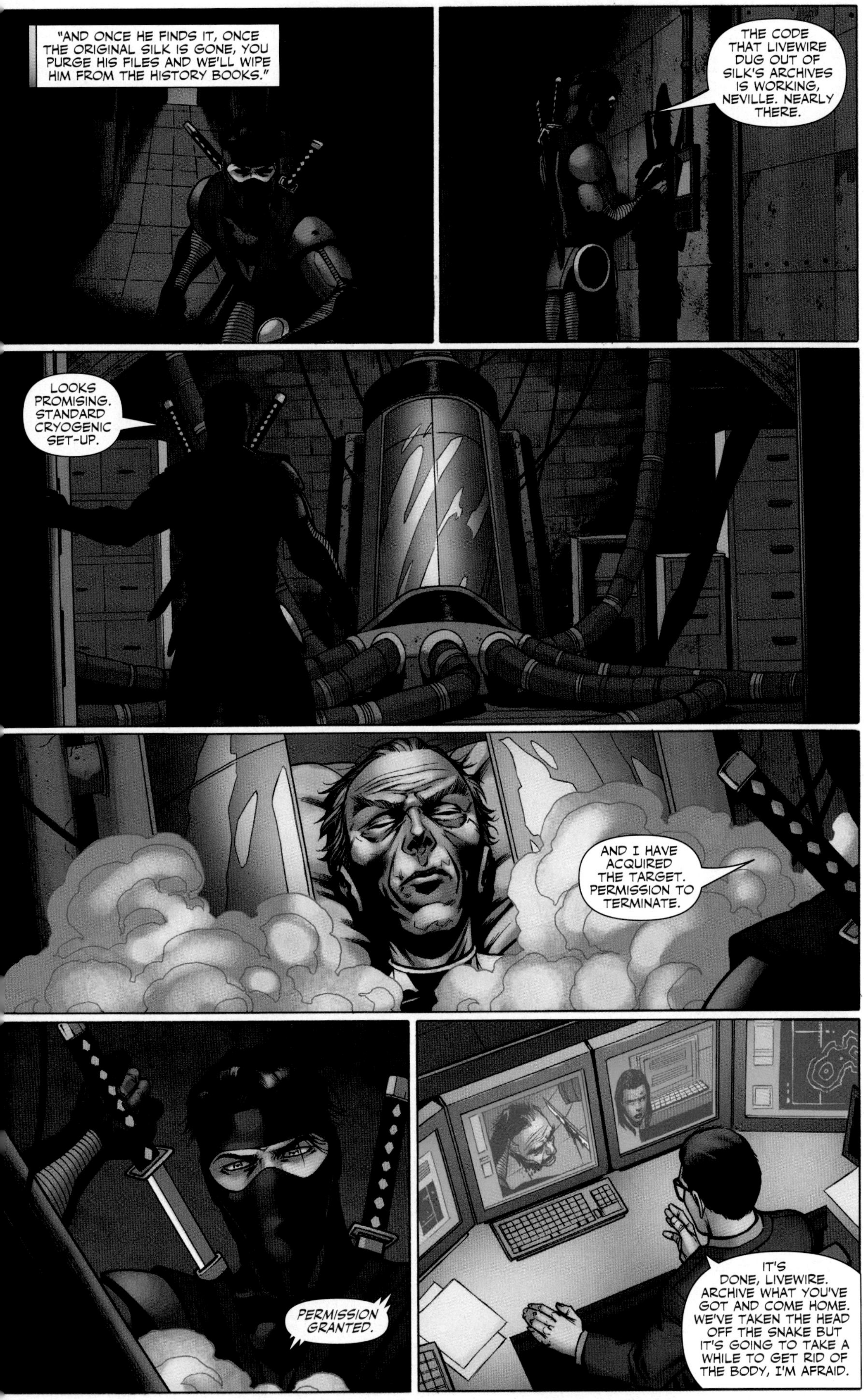
"AND ONCE HE FINDS IT, ONCE THE ORIGINAL SILK IS GONE, YOU PURGE HIS FILES AND WE'LL WIPE HIM FROM THE HISTORY BOOKS."
THE CODE THAT LIVEWIRE DUG OUT OF SILK'S ARCHIVES IS WORKING, NEVILLE. NEARLY THERE.
LOOKS PROMISING. STANDARD CRYOGENIC SET-UP.
AND I HAVE ACQUIRED THE TARGET. PERMISSION TO TERMINATE.
PERMISSION GRANTED.
IT'S DONE, LIVEWIRE. ARCHIVE WHAT YOU'VE GOT AND COME HOME. WE'VE TAKEN THE HEAD OFF THE SNAKE BUT IT'S GOING TO TAKE A WHILE TO GET RID OF THE BODY, I'M AFRAID.

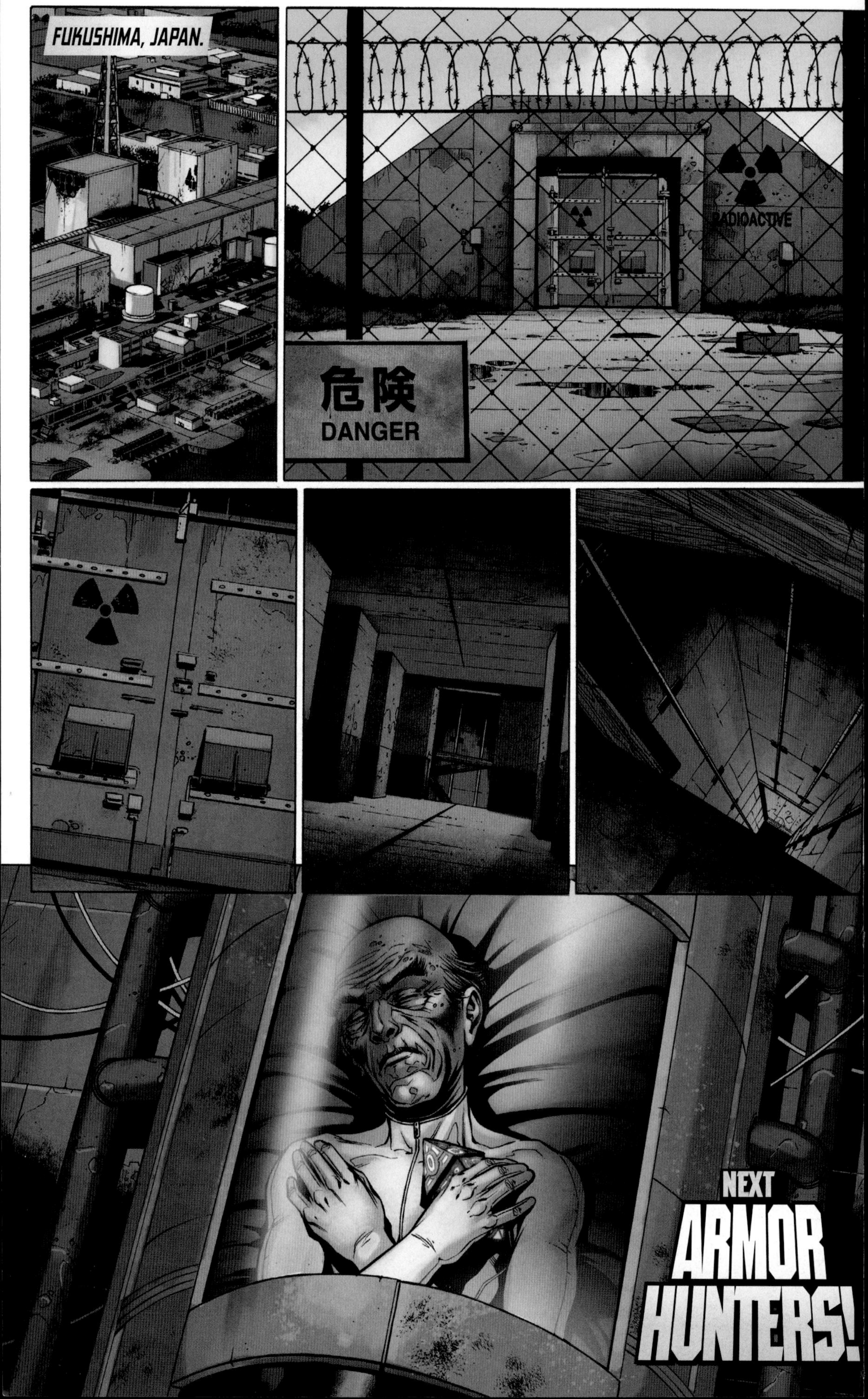
FUKUSHIMA, JAPAN.
RADIOACTIVE
危険
DANGER
NEXT
ARMOR HUNTERS!

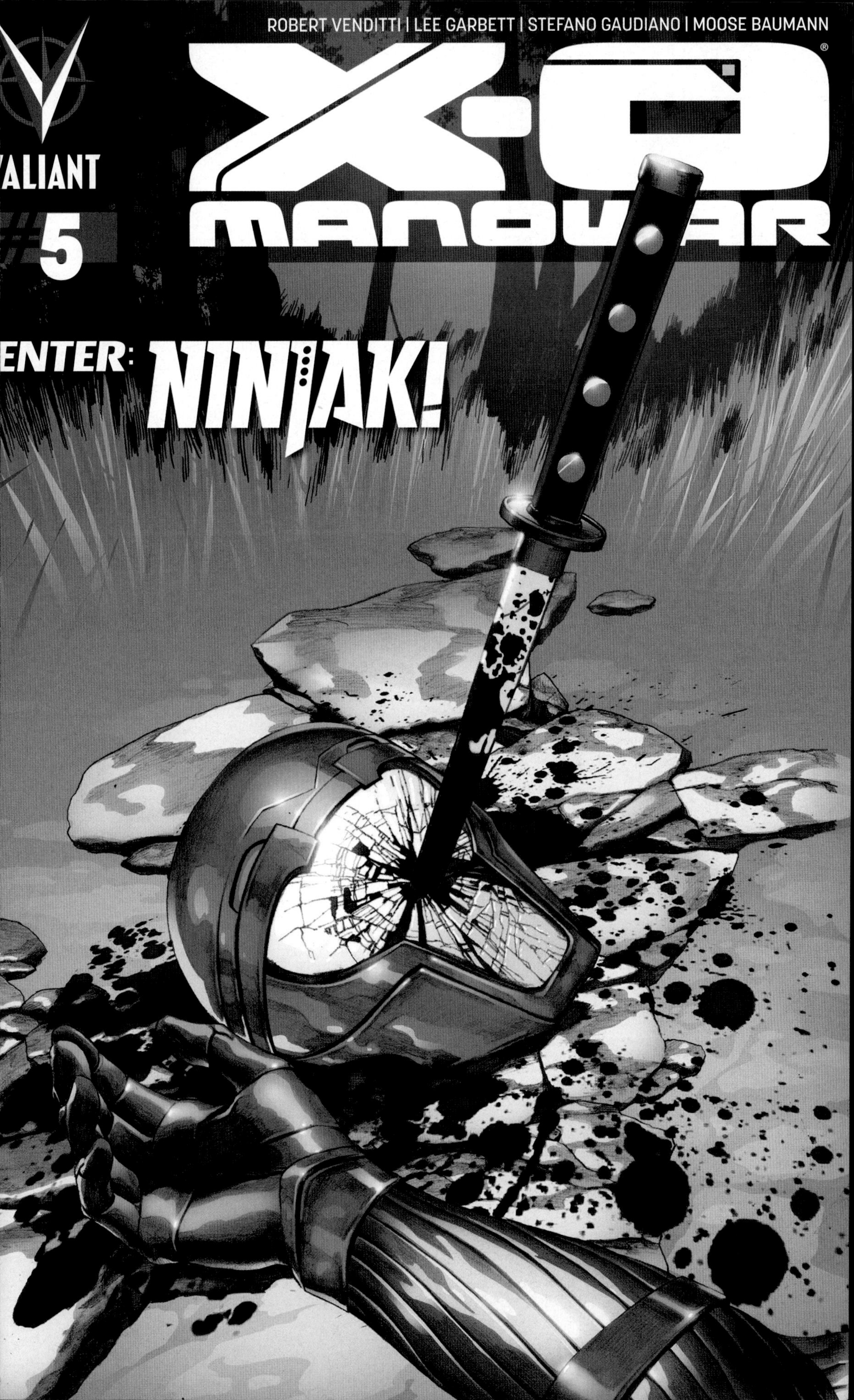

ROBERT VENDITTI | LEE GARBETT | STEFANO GAUDIANO | MOOSE BAUMANN
VALIANT
X-O MANOWAR
#5
ENTER: NINJAK!

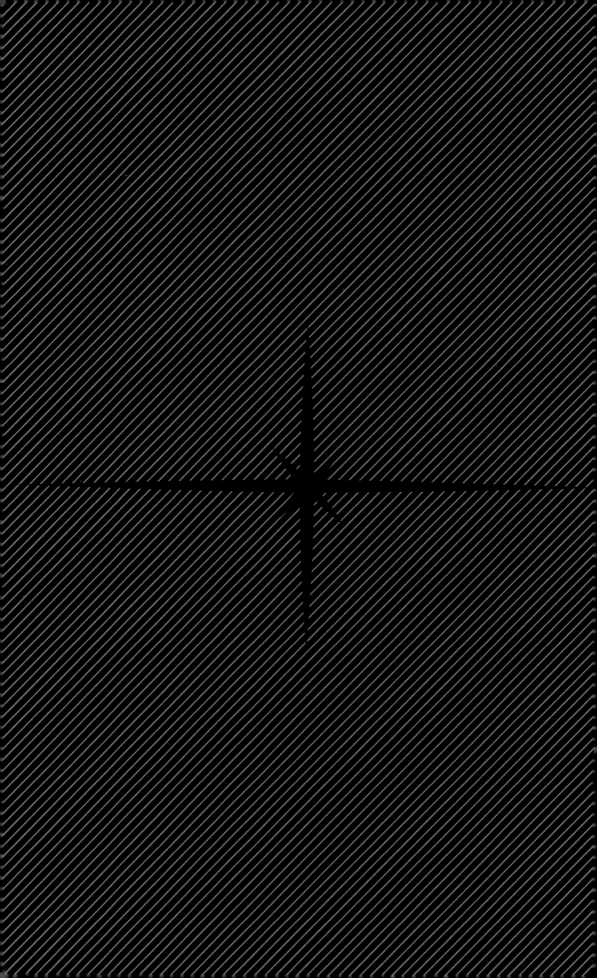

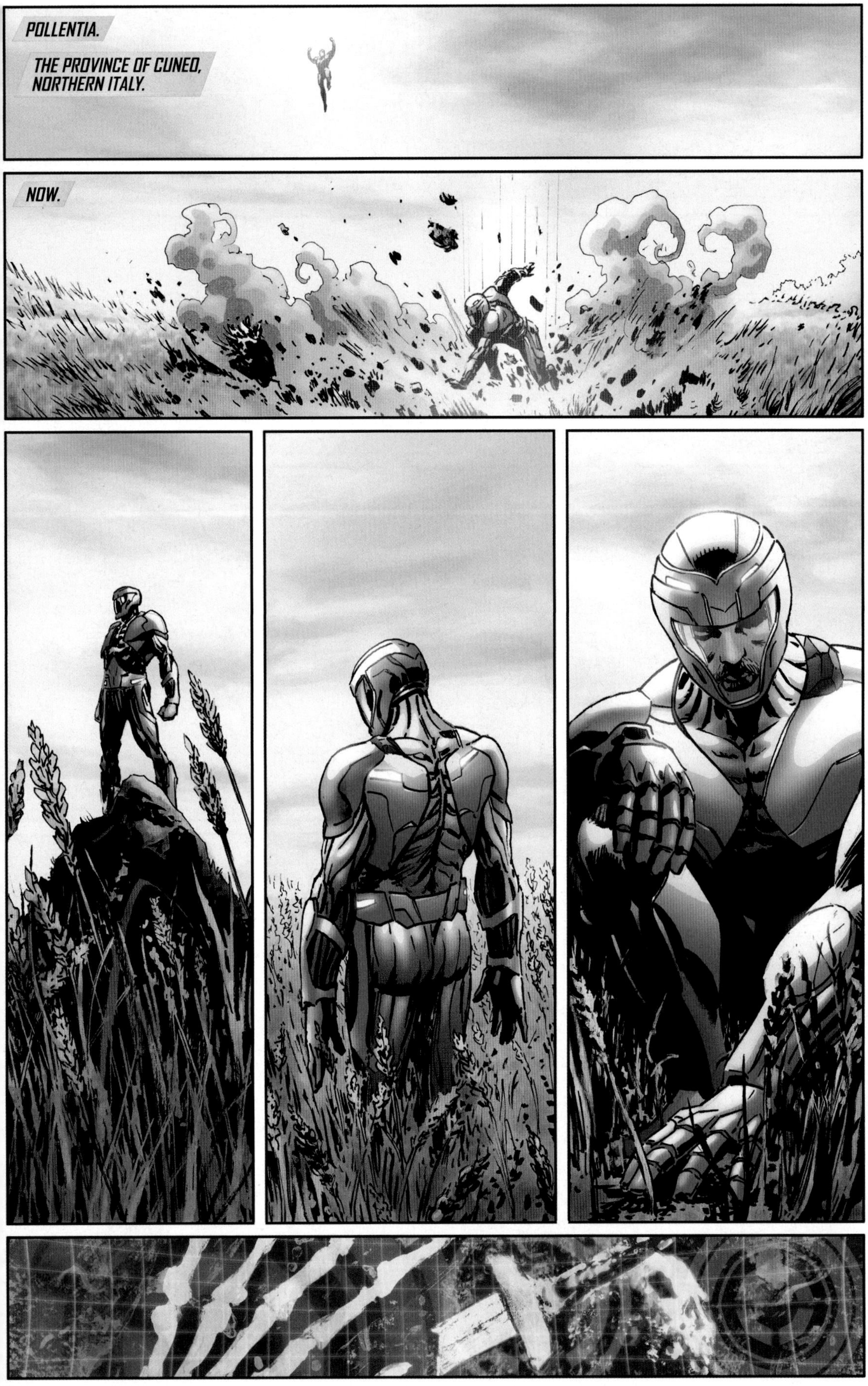
POLLENTIA.
THE PROVINCE OF CUNEO, NORTHERN ITALY.
NOW.

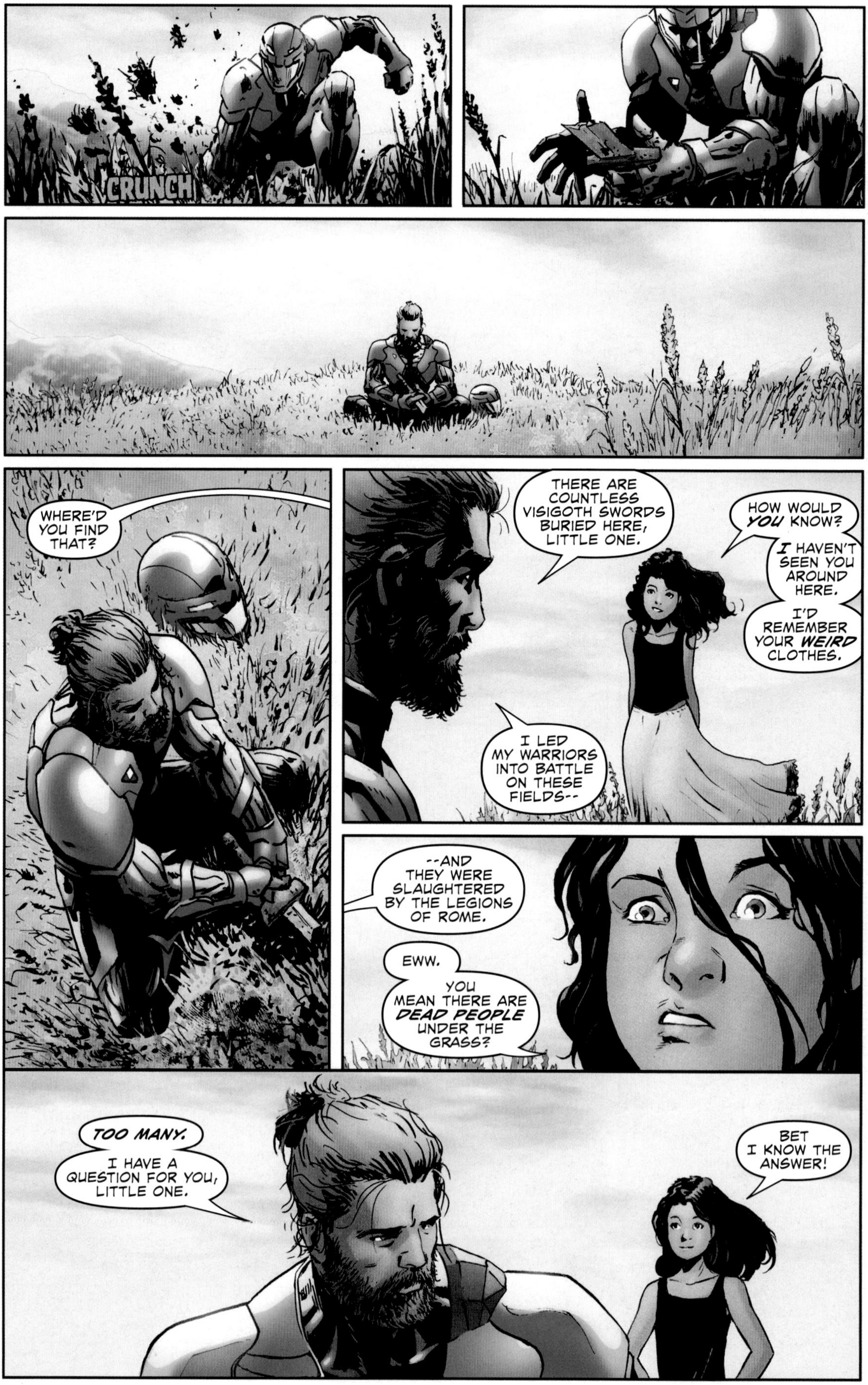
CRUNCH
WHERE'D YOU FIND THAT?
THERE ARE COUNTLESS VISIGOTH SWORDS BURIED HERE, LITTLE ONE.
HOW WOULD YOU KNOW?
I HAVEN'T SEEN YOU AROUND HERE.
I'D REMEMBER YOUR WEIRD CLOTHES.
I LED MY WARRIORS INTO BATTLE ON THESE FIELDS--
--AND THEY WERE SLAUGHTERED BY THE LEGIONS OF ROME.
EWW.
YOU MEAN THERE ARE DEAD PEOPLE UNDER THE GRASS?
TOO MANY.
I HAVE A QUESTION FOR YOU, LITTLE ONE.
BET I KNOW THE ANSWER!

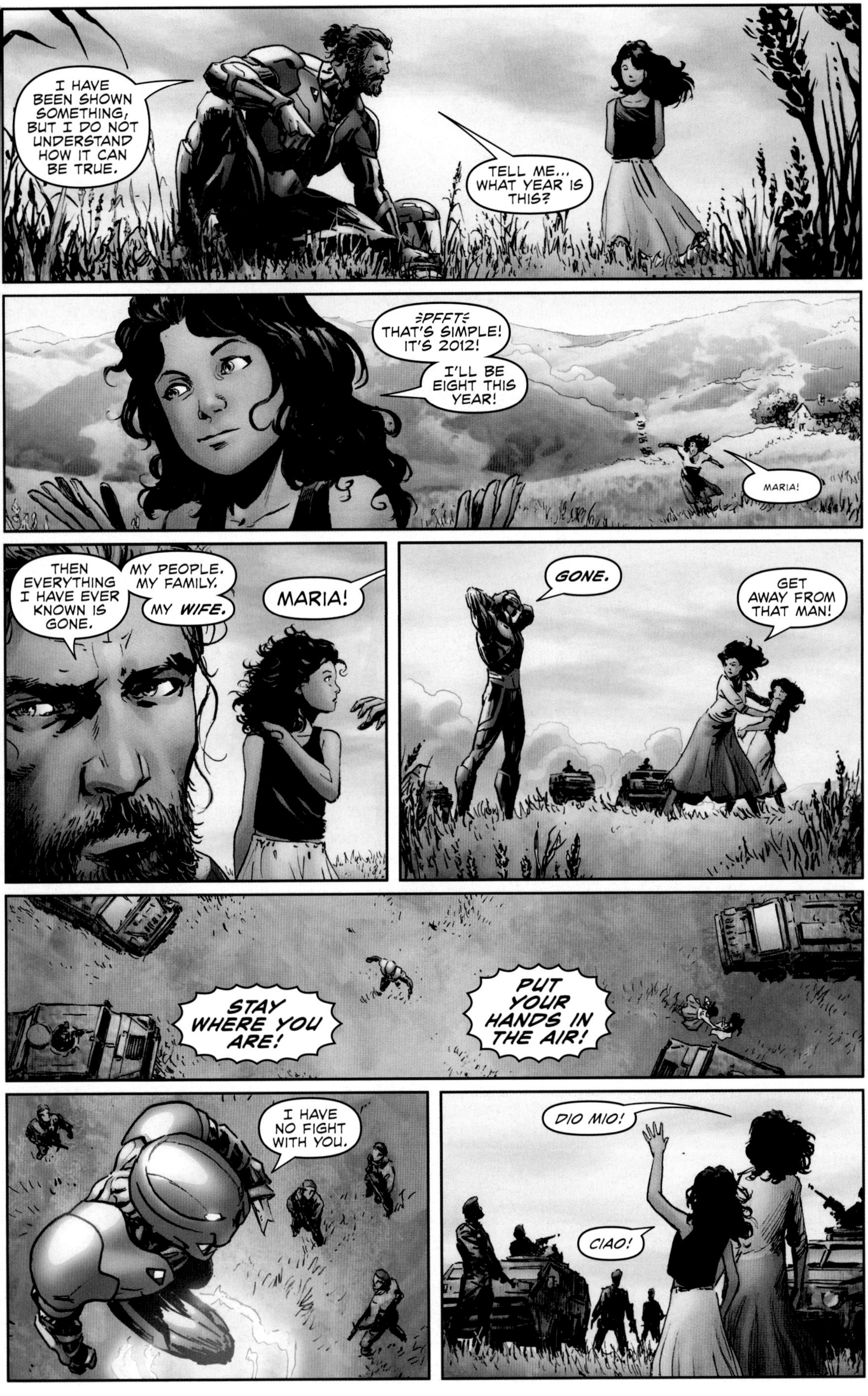
I HAVE BEEN SHOWN SOMETHING, BUT I DO NOT UNDERSTAND HOW IT CAN BE TRUE.
TELL ME... WHAT YEAR IS THIS?
=PFFT= THAT'S SIMPLE! IT'S 2012!
I'LL BE EIGHT THIS YEAR!
MARIA!
THEN EVERYTHING I HAVE EVER KNOWN IS GONE.
MY PEOPLE. MY FAMILY.
MY WIFE.
MARIA!
GONE.
GET AWAY FROM THAT MAN!
STAY WHERE YOU ARE!
PUT YOUR HANDS IN THE AIR!
I HAVE NO FIGHT WITH YOU.
DIO MIO!
CIAO!

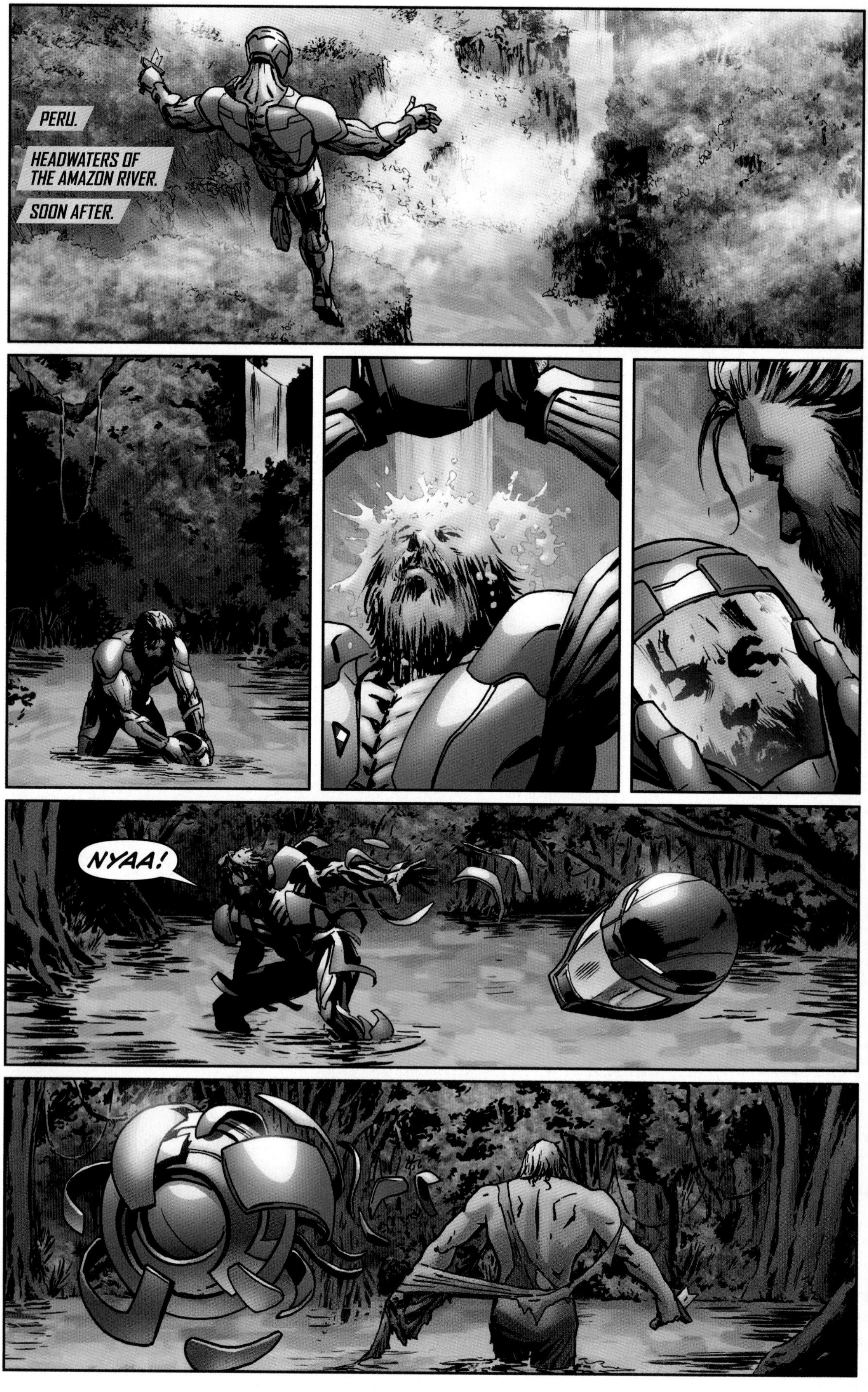
PERU.
HEADWATERS OF THE AMAZON RIVER.
SOON AFTER.
NYAA!

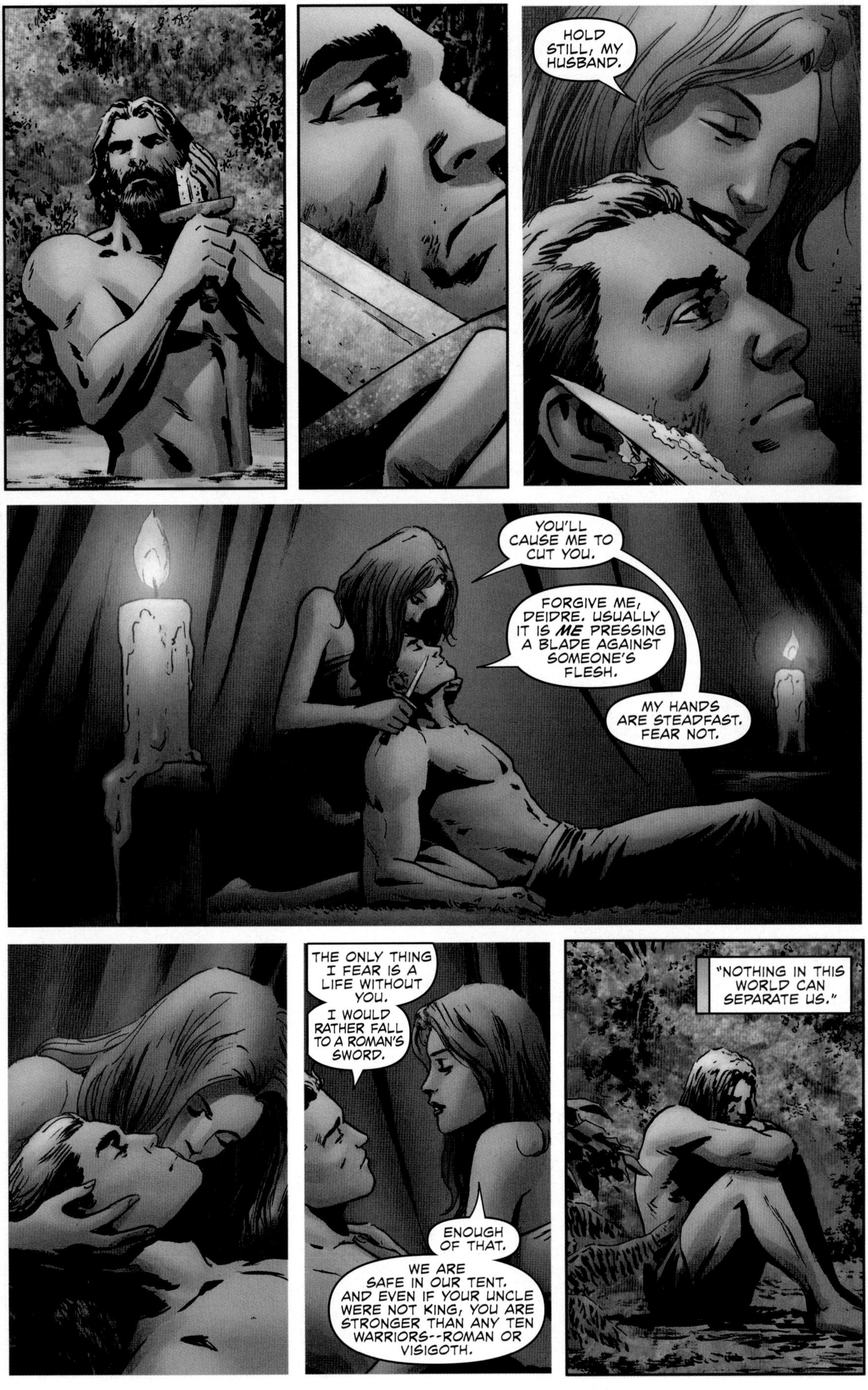
HOLD STILL, MY HUSBAND.
YOU'LL CAUSE ME TO CUT YOU.
FORGIVE ME, DEIDRE. USUALLY IT IS ME PRESSING A BLADE AGAINST SOMEONE'S FLESH.
MY HANDS ARE STEADFAST. FEAR NOT.
THE ONLY THING I FEAR IS A LIFE WITHOUT YOU.
I WOULD RATHER FALL TO A ROMAN'S SWORD.
ENOUGH OF THAT.
WE ARE SAFE IN OUR TENT. AND EVEN IF YOUR UNCLE WERE NOT KING, YOU ARE STRONGER THAN ANY TEN WARRIORS--ROMAN OR VISIGOTH.
"NOTHING IN THIS WORLD CAN SEPARATE US."

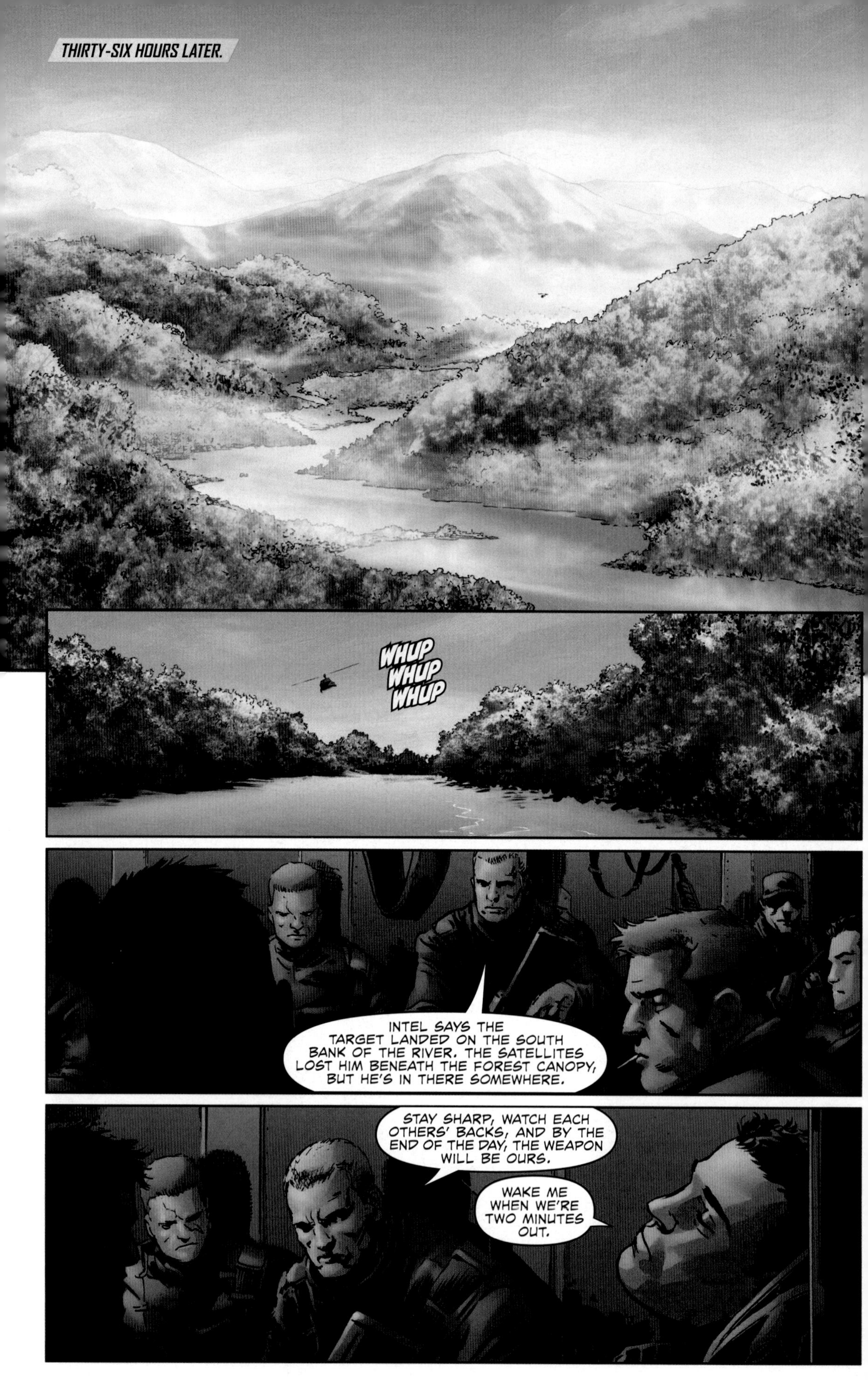
THIRTY-SIX HOURS LATER.
WHUP WHUP WHUP
INTEL SAYS THE TARGET LANDED ON THE SOUTH BANK OF THE RIVER. THE SATELLITES LOST HIM BENEATH THE FOREST CANOPY, BUT HE'S IN THERE SOMEWHERE.
STAY SHARP, WATCH EACH OTHERS' BACKS, AND BY THE END OF THE DAY, THE WEAPON WILL BE OURS.
WAKE ME WHEN WE'RE TWO MINUTES OUT.

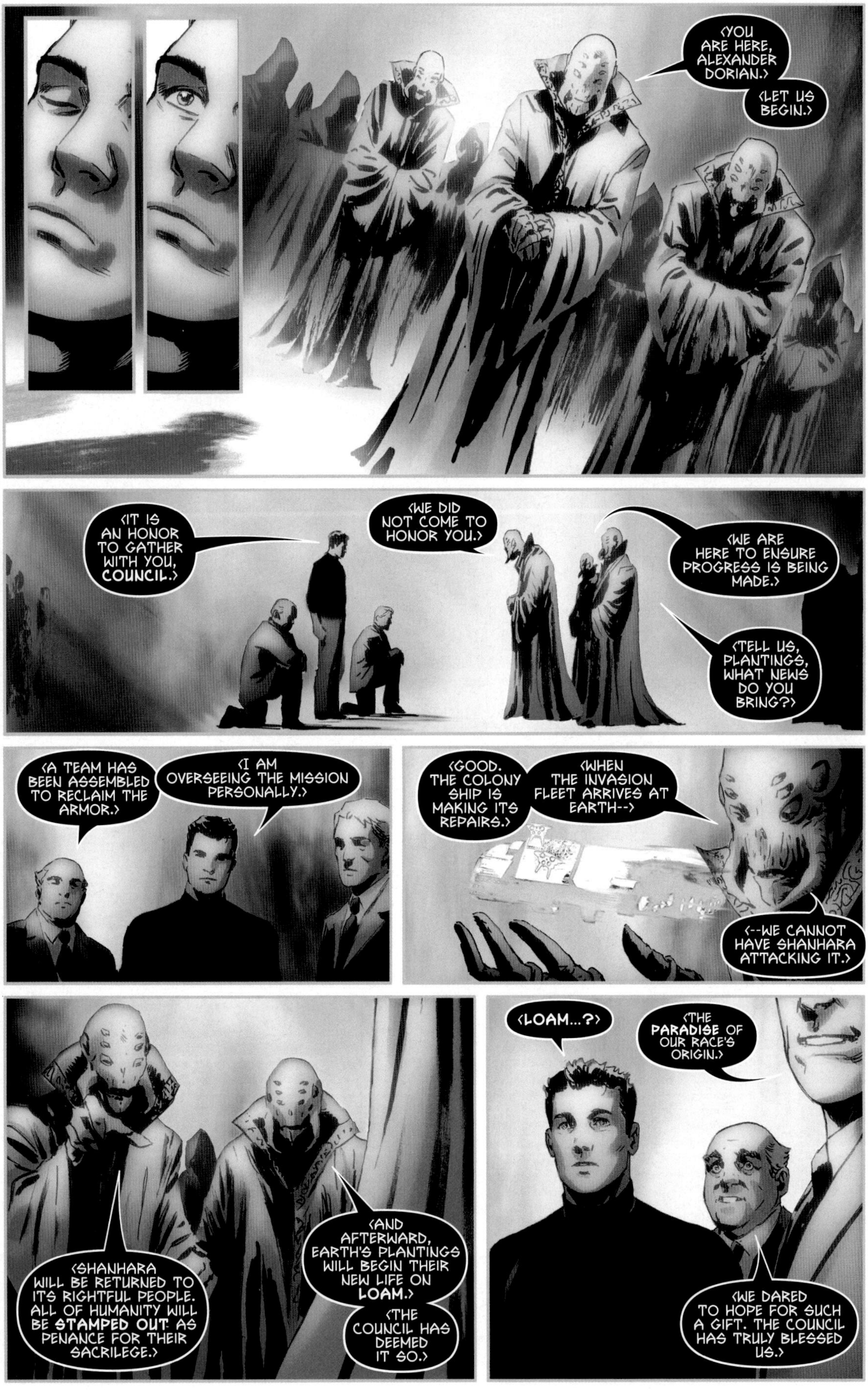
‹YOU ARE HERE, ALEXANDER DORIAN.›
‹LET US BEGIN.›
‹IT IS AN HONOR TO GATHER WITH YOU, **COUNCIL**.›
‹WE DID NOT COME TO HONOR YOU.›
‹WE ARE HERE TO ENSURE PROGRESS IS BEING MADE.›
‹TELL US, PLANTINGS, WHAT NEWS DO YOU BRING?›
‹A TEAM HAS BEEN ASSEMBLED TO RECLAIM THE ARMOR.›
‹I AM OVERSEEING THE MISSION PERSONALLY.›
‹GOOD. THE COLONY SHIP IS MAKING ITS REPAIRS.›
‹WHEN THE INVASION FLEET ARRIVES AT EARTH--›
‹--WE CANNOT HAVE SHANHARA ATTACKING IT.›
‹SHANHARA WILL BE RETURNED TO ITS RIGHTFUL PEOPLE. ALL OF HUMANITY WILL BE **STAMPED OUT** AS PENANCE FOR THEIR SACRILEGE.›
‹AND AFTERWARD, EARTH'S PLANTINGS WILL BEGIN THEIR NEW LIFE ON **LOAM**.›
‹THE COUNCIL HAS DEEMED IT SO.›
‹**LOAM**...?›
‹THE **PARADISE** OF OUR RACE'S ORIGIN.›
‹WE DARED TO HOPE FOR SUCH A GIFT. THE COUNCIL HAS TRULY BLESSED US.›

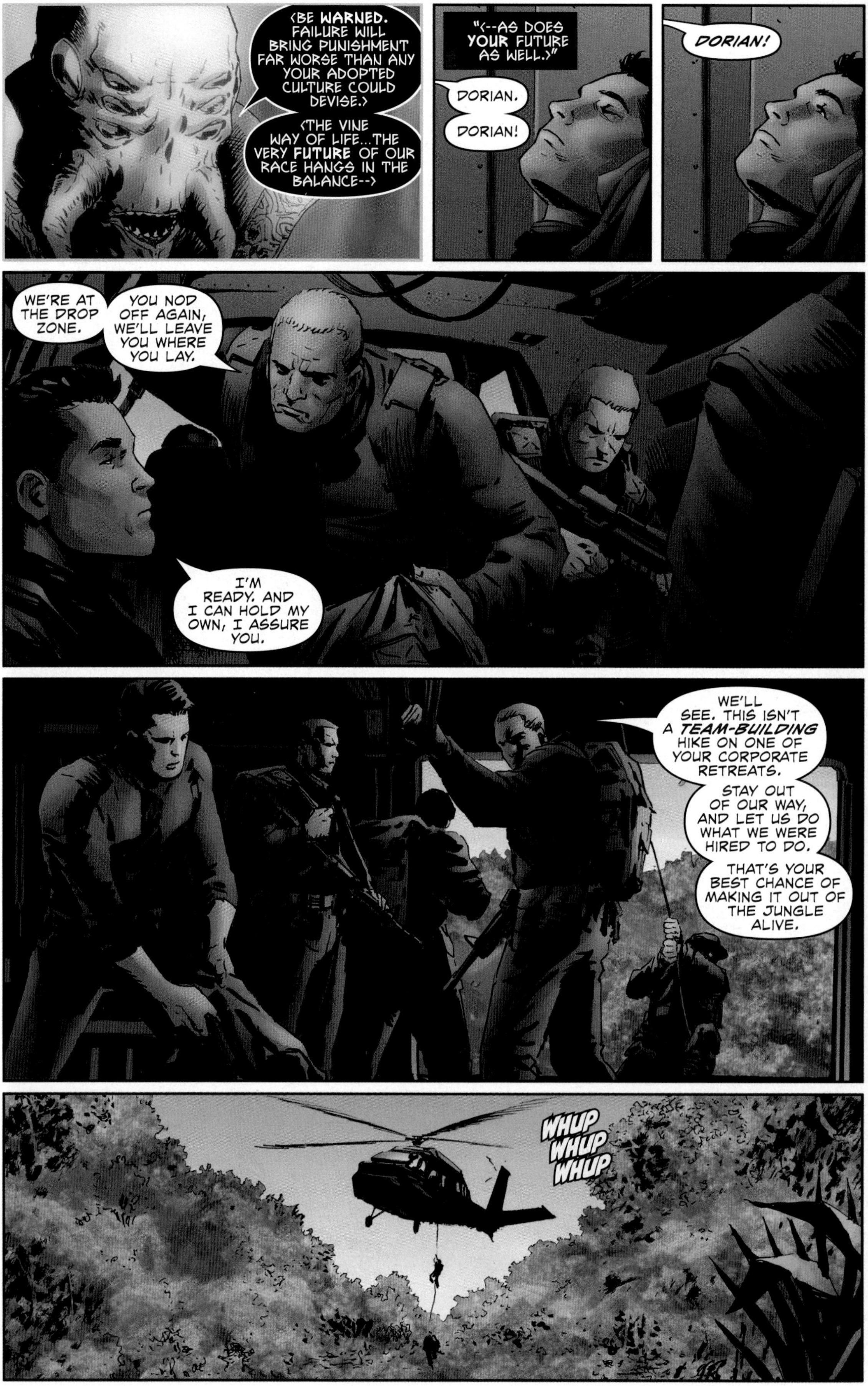
‹BE WARNED. FAILURE WILL BRING PUNISHMENT FAR WORSE THAN ANY YOUR ADOPTED CULTURE COULD DEVISE.›
‹THE VINE WAY OF LIFE...THE VERY FUTURE OF OUR RACE HANGS IN THE BALANCE--›
"‹--AS DOES YOUR FUTURE AS WELL.›"
DORIAN.
DORIAN!
DORIAN!
WE'RE AT THE DROP ZONE.
YOU NOD OFF AGAIN, WE'LL LEAVE YOU WHERE YOU LAY.
I'M READY. AND I CAN HOLD MY OWN, I ASSURE YOU.
WE'LL SEE. THIS ISN'T A TEAM-BUILDING HIKE ON ONE OF YOUR CORPORATE RETREATS.
STAY OUT OF OUR WAY, AND LET US DO WHAT WE WERE HIRED TO DO.
THAT'S YOUR BEST CHANCE OF MAKING IT OUT OF THE JUNGLE ALIVE.
WHUP WHUP WHUP

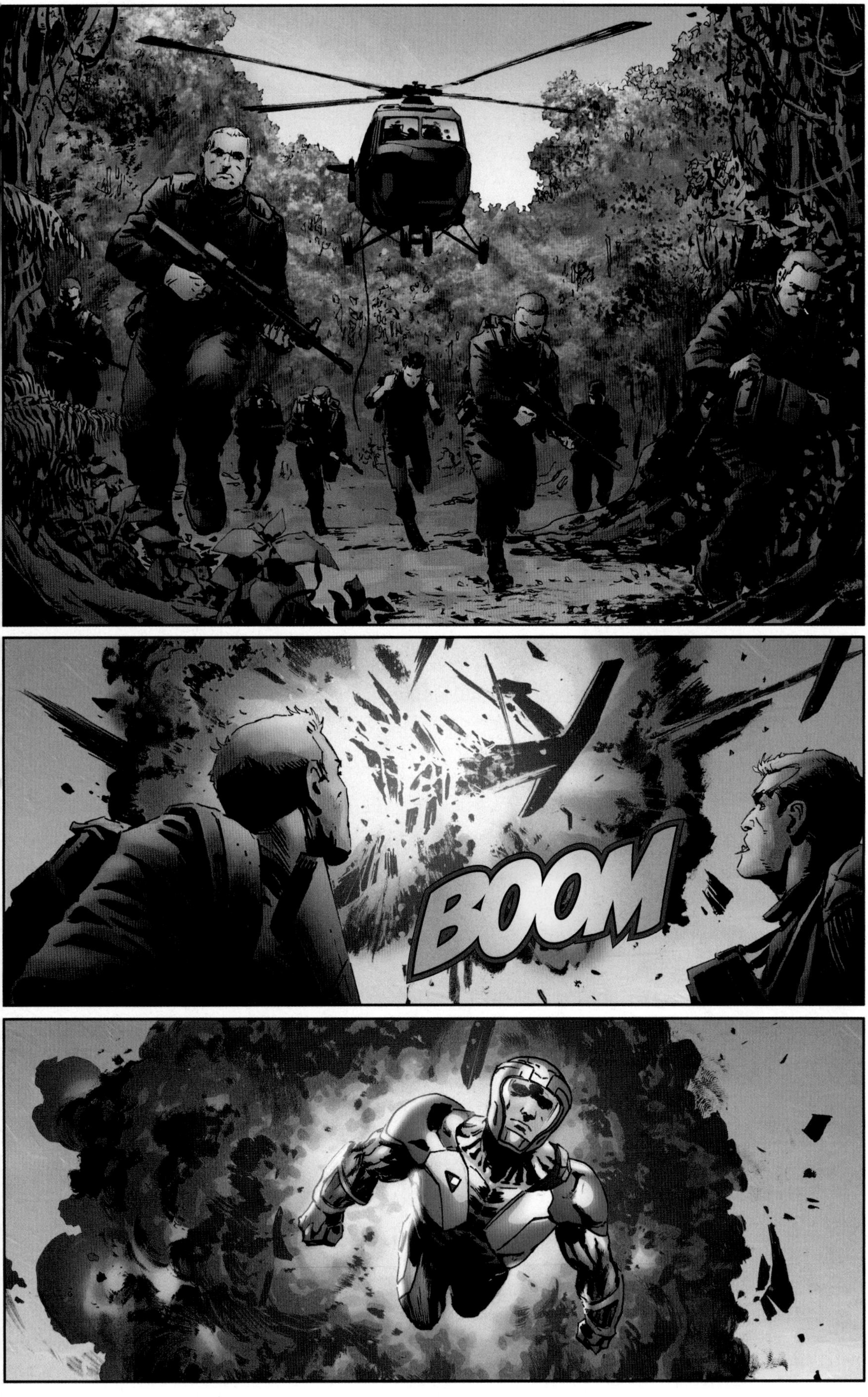
BOOM

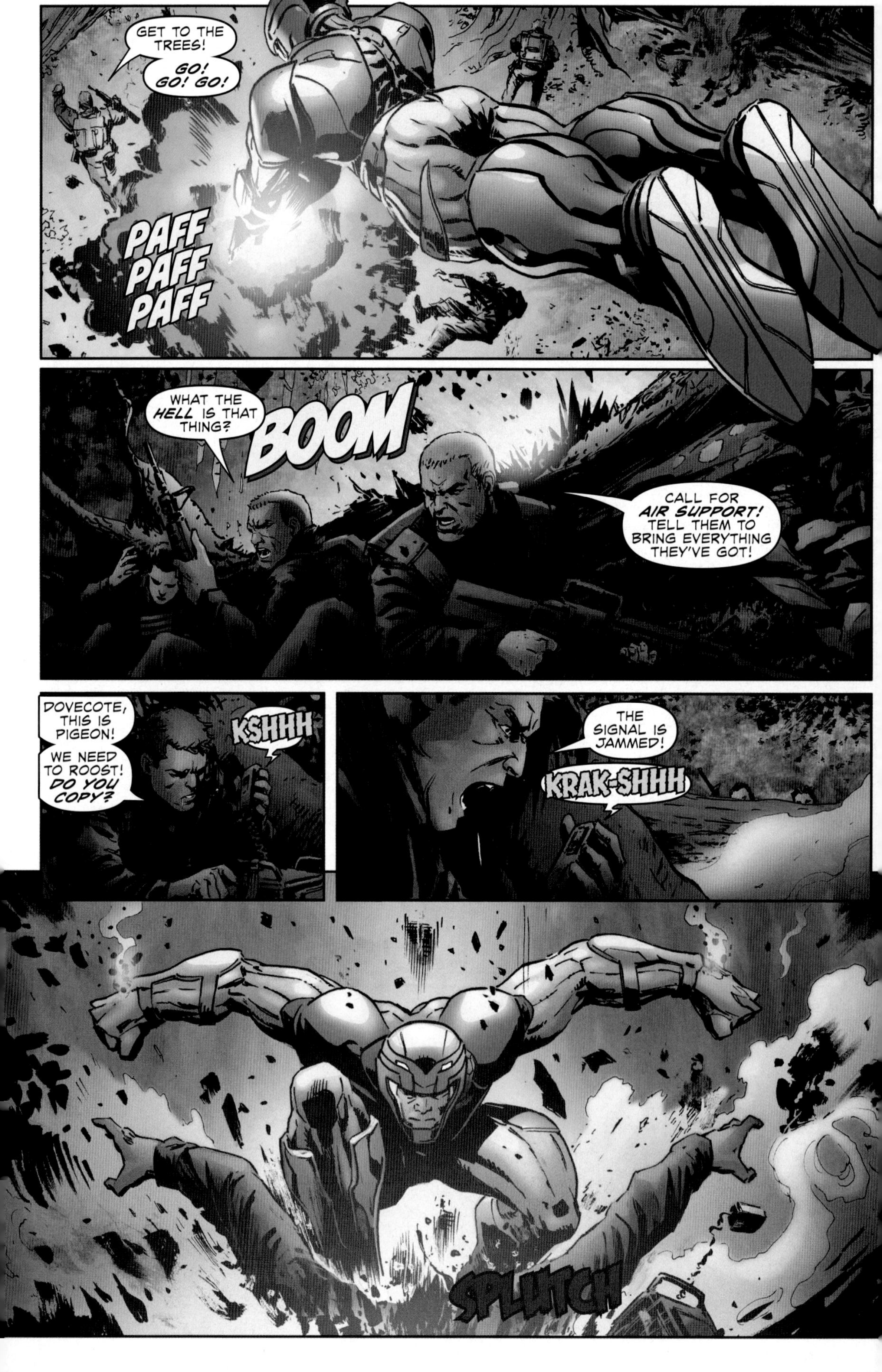

GET TO THE TREES!
GO! GO! GO!
PAFF PAFF PAFF
WHAT THE HELL IS THAT THING?
BOOM
CALL FOR AIR SUPPORT! TELL THEM TO BRING EVERYTHING THEY'VE GOT!
DOVECOTE, THIS IS PIGEON!
WE NEED TO ROOST! DO YOU COPY?
KSHHH
THE SIGNAL IS JAMMED!
KRAK-SHHH
SPLUTCH

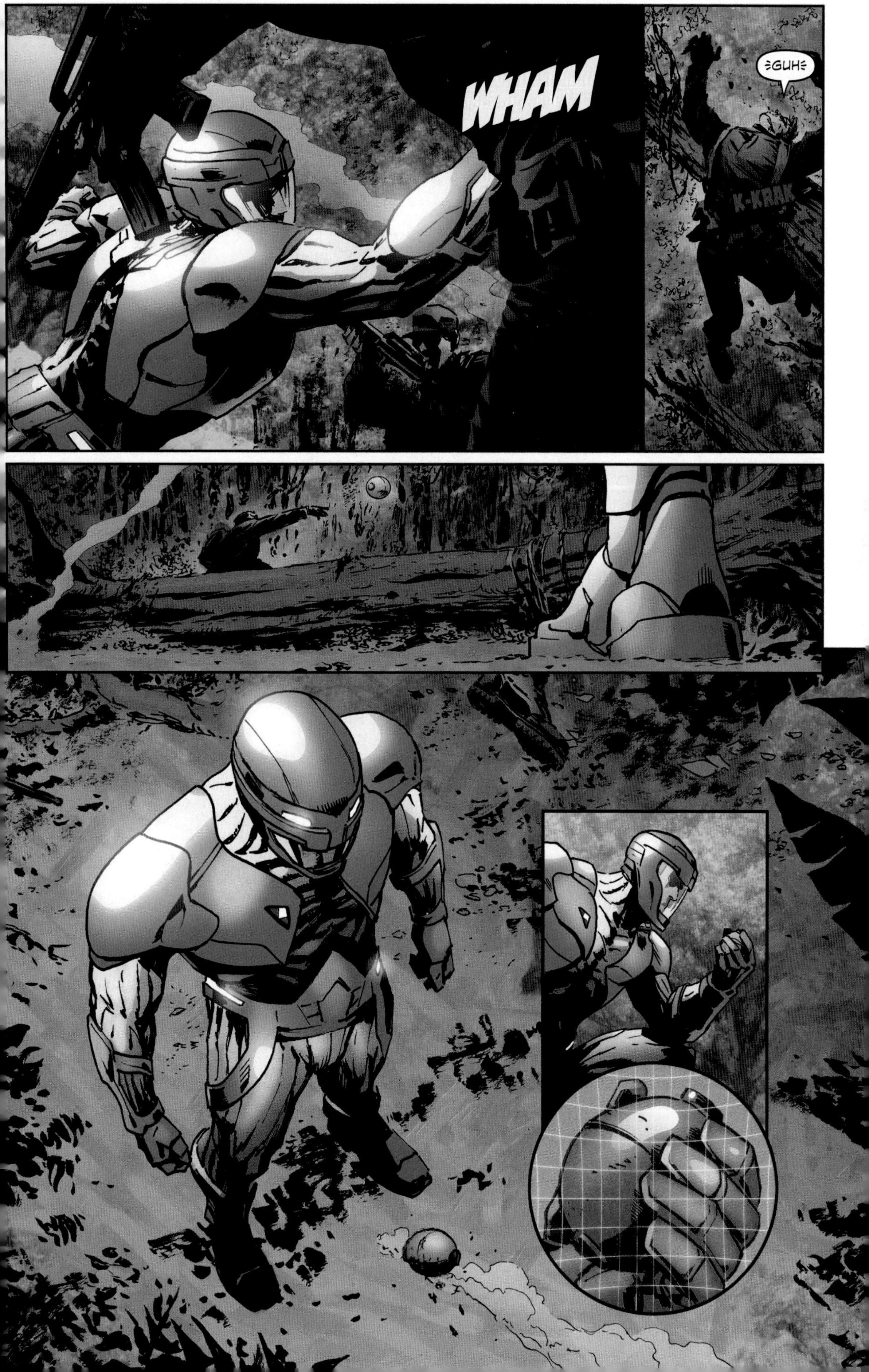
WHAM
GUH
K-KRAK

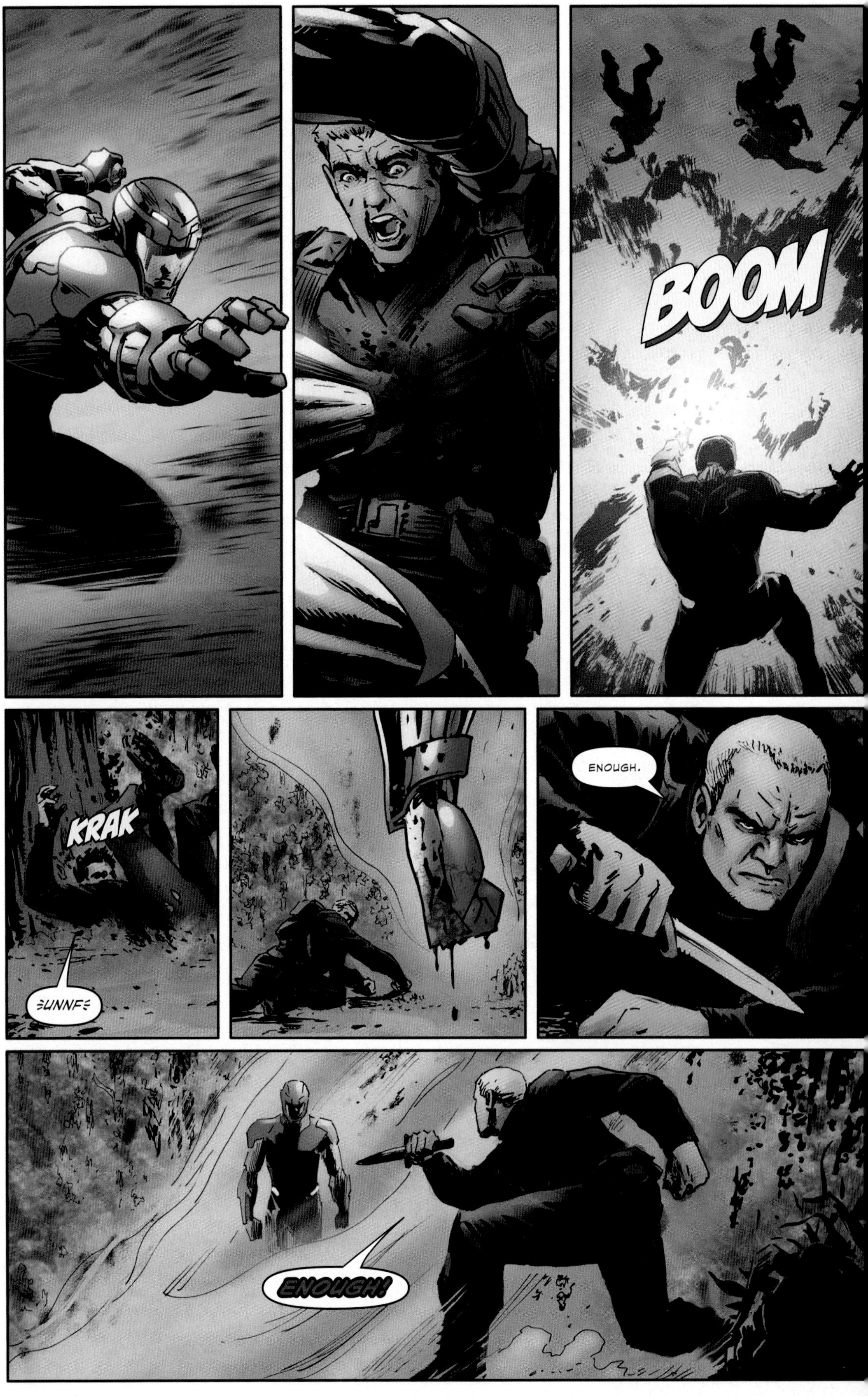
BOOM
KRAK
UNNF
ENOUGH.
ENOUGH!

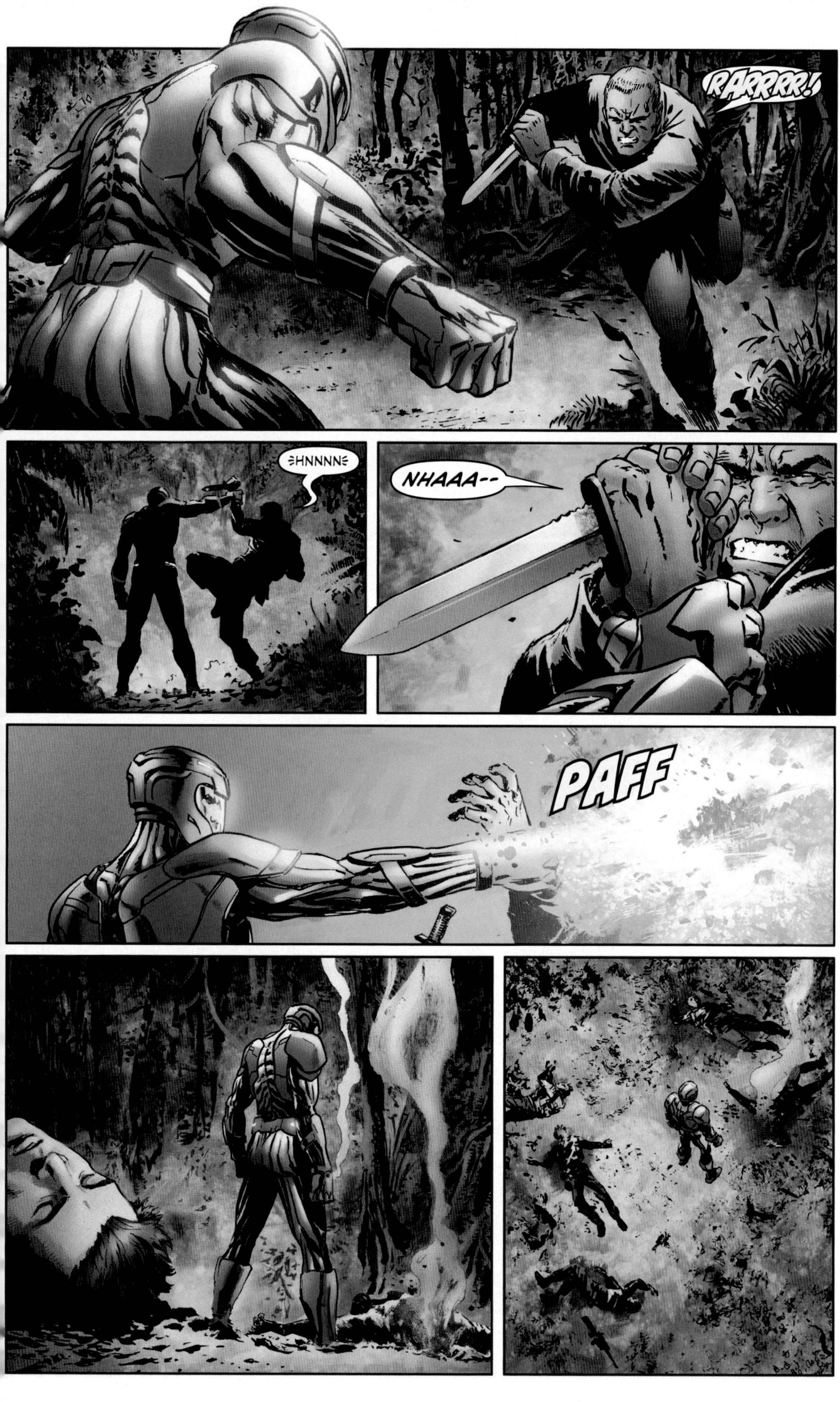
RARRRR!
HNNNN
NHAAA--
PAFF

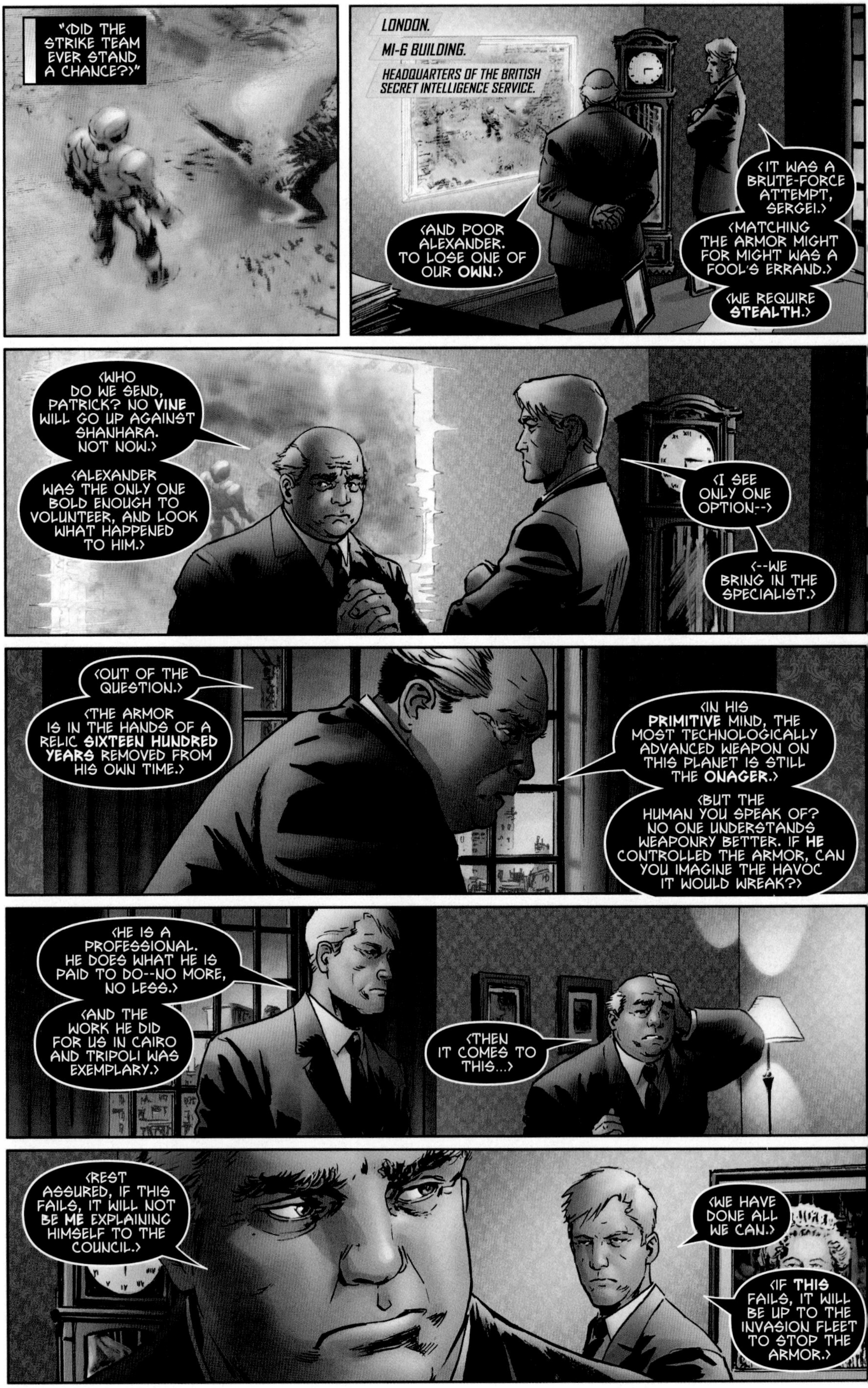
"‹DID THE STRIKE TEAM EVER STAND A CHANCE?›"
LONDON.
MI-6 BUILDING.
HEADQUARTERS OF THE BRITISH SECRET INTELLIGENCE SERVICE.
‹AND POOR ALEXANDER. TO LOSE ONE OF OUR OWN.›
‹IT WAS A BRUTE-FORCE ATTEMPT, SERGEI.›
‹MATCHING THE ARMOR MIGHT FOR MIGHT WAS A FOOL'S ERRAND.›
‹WE REQUIRE STEALTH.›
‹WHO DO WE SEND, PATRICK? NO VINE WILL GO UP AGAINST SHANHARA. NOT NOW.›
‹ALEXANDER WAS THE ONLY ONE BOLD ENOUGH TO VOLUNTEER, AND LOOK WHAT HAPPENED TO HIM.›
‹I SEE ONLY ONE OPTION--›
‹--WE BRING IN THE SPECIALIST.›
‹OUT OF THE QUESTION.›
‹THE ARMOR IS IN THE HANDS OF A RELIC SIXTEEN HUNDRED YEARS REMOVED FROM HIS OWN TIME.›
‹IN HIS PRIMITIVE MIND, THE MOST TECHNOLOGICALLY ADVANCED WEAPON ON THIS PLANET IS STILL THE ONAGER.›
‹BUT THE HUMAN YOU SPEAK OF? NO ONE UNDERSTANDS WEAPONRY BETTER. IF HE CONTROLLED THE ARMOR, CAN YOU IMAGINE THE HAVOC IT WOULD WREAK?›
‹HE IS A PROFESSIONAL. HE DOES WHAT HE IS PAID TO DO--NO MORE, NO LESS.›
‹AND THE WORK HE DID FOR US IN CAIRO AND TRIPOLI WAS EXEMPLARY.›
‹THEN IT COMES TO THIS...›
‹REST ASSURED, IF THIS FAILS, IT WILL NOT BE ME EXPLAINING HIMSELF TO THE COUNCIL.›
‹WE HAVE DONE ALL WE CAN.›
‹IF THIS FAILS, IT WILL BE UP TO THE INVASION FLEET TO STOP THE ARMOR.›

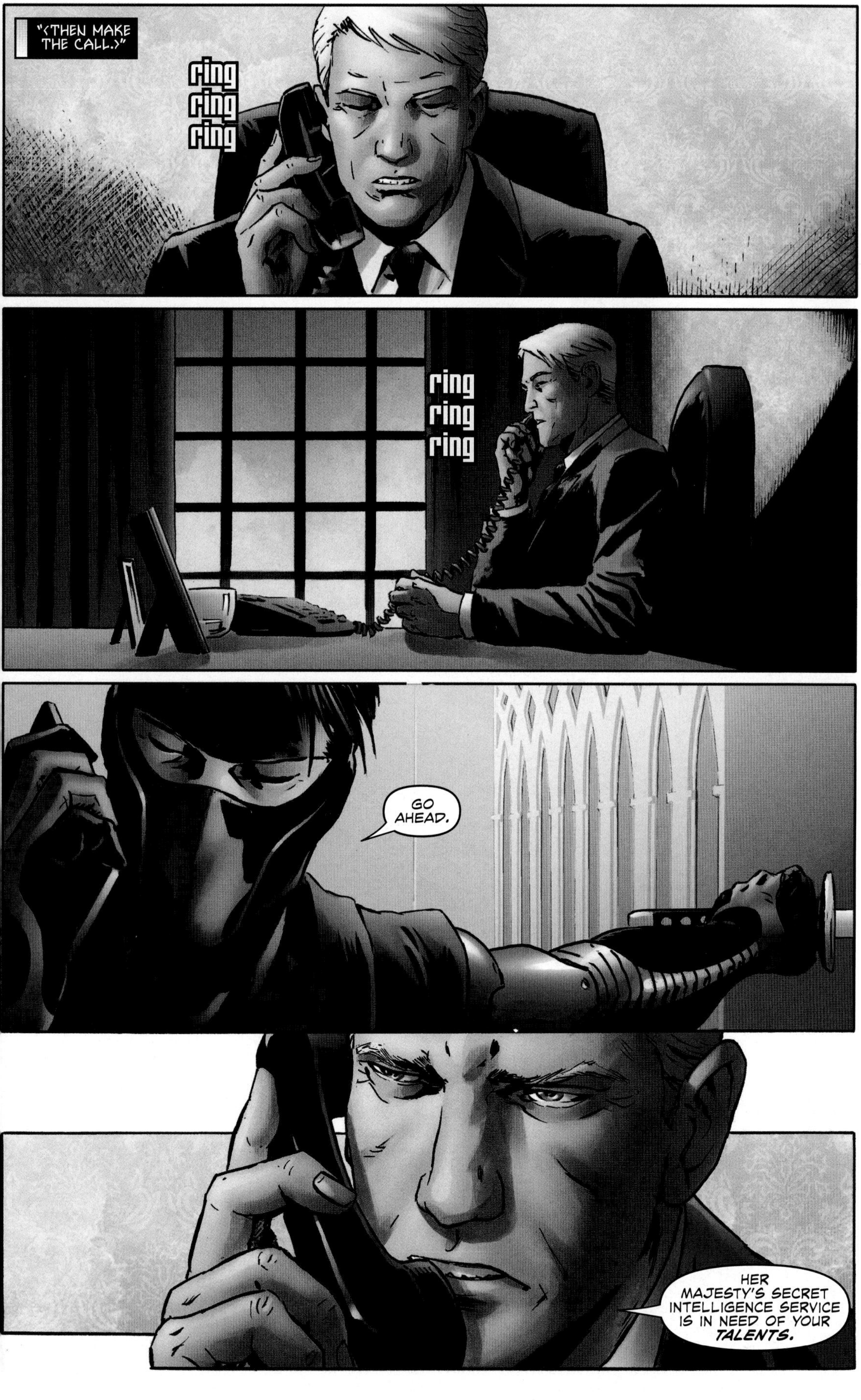
"‹THEN MAKE THE CALL.›"
ring ring ring
ring ring ring
GO AHEAD.
HER MAJESTY'S SECRET INTELLIGENCE SERVICE IS IN NEED OF YOUR *TALENTS.*

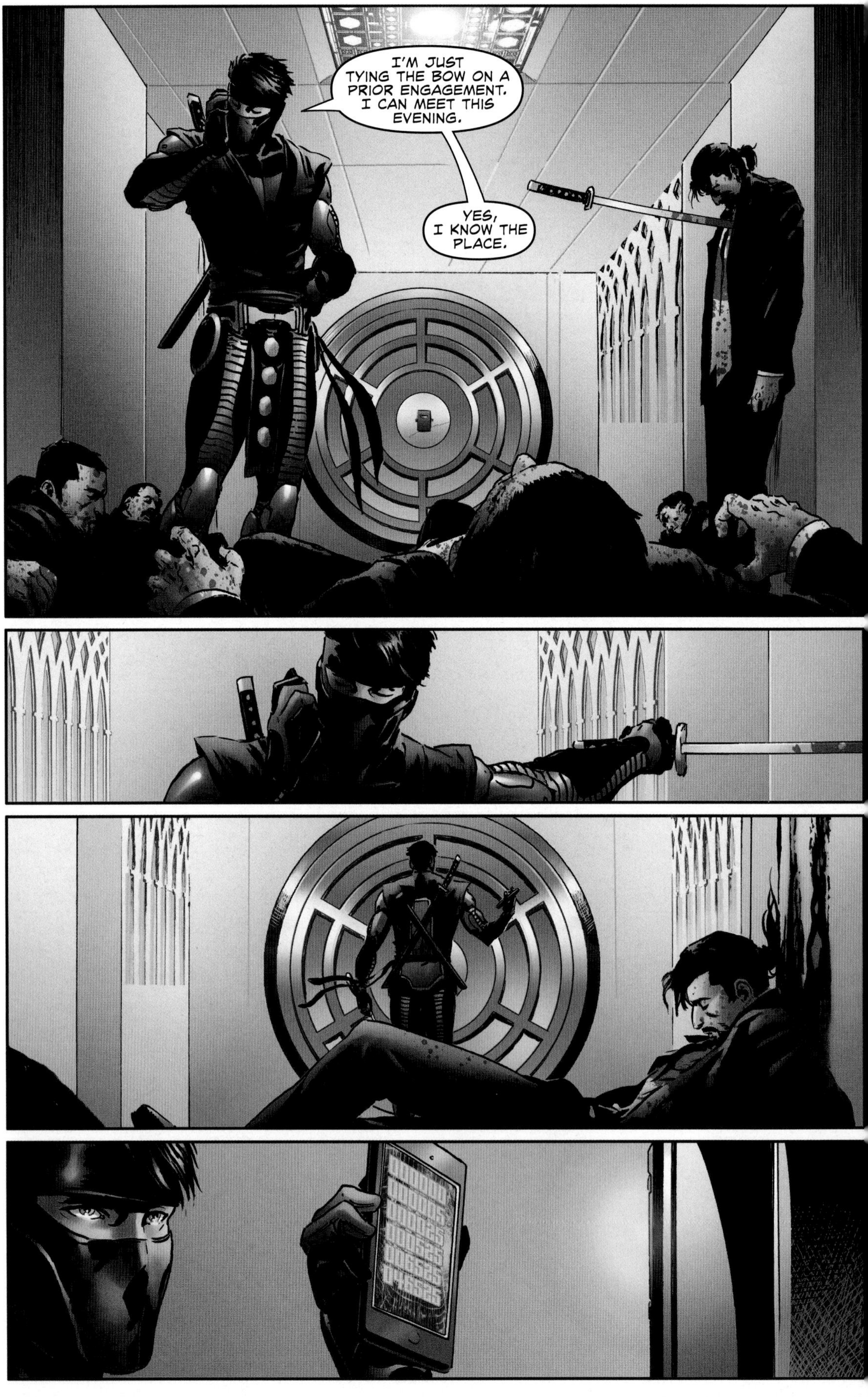
I'M JUST TYING THE BOW ON A PRIOR ENGAGEMENT. I CAN MEET THIS EVENING.
YES, I KNOW THE PLACE.

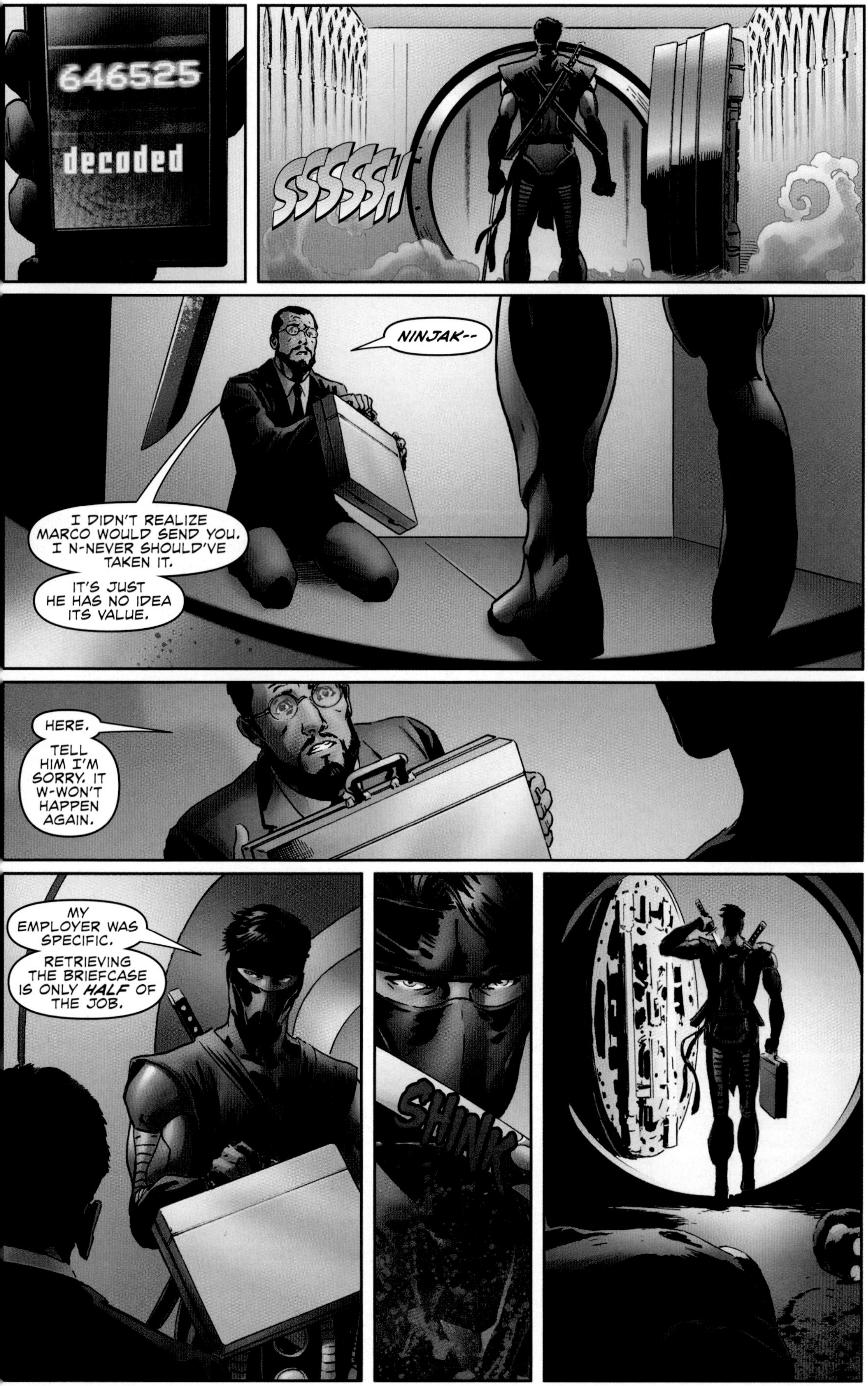
646525
decoded
SSSSSH
NINJAK--
I DIDN'T REALIZE MARCO WOULD SEND YOU. I N-NEVER SHOULD'VE TAKEN IT.
IT'S JUST HE HAS NO IDEA ITS VALUE.
HERE.
TELL HIM I'M SORRY. IT W-WON'T HAPPEN AGAIN.
MY EMPLOYER WAS SPECIFIC.
RETRIEVING THE BRIEFCASE IS ONLY HALF OF THE JOB.
SHINK

LONDON.

TILBURY DOCKS.

EIGHT HOURS LATER.

I DIDN'T EXPECT A CALL FROM YOU AGAIN WITH THE LATEST ROUND OF AUSTERITY COMING OUT OF PARLIAMENT.

I WAS WORRIED MY LAST JOB BROKE YOUR BANK.

SOME THINGS AREN'T SUSCEPTIBLE TO BUDGETARY RESTRAINT.

LIKE THE RECENT TERRORIST ATTACKS IN ROME.

THE PRESS HAS A FEW TOURIST PHOTOS, BUT MY *SOURCES* INSIDE THE ITALIAN GOVERNMENT WERE ABLE TO SUPPLY THESE HI-RES IMAGES.

THE TERRORIST WORE A HIGHLY ADVANCED BATTLE SUIT OF SOME UNKNOWN DESIGN.

ITS CAPABILITIES ARE *FAR BEYOND* ANYTHING WE'VE TESTED.

EVEN THE ITALIAN AIR FORCE WAS NO MATCH FOR IT.

SINCE WHEN HAVE THE ITALIANS BEEN A MATCH FOR ANYTHING?

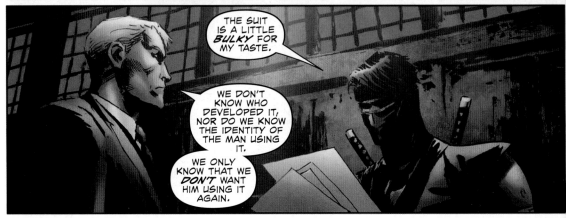

THE SUIT IS A LITTLE *BULKY* FOR MY TASTE.

WE DON'T KNOW WHO DEVELOPED IT, NOR DO WE KNOW THE IDENTITY OF THE MAN USING IT.

WE ONLY KNOW THAT WE *DON'T* WANT HIM USING IT AGAIN.

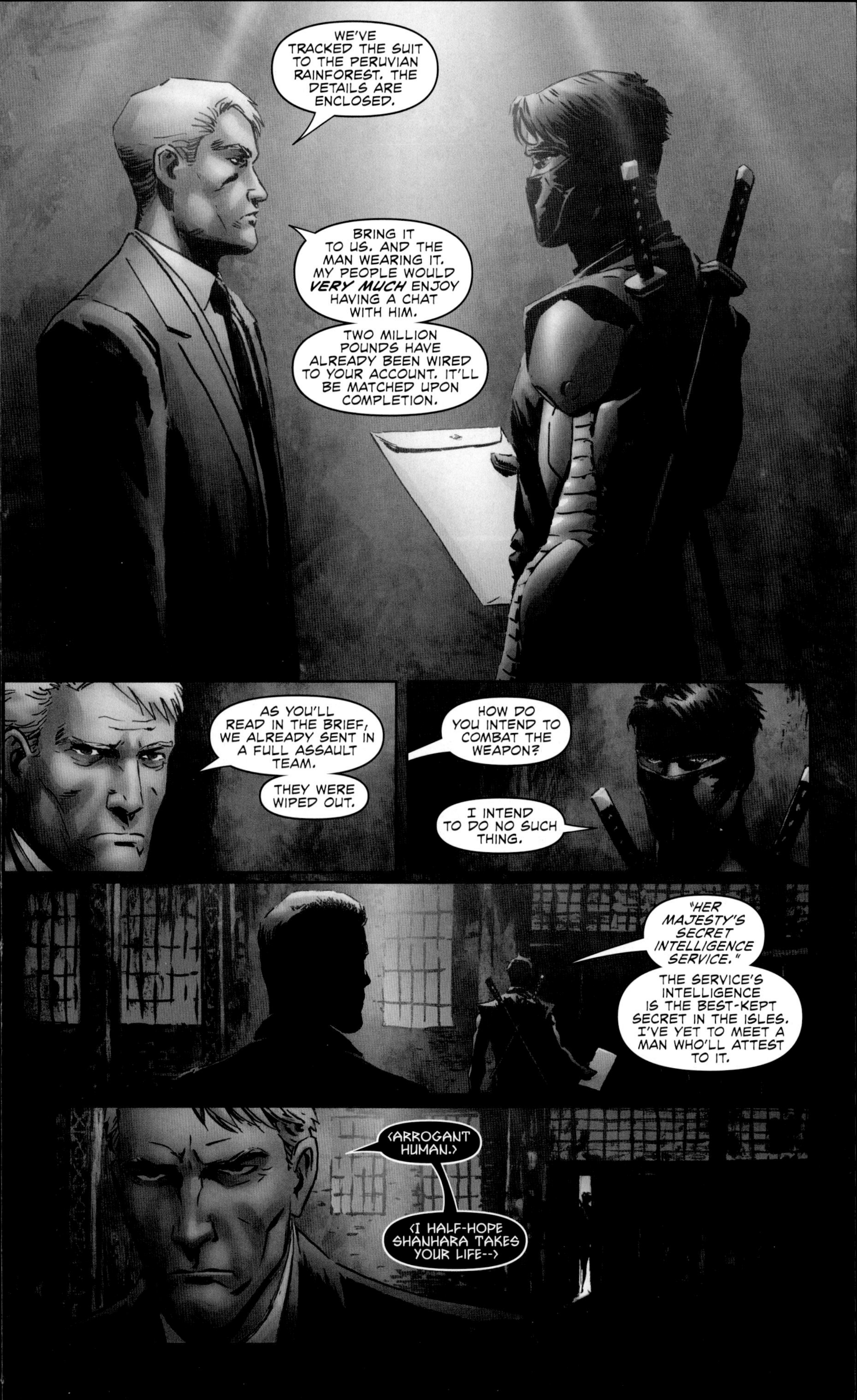
WE'VE TRACKED THE SUIT TO THE PERUVIAN RAINFOREST. THE DETAILS ARE ENCLOSED.
BRING IT TO US. AND THE MAN WEARING IT. MY PEOPLE WOULD *VERY MUCH* ENJOY HAVING A CHAT WITH HIM.
TWO MILLION POUNDS HAVE ALREADY BEEN WIRED TO YOUR ACCOUNT. IT'LL BE MATCHED UPON COMPLETION.
AS YOU'LL READ IN THE BRIEF, WE ALREADY SENT IN A FULL ASSAULT TEAM.
THEY WERE WIPED OUT.
HOW DO YOU INTEND TO COMBAT THE WEAPON?
I INTEND TO DO NO SUCH THING.
"HER MAJESTY'S SECRET INTELLIGENCE SERVICE."
THE SERVICE'S INTELLIGENCE IS THE BEST-KEPT SECRET IN THE ISLES. I'VE YET TO MEET A MAN WHO'LL ATTEST TO IT.
‹ARROGANT HUMAN.›
‹I HALF-HOPE SHANHARA TAKES YOUR LIFE--›

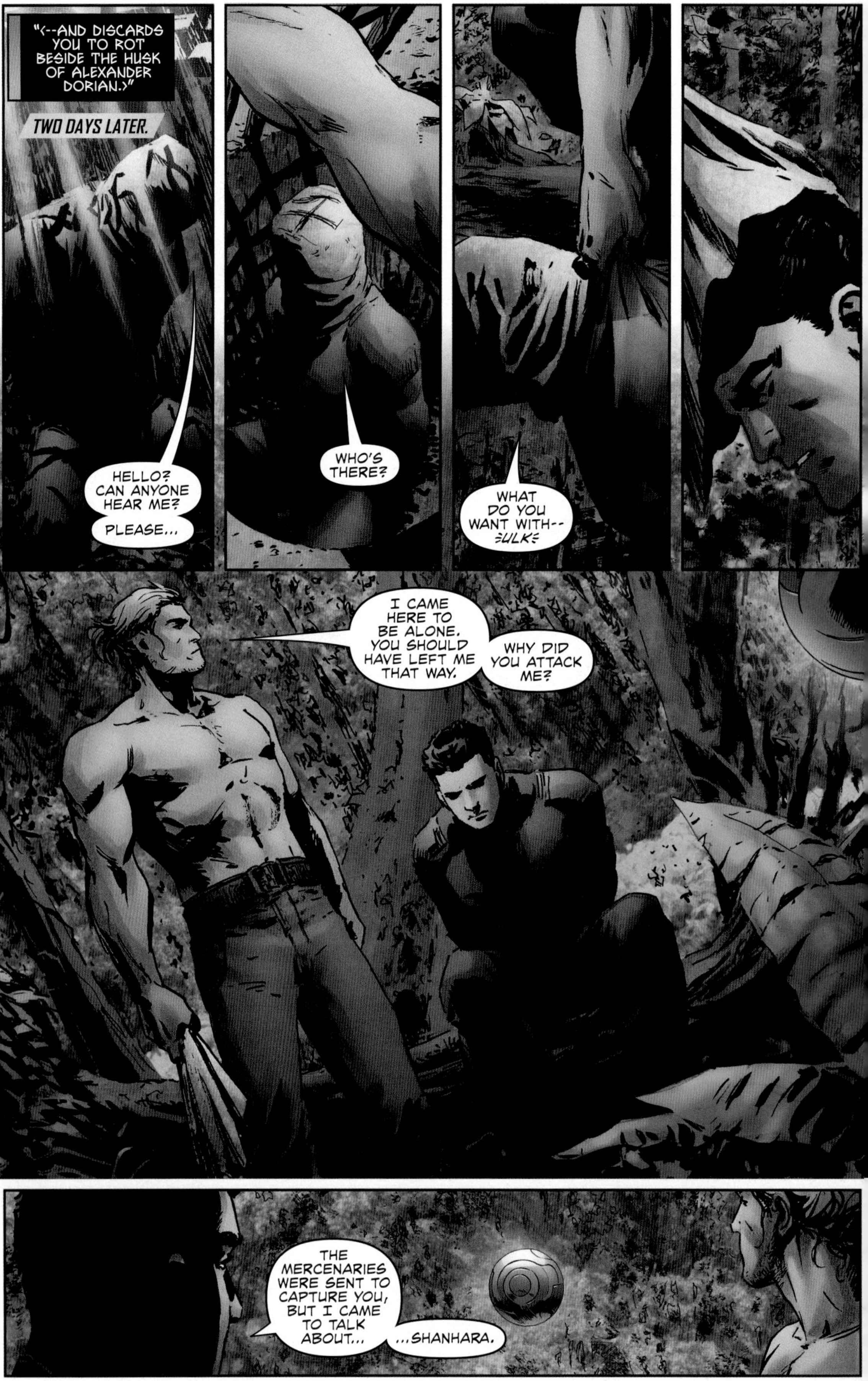
"‹--AND DISCARDS YOU TO ROT BESIDE THE HUSK OF ALEXANDER DORIAN.›"
TWO DAYS LATER.
HELLO? CAN ANYONE HEAR ME?
PLEASE...
WHO'S THERE?
WHAT DO YOU WANT WITH--
ULK
I CAME HERE TO BE ALONE. YOU SHOULD HAVE LEFT ME THAT WAY.
WHY DID YOU ATTACK ME?
THE MERCENARIES WERE SENT TO CAPTURE YOU, BUT I CAME TO TALK ABOUT...
...SHANHARA.

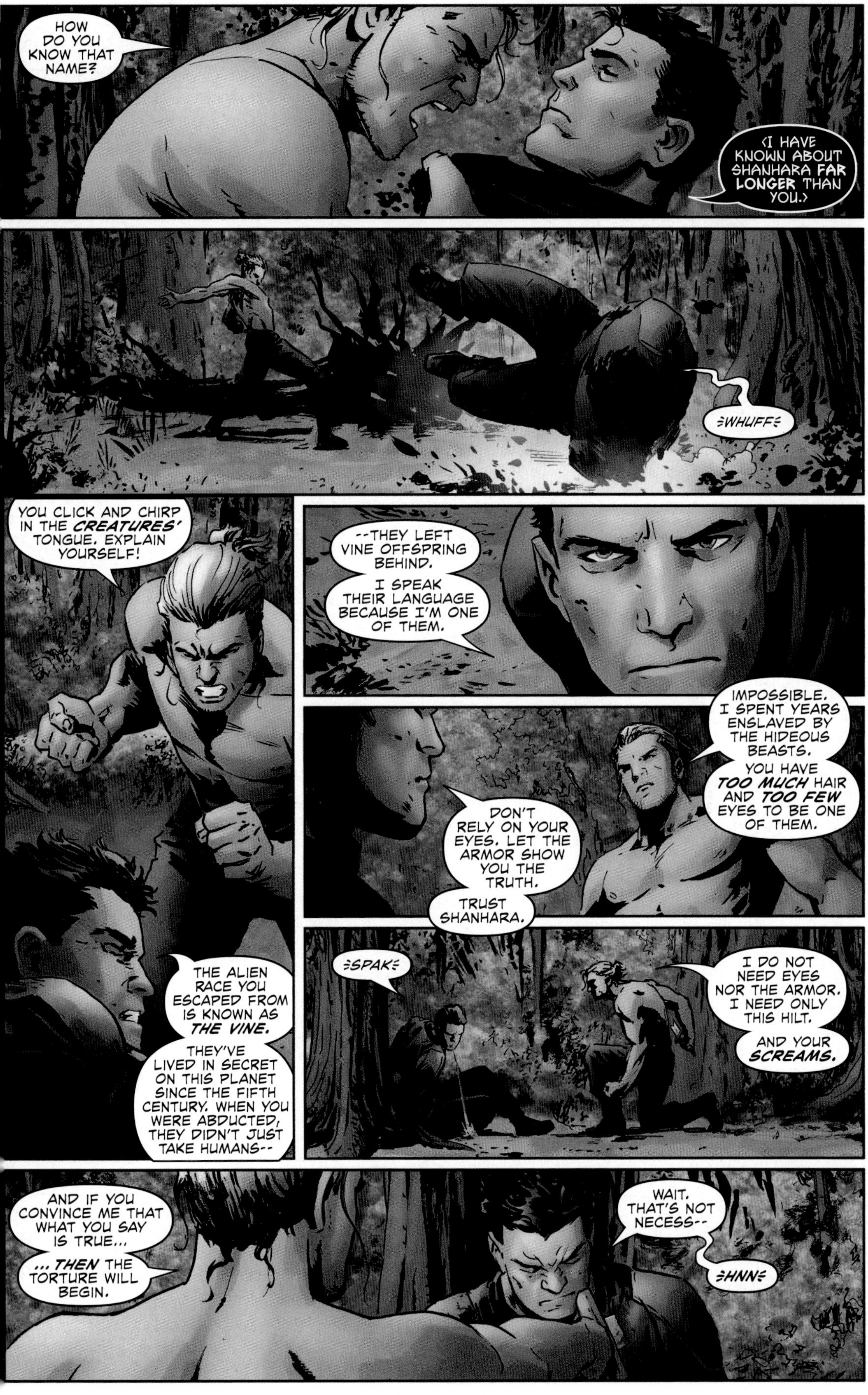
HOW DO YOU KNOW THAT NAME?
<I HAVE KNOWN ABOUT SHANHARA **FAR LONGER** THAN YOU.>
=WHUFF=
YOU CLICK AND CHIRP IN THE ***CREATURES'*** TONGUE. EXPLAIN YOURSELF!
THE ALIEN RACE YOU ESCAPED FROM IS KNOWN AS ***THE VINE.***
THEY'VE LIVED IN SECRET ON THIS PLANET SINCE THE FIFTH CENTURY. WHEN YOU WERE ABDUCTED, THEY DIDN'T JUST TAKE HUMANS--
--THEY LEFT VINE OFFSPRING BEHIND.
I SPEAK THEIR LANGUAGE BECAUSE I'M ONE OF THEM.
IMPOSSIBLE. I SPENT YEARS ENSLAVED BY THE HIDEOUS BEASTS.
YOU HAVE ***TOO MUCH*** HAIR AND ***TOO FEW*** EYES TO BE ONE OF THEM.
DON'T RELY ON YOUR EYES. LET THE ARMOR SHOW YOU THE TRUTH.
TRUST SHANHARA.
=SPAK=
I DO NOT NEED EYES NOR THE ARMOR. I NEED ONLY THIS HILT.
AND YOUR ***SCREAMS.***
AND IF YOU CONVINCE ME THAT WHAT YOU SAY IS TRUE...
...THEN THE TORTURE WILL BEGIN.
WAIT. THAT'S NOT NECESS--
=HNN=

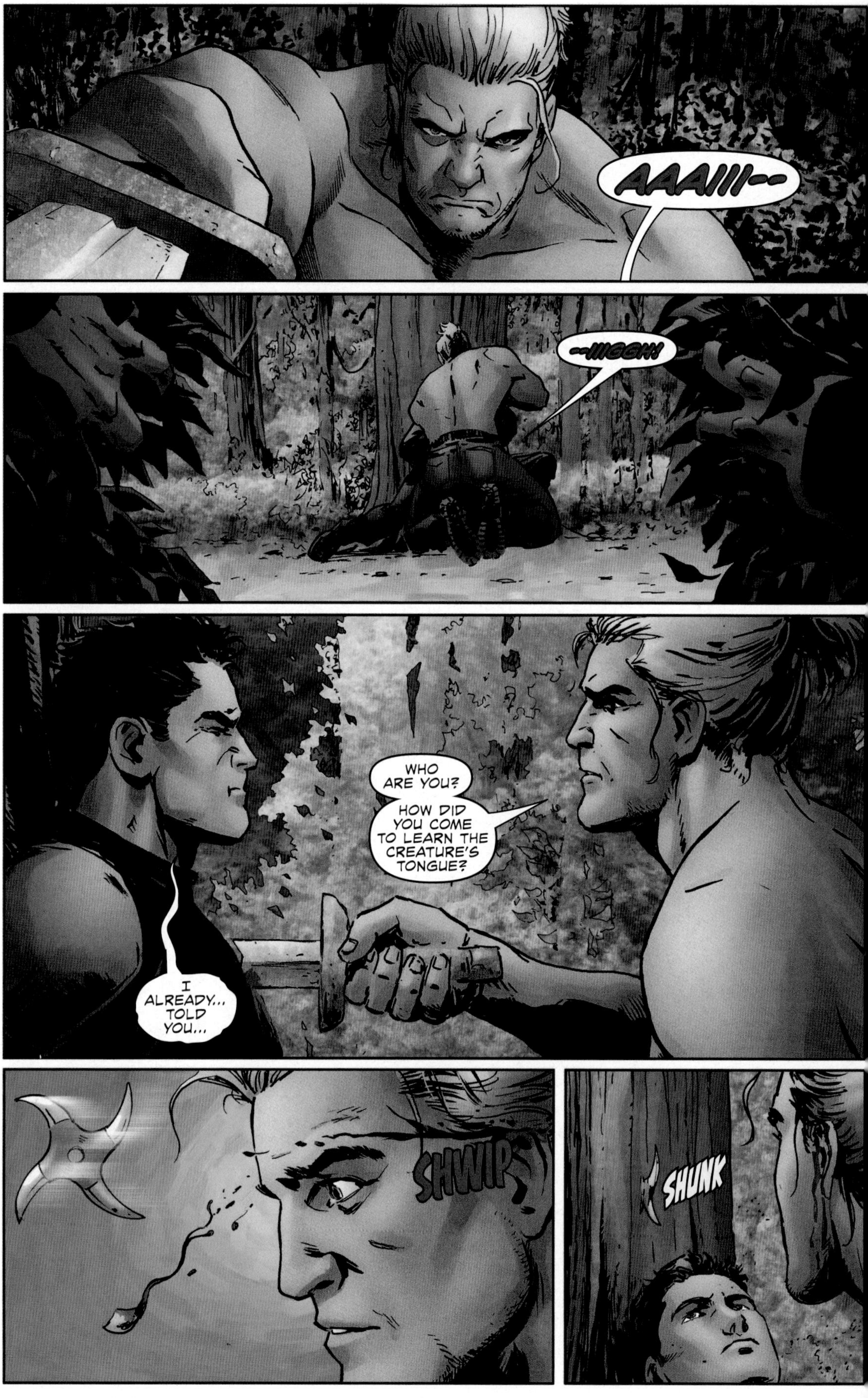
AAAIII--
--IIIGGH!
WHO ARE YOU?
HOW DID YOU COME TO LEARN THE CREATURE'S TONGUE?
I ALREADY... TOLD YOU...
SHWIP
SHUNK

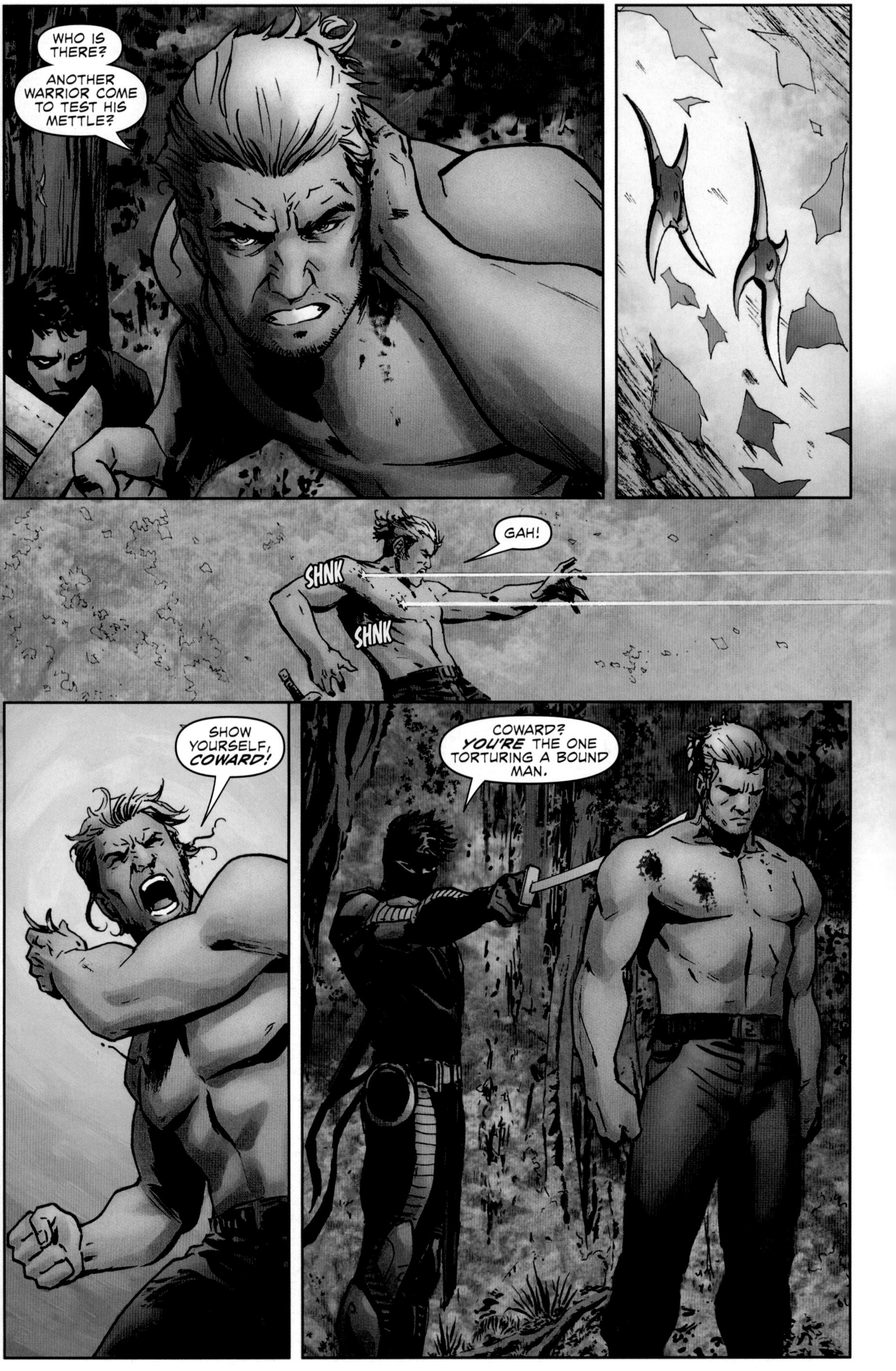

WHO IS THERE?
ANOTHER WARRIOR COME TO TEST HIS METTLE?
GAH!
SHNK
SHNK
SHOW YOURSELF, *COWARD!*
COWARD? *YOU'RE* THE ONE TORTURING A BOUND MAN.

I HAVE SEEN WOMEN *TRIM THEIR HAIR* WITH LARGER BLADES.

I AM ARIC OF DACIA. I CUT MY TEETH ON SWORDS.

TOO BAD YOU DIDN'T CUT YOUR *TONGUE.*

AND YOUR RUSTY ANTIQUE IS NOTHING TO BRAG ABOUT.

I WILL SHOW YOU *MUCH MORE--*

--THAN A...
...KILL YOU...

DROWSY? THAT WOULD BE THE TRANQUILIZER FOGGING YOUR BRAIN.

SEE, THE THING ABOUT ME IS, WHEN I FIGHT SOMEONE--

WHUMP

--THEY DON'T REALIZE IT, UNTIL IT'S OVER.

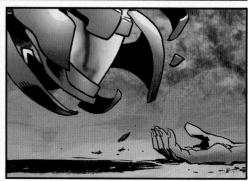

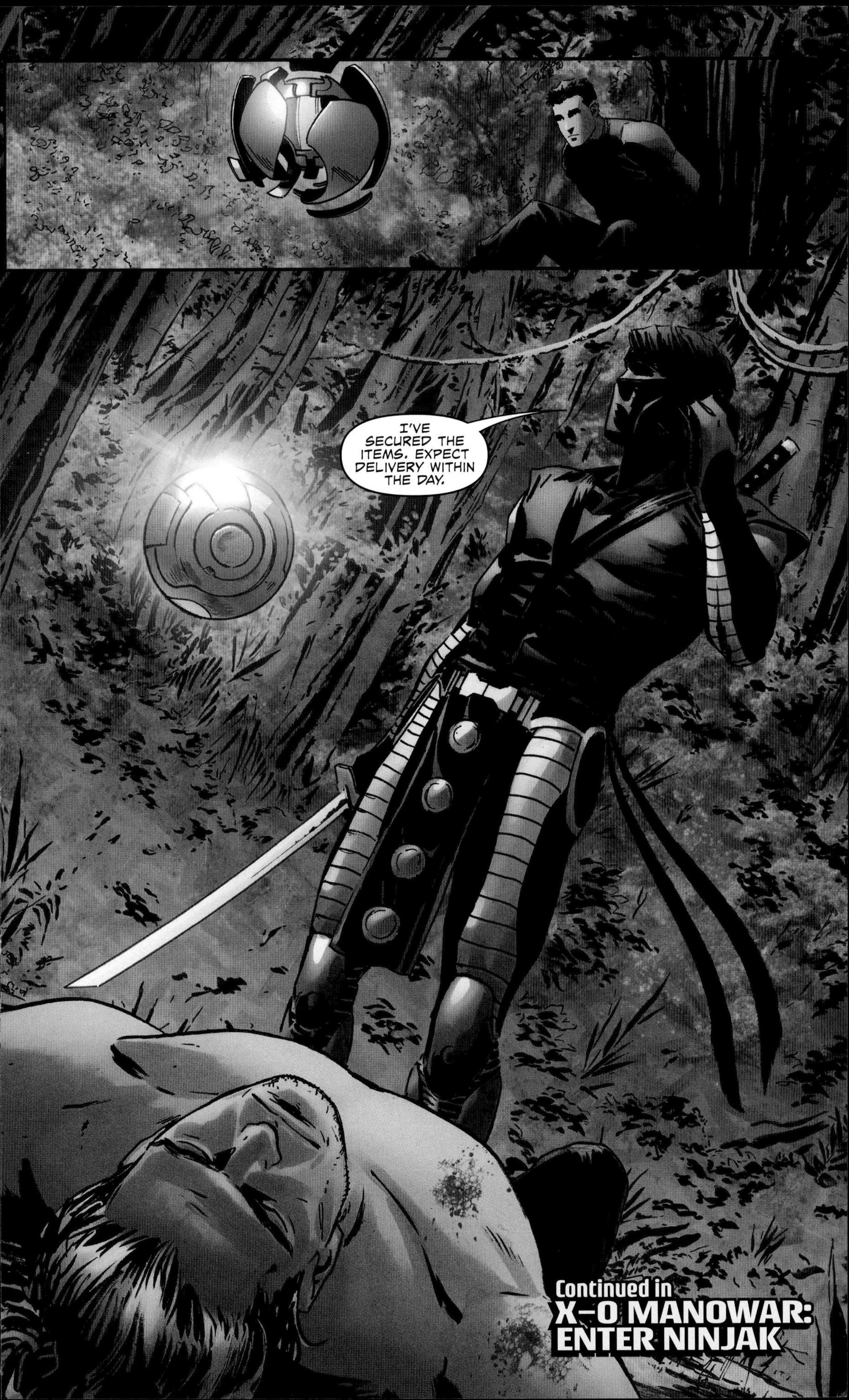
I'VE SECURED THE ITEMS. EXPECT DELIVERY WITHIN THE DAY.
Continued in X-O MANOWAR: ENTER NINJAK

GALLERY

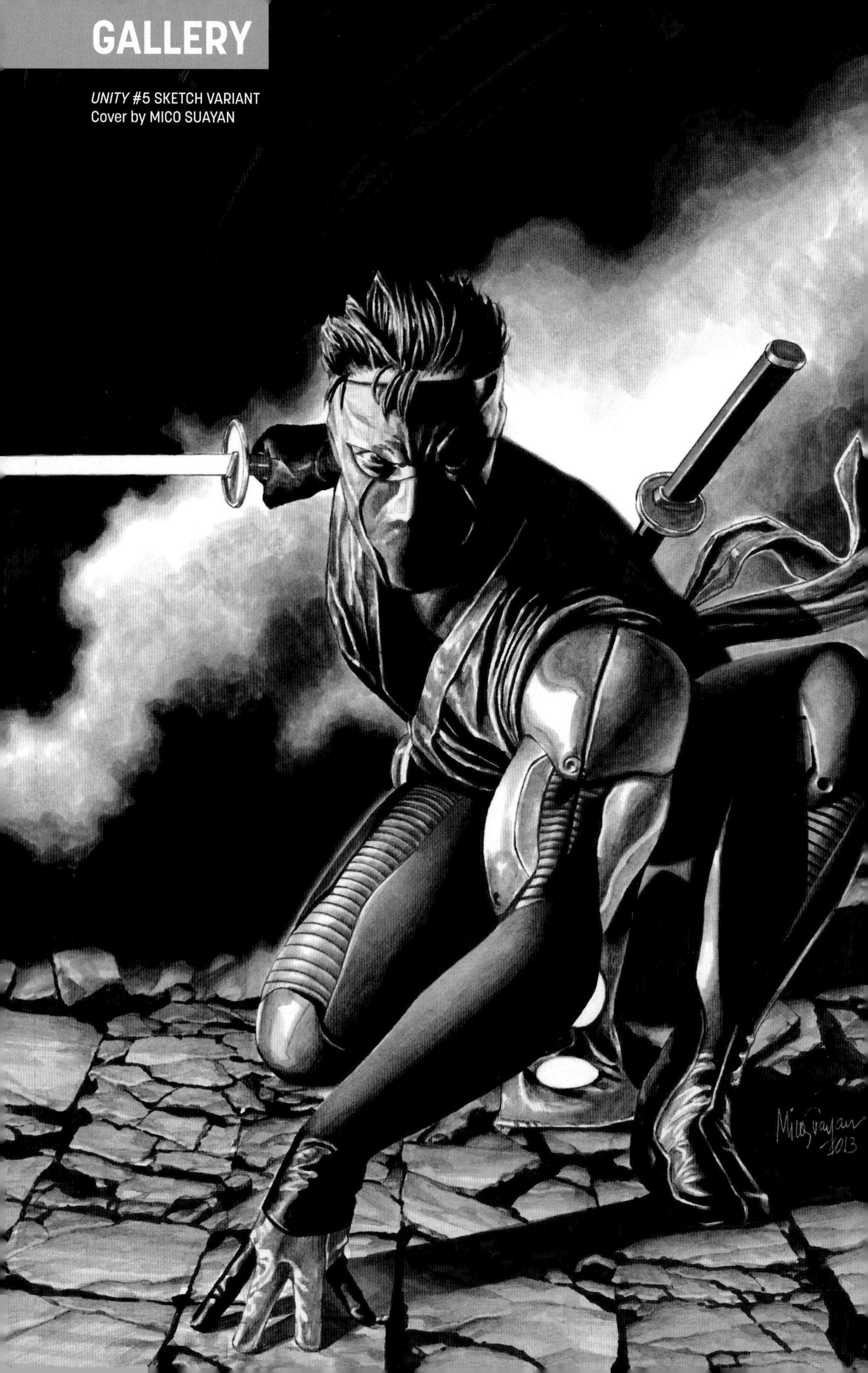

UNITY #5 SKETCH VARIANT
Cover by MICO SUAYAN

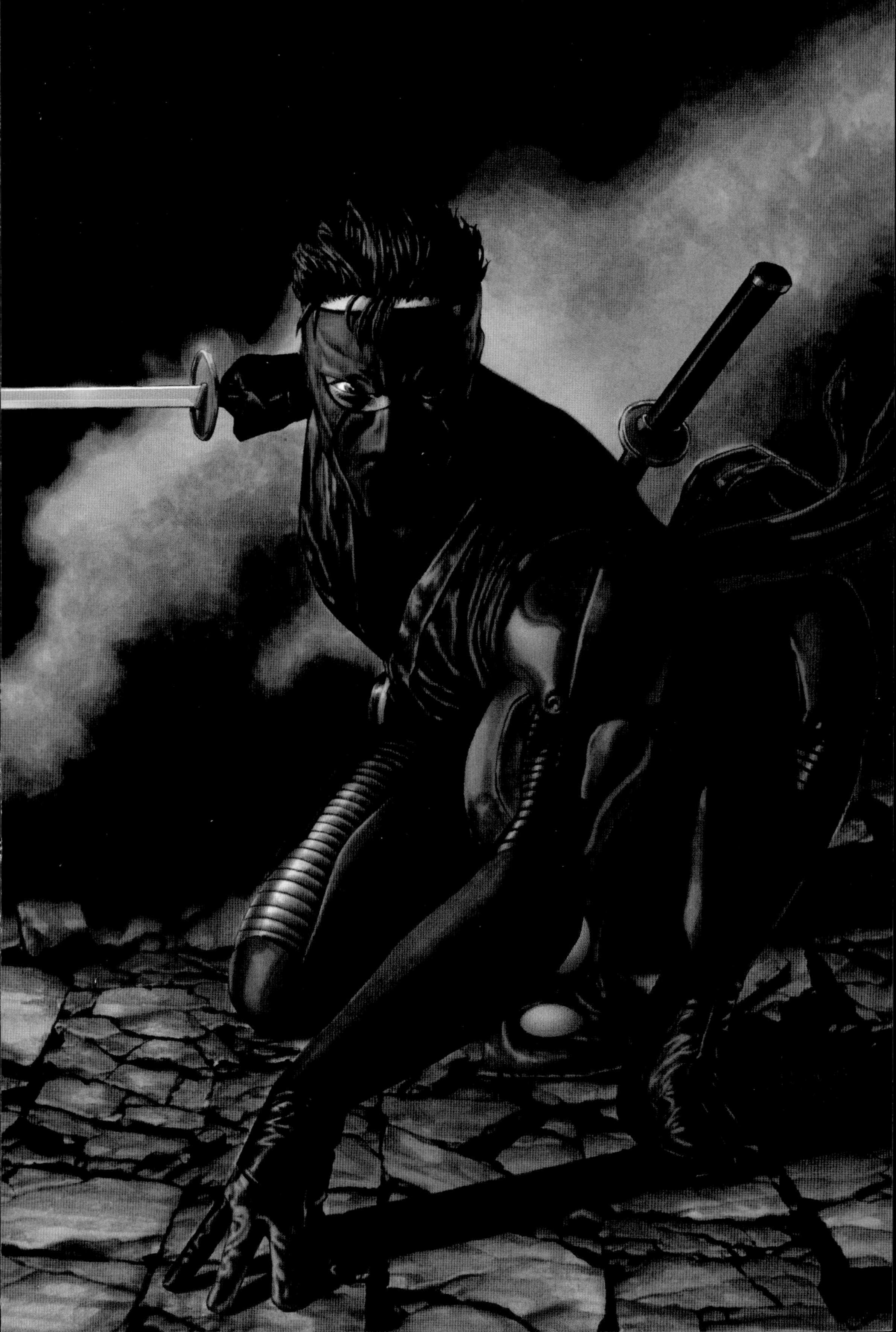

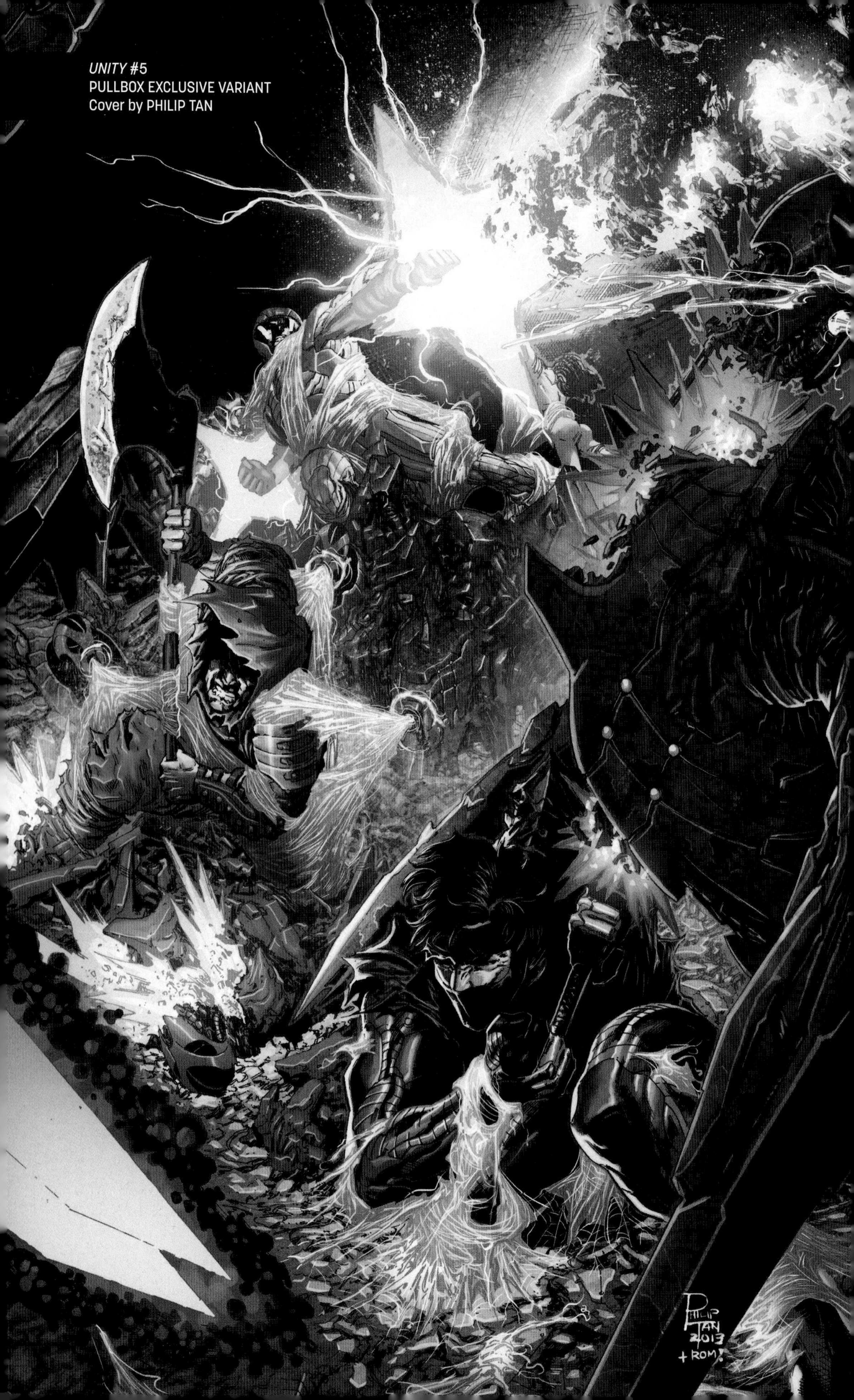
PHILIP TAN 2013 + ROM

UNITY #5
PULLBOX EXCLUSIVE VARIANT
Cover by PHILIP TAN

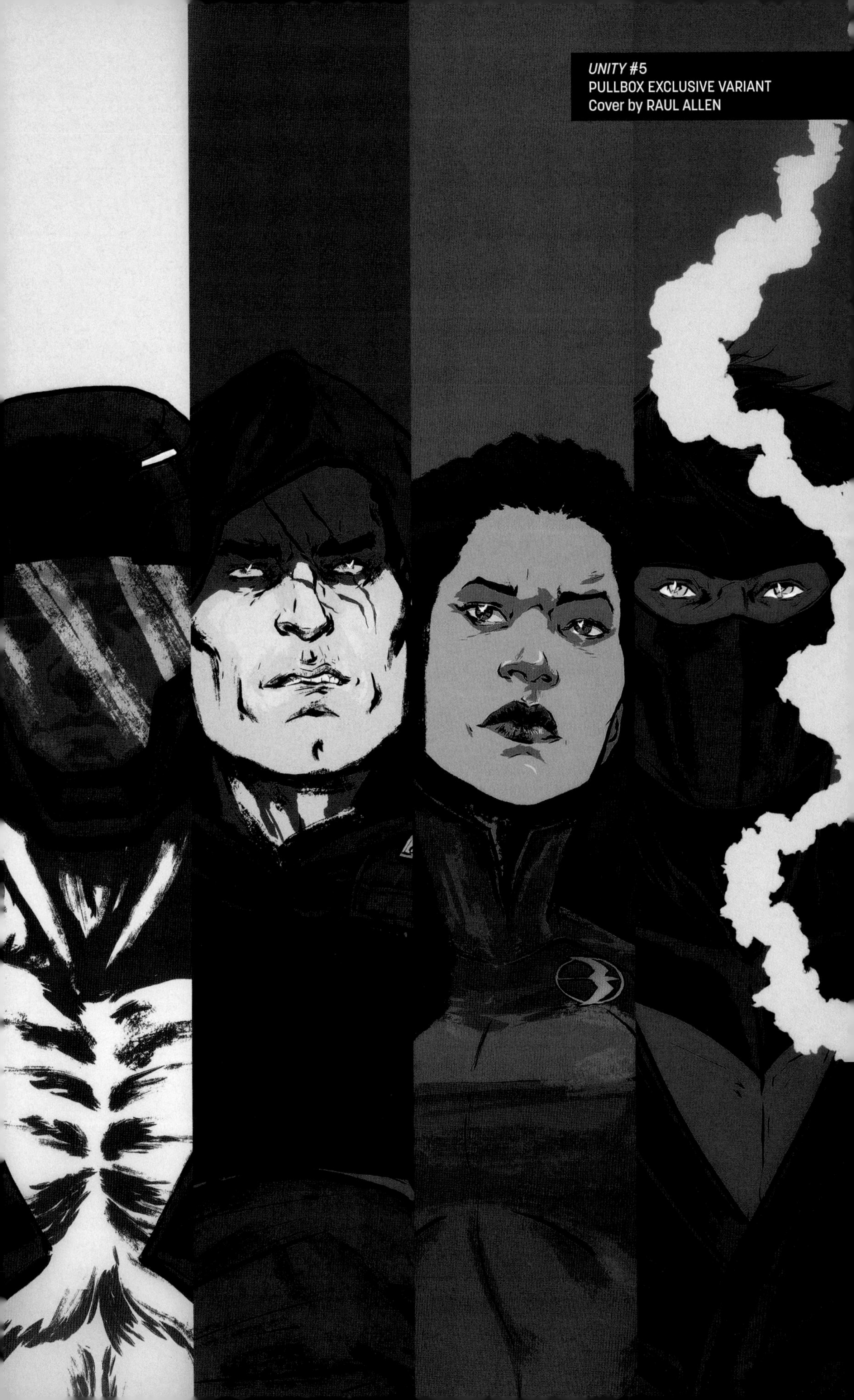

UNITY #5
PULLBOX EXCLUSIVE VARIANT
Cover by RAUL ALLEN

UNITY #5
PULLBOX EXCLUSIVE VARIANT
Cover by DIEGO BERNARD with
ALEJANDRO SICAT

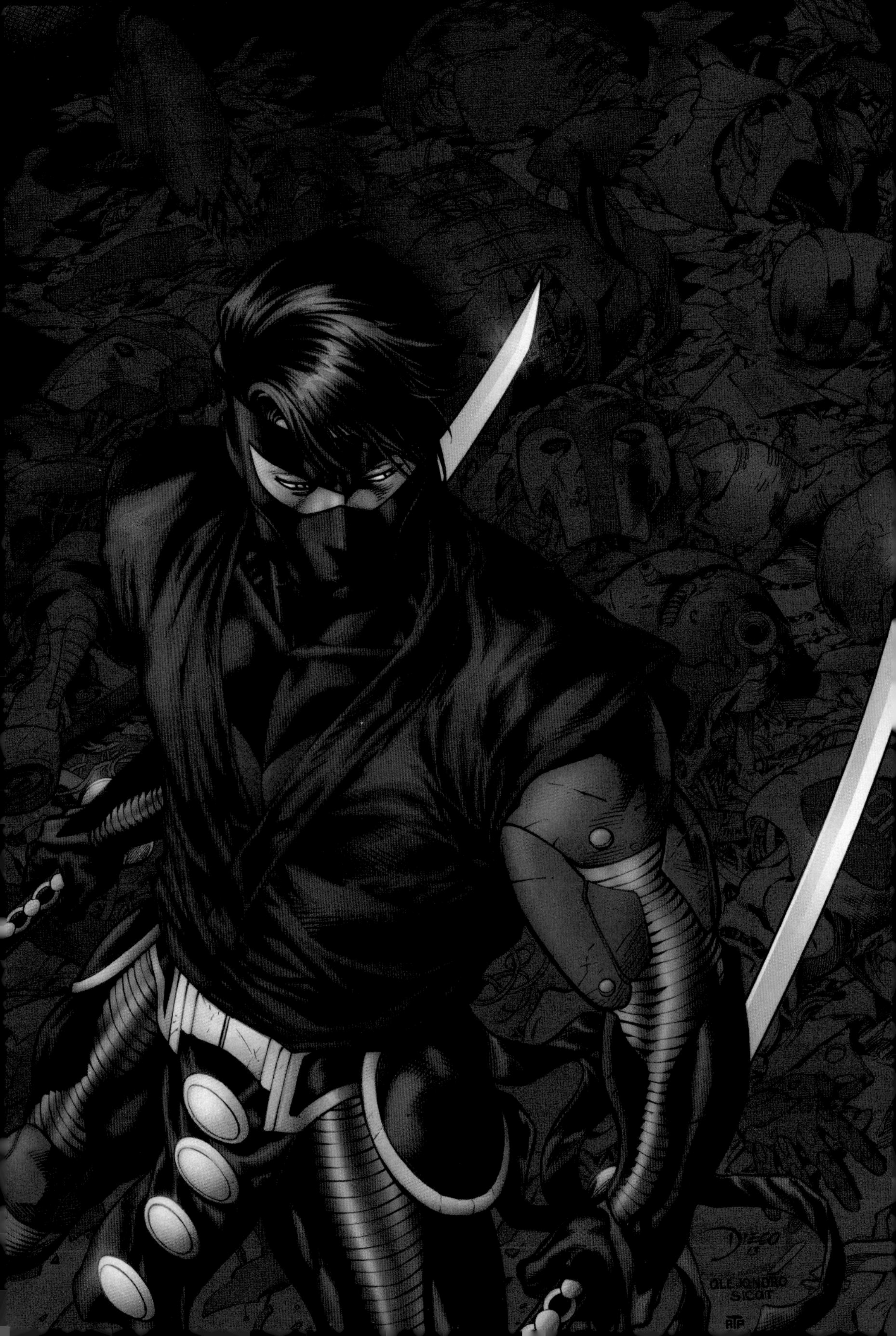

UNITY #5 VARIANT
Cover by MATT KINDT

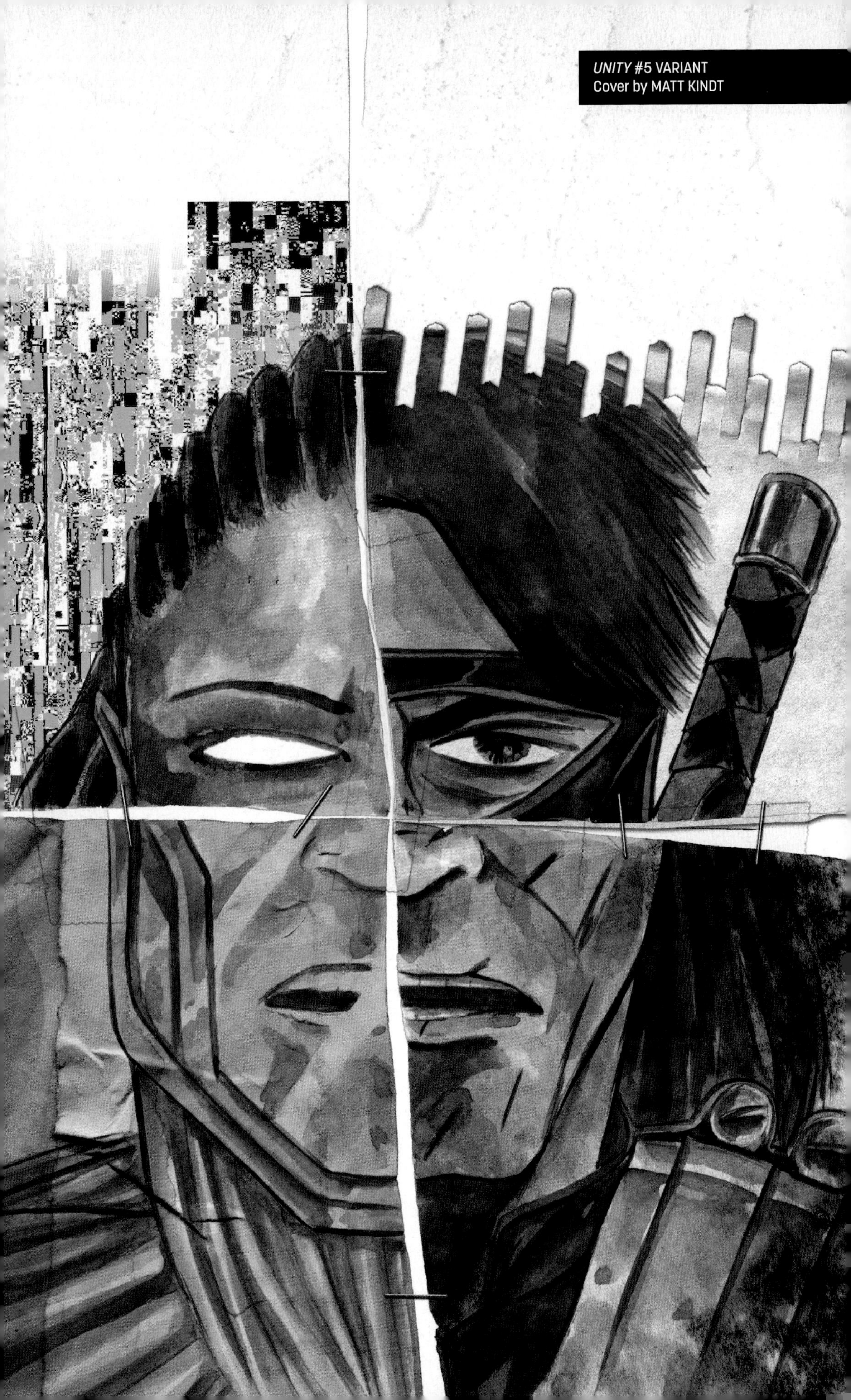

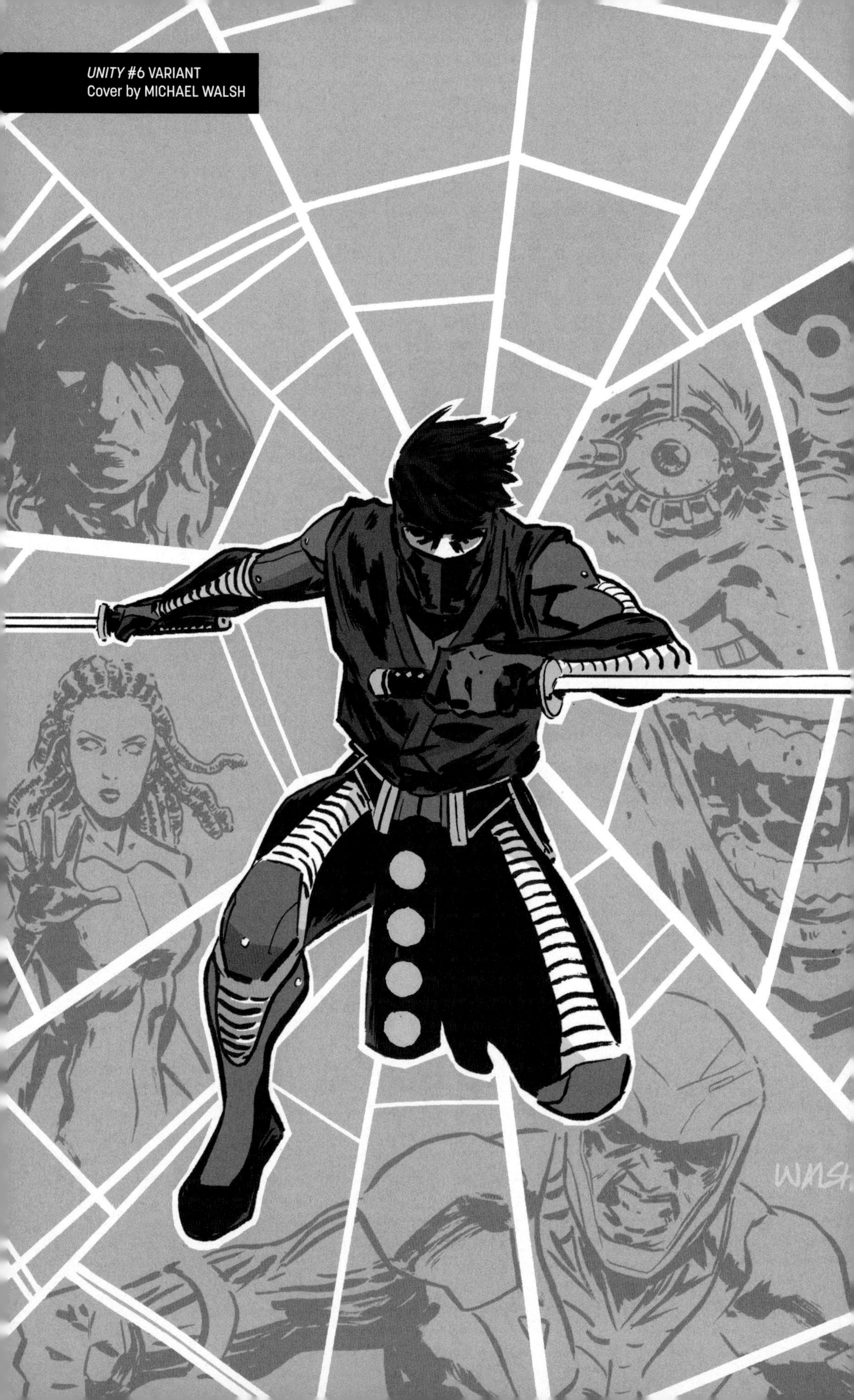

UNITY #6 VARIANT
Cover by MICHAEL WALSH

UNITY #6 VARIANT
Cover by RAUL ALLEN

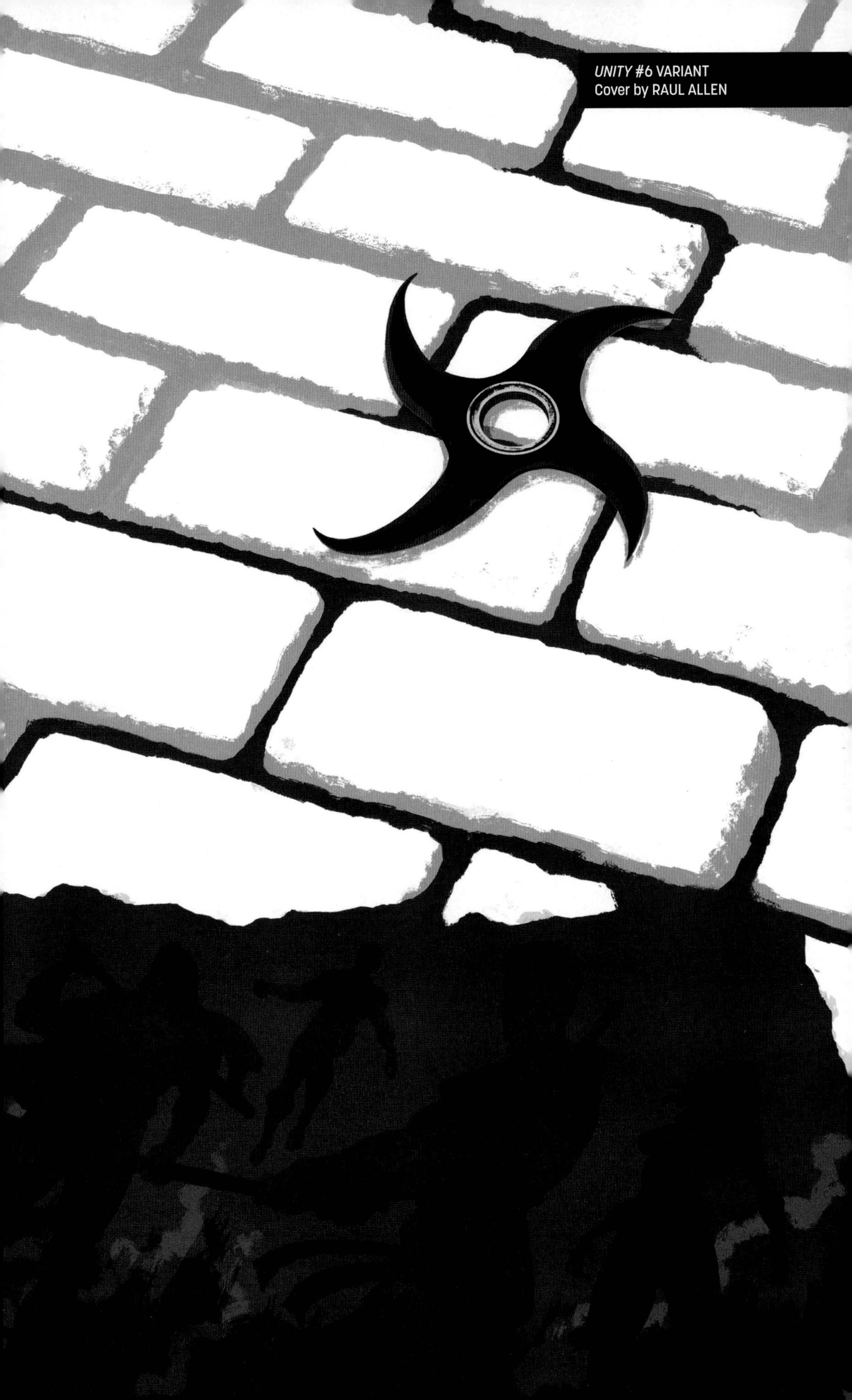

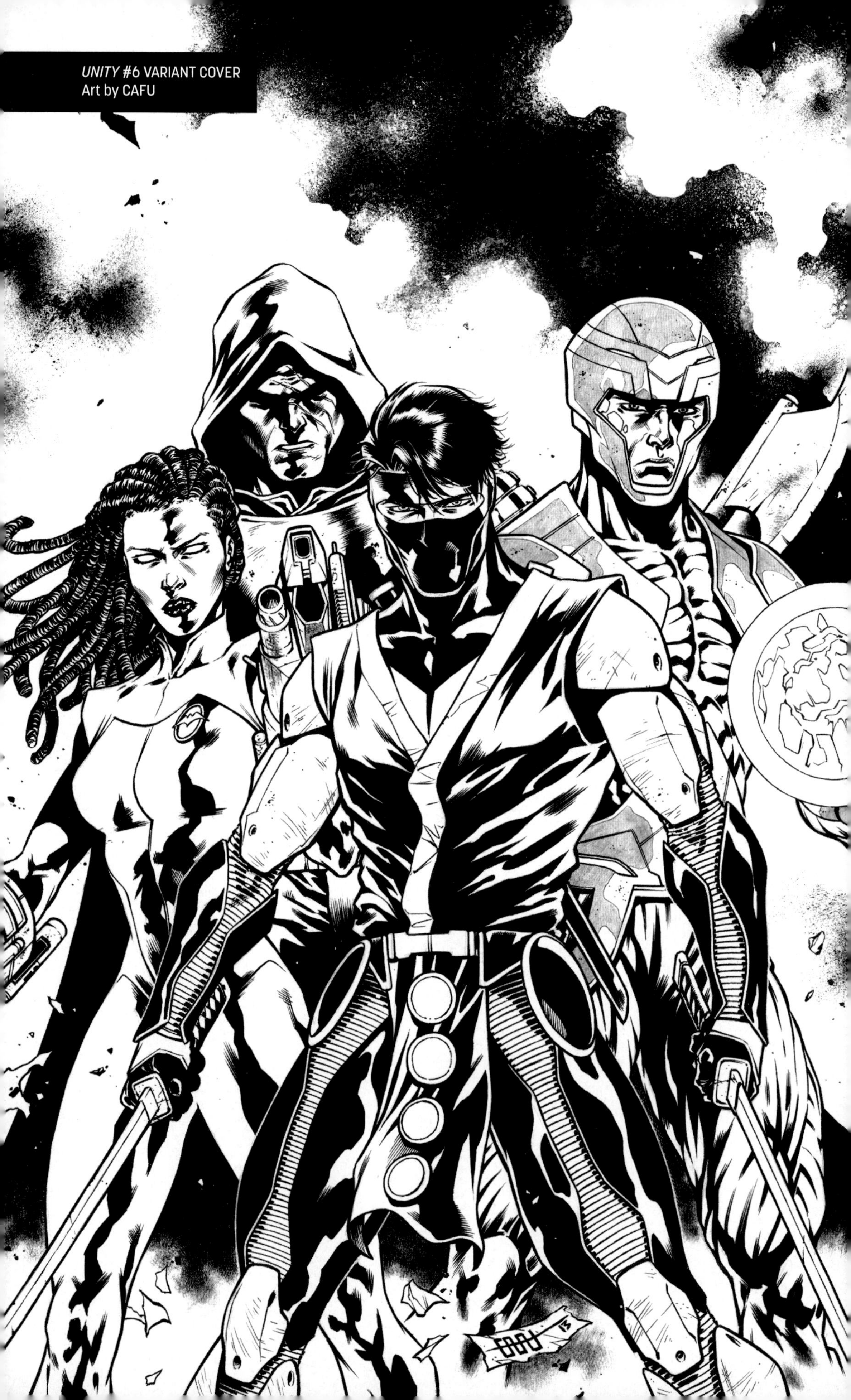

UNITY #6 VARIANT COVER
Art by CAFU

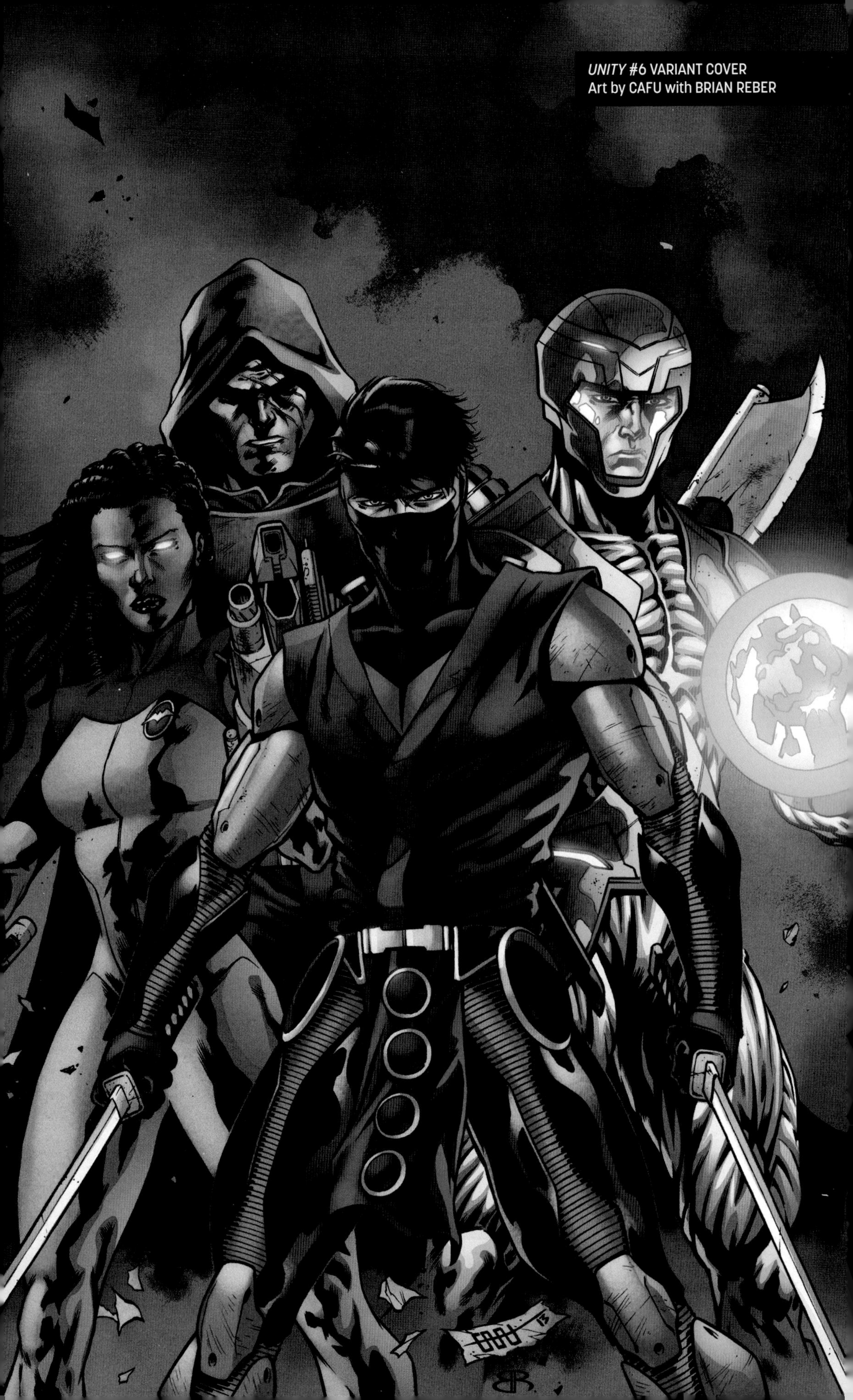

UNITY #6 VARIANT COVER
Art by CAFU with BRIAN REBER

UNITY #7 VARIANT
Cover by RAUL ALLEN

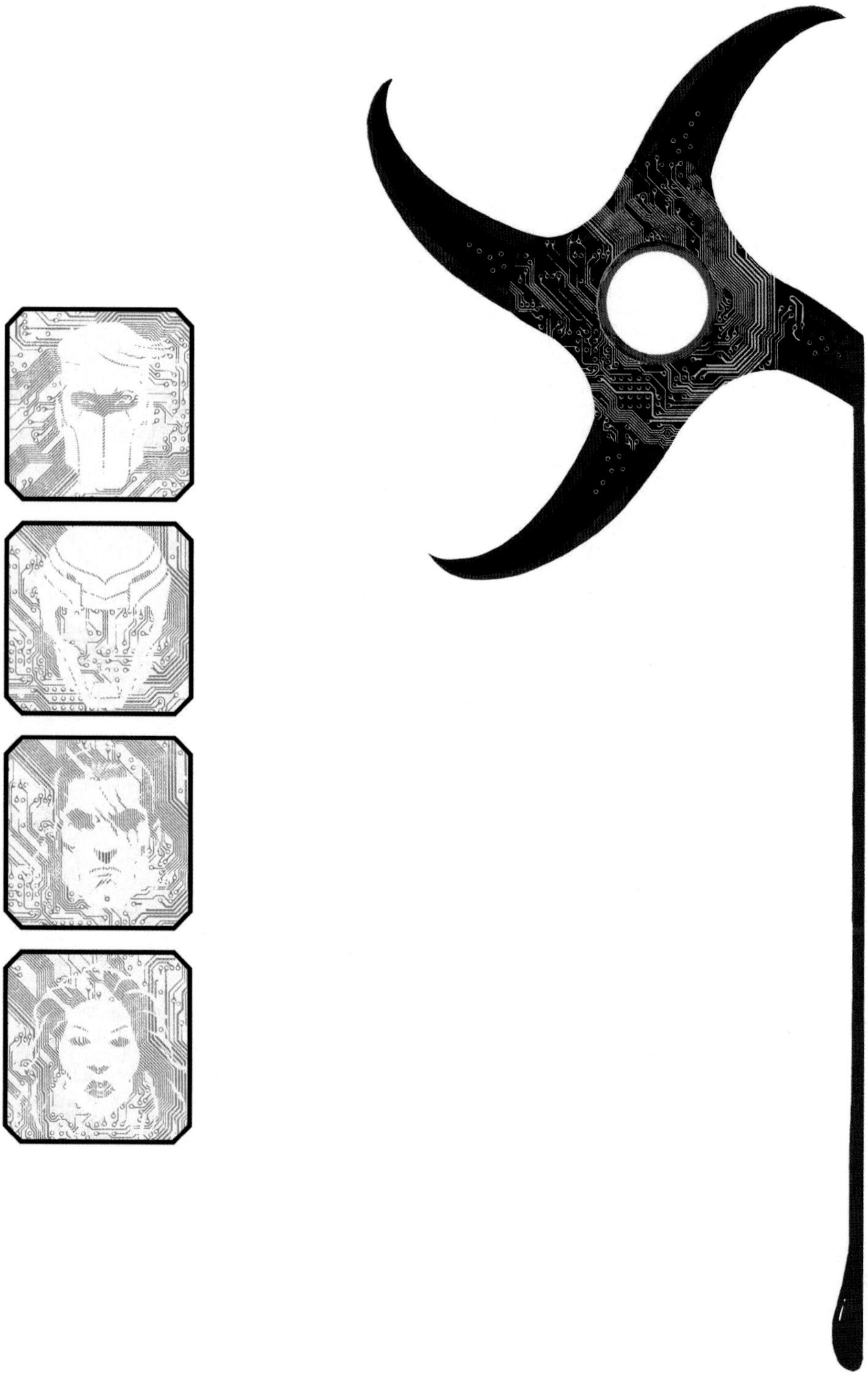

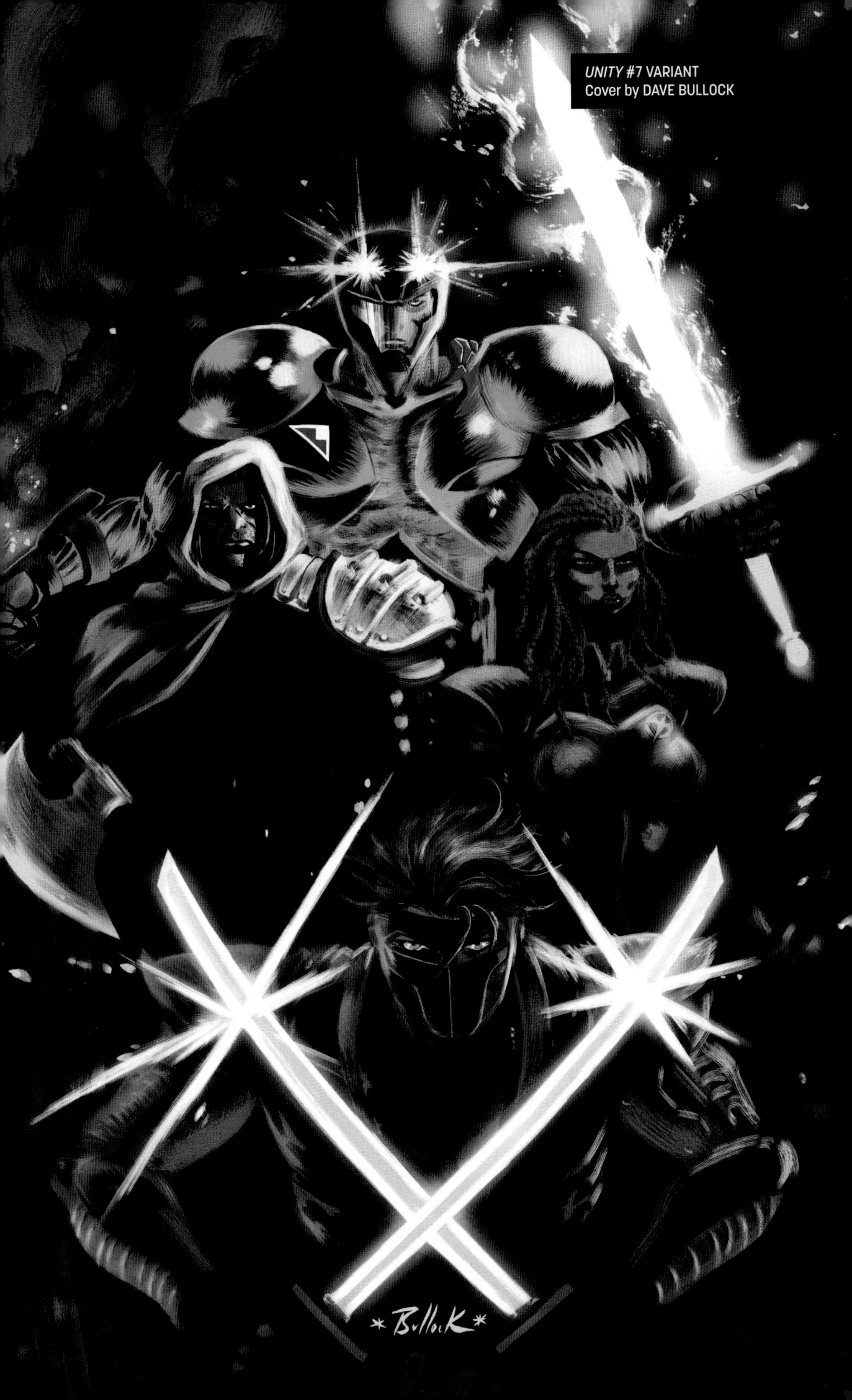
Bullock

UNITY #7 VARIANT
Cover by DAVE BULLOCK

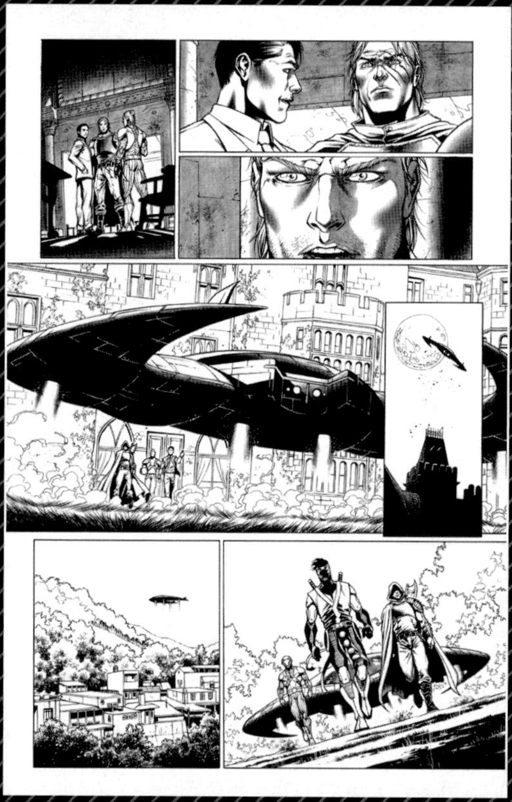

UNITY #5, p. 12
Art by CAFU

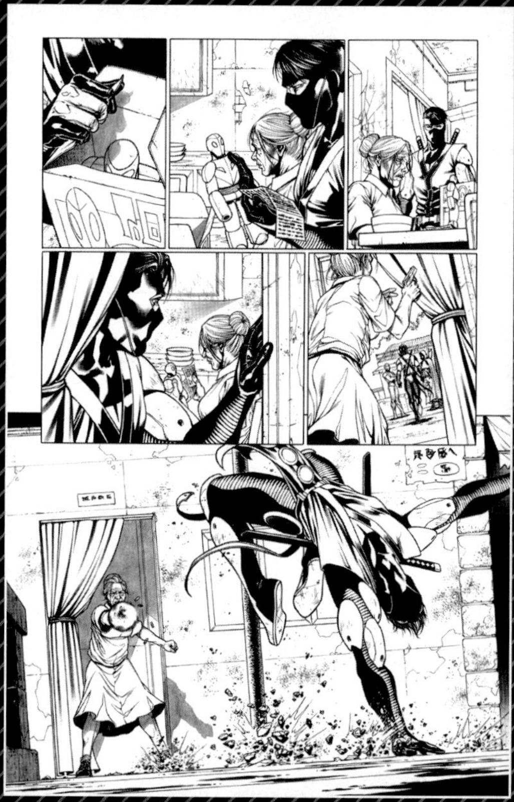

UNITY #5, p. 14
Art by CAFU

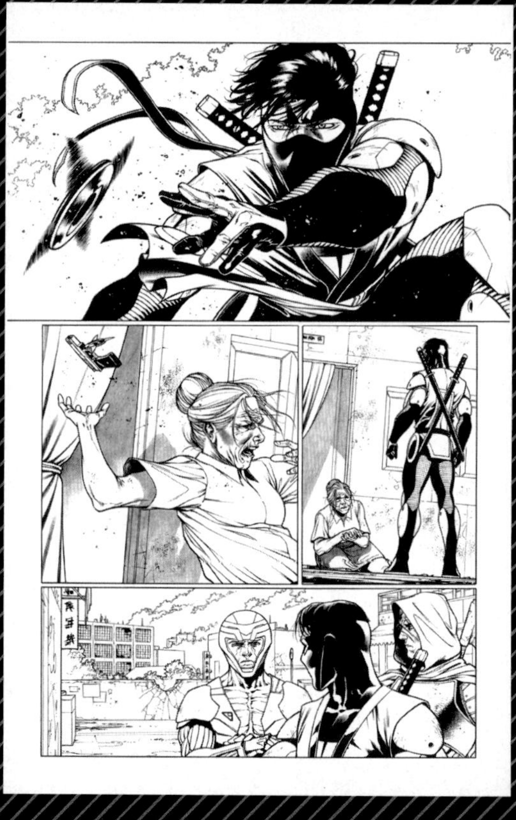

UNITY #5, p. 15
Art by CAFU

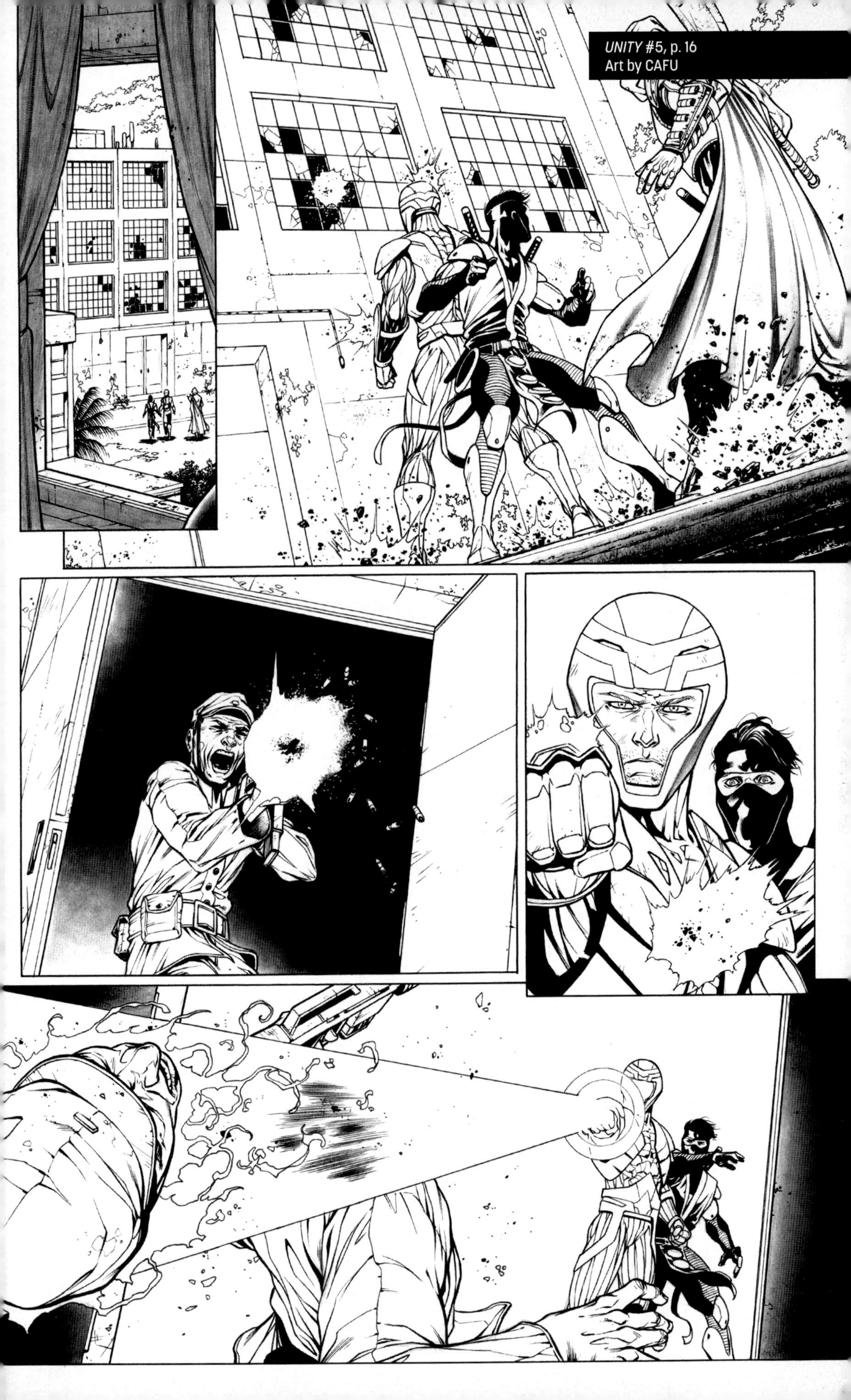
UNITY #5, p. 16
Art by CAFU

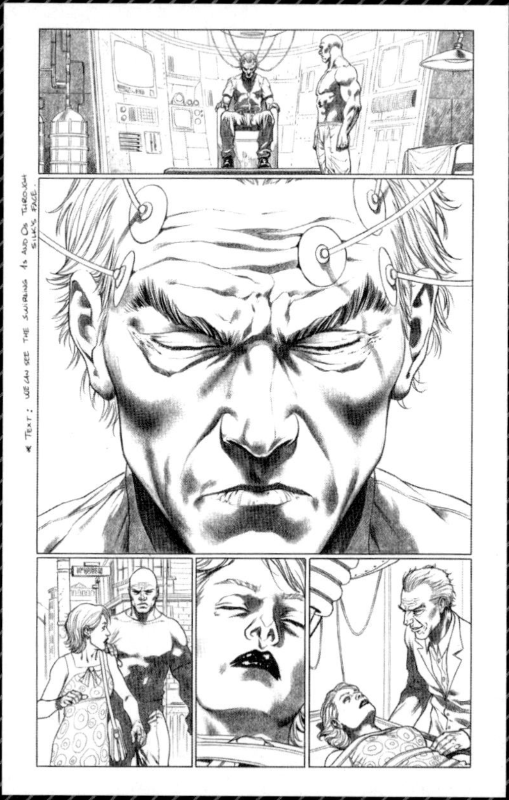
* TEXT: WE CAN SEE THE SWIRLING 1s AND 0s THROUGH SILK'S FACE.

UNITY #6, p. 12
Pencils by CAFU

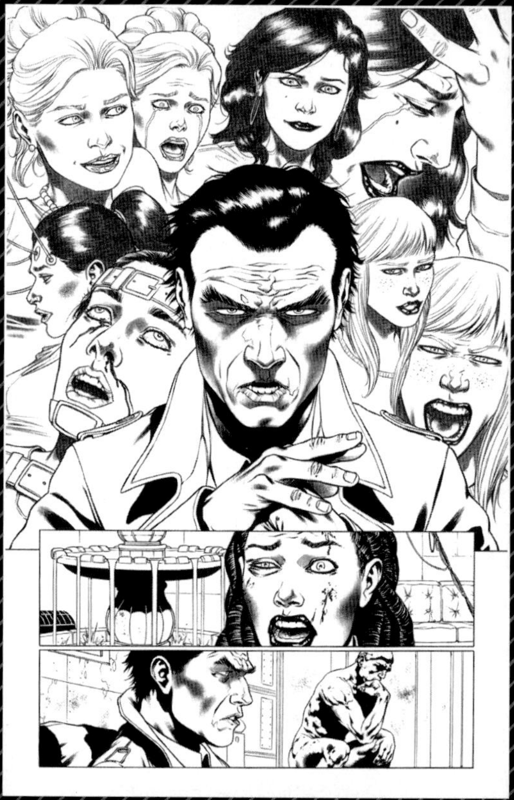

UNITY #6, p. 15
Art by CAFU

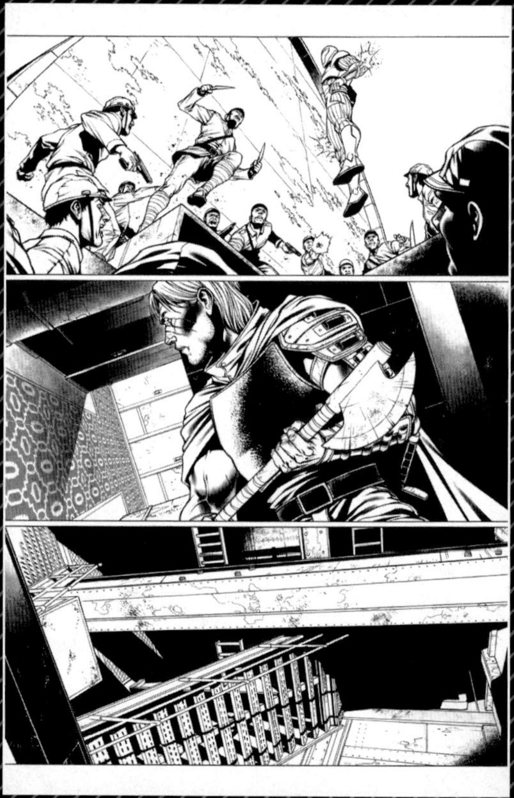

UNITY #6, p. 17
Art by CAFU

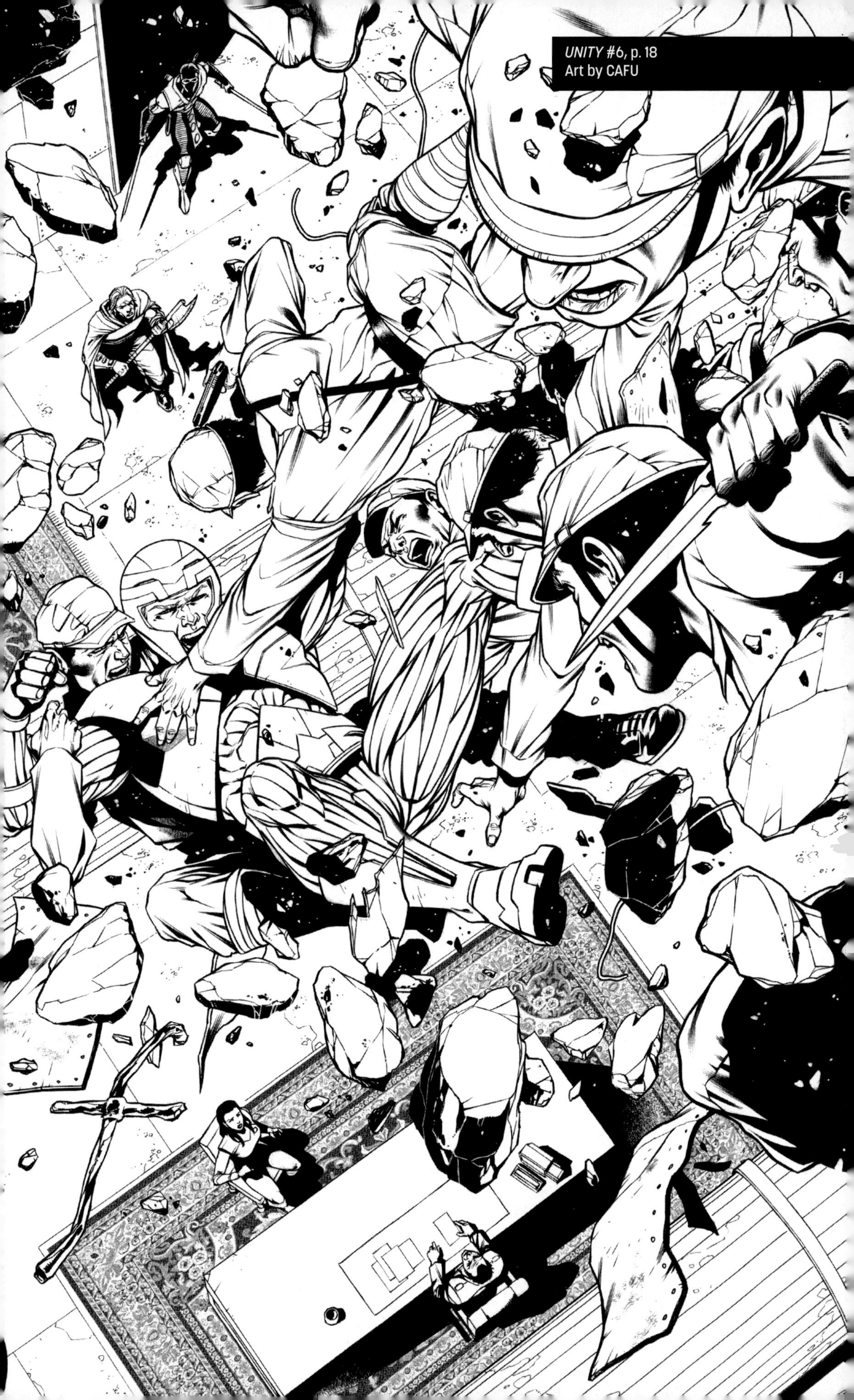

UNITY #6, p. 18
Art by CAFU

UNITY #7, p. 4
Art by CAFU

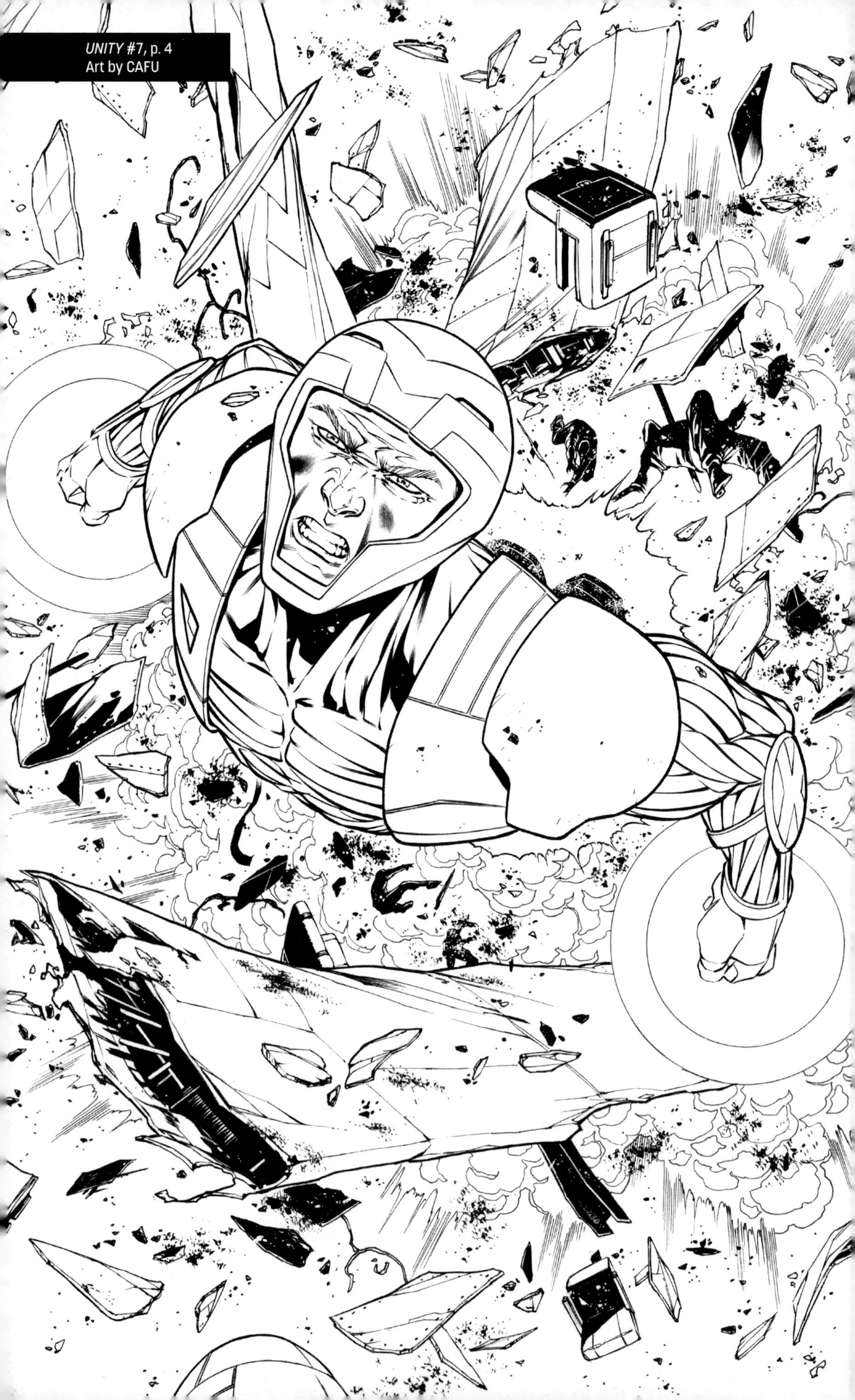

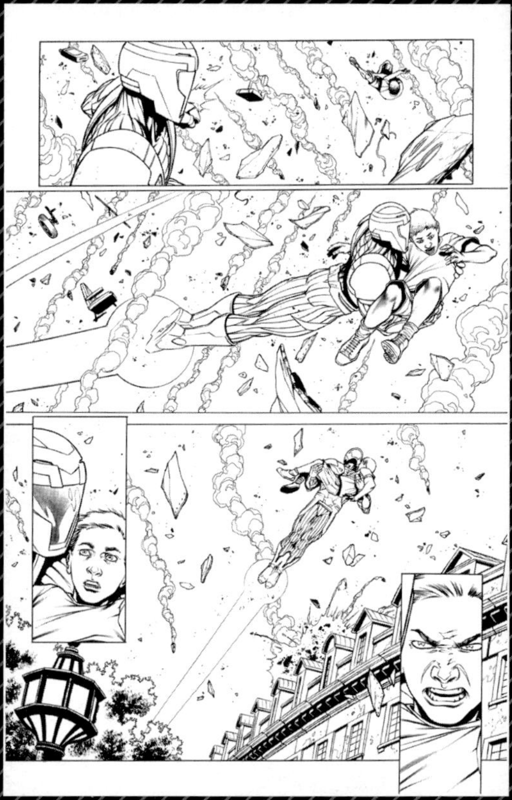

UNITY #7, p. 5
Art by CAFU

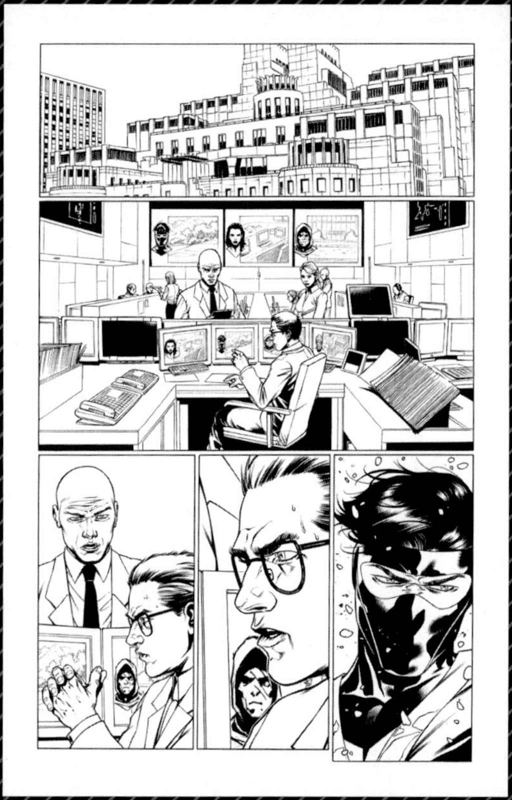

UNITY #7, p. 6
Art by CAFU

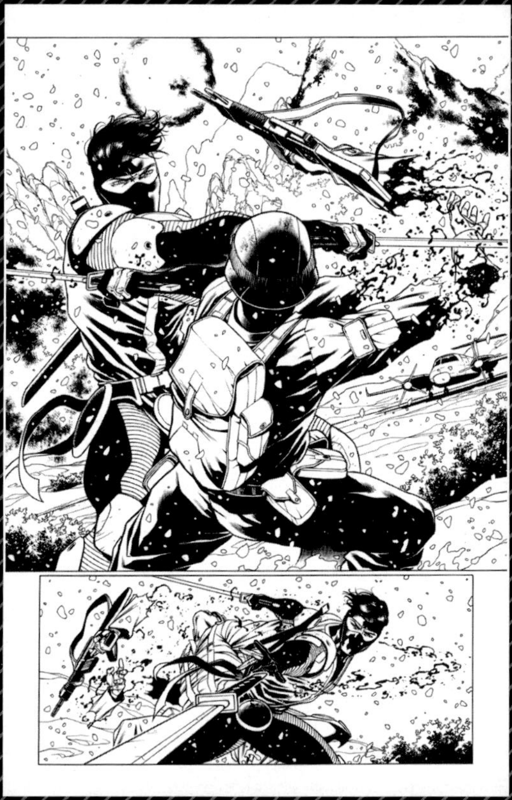

UNITY #7, p. 7
Art by CAFU

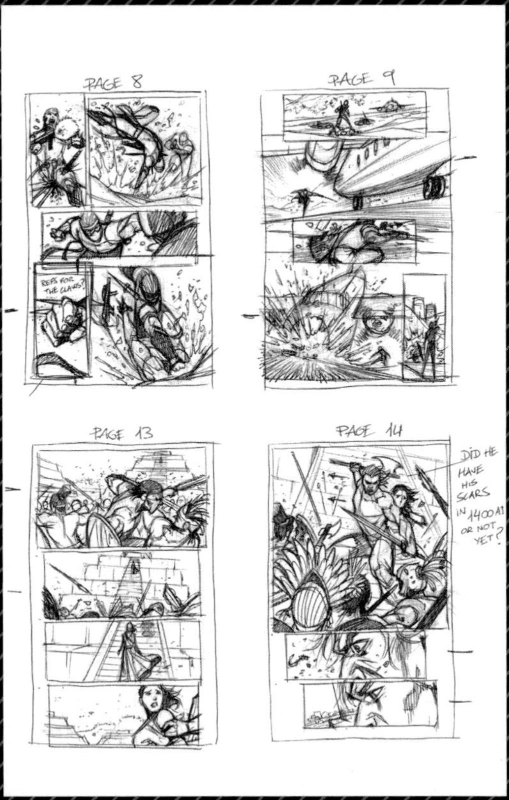
PAGE 8
PAGE 9
REFS FOR THE CLAWS?
PAGE 13
PAGE 14
DID HE HAVE HIS SCARS IN 1400 AD OR NOT YET?

UNITY #7
Interior thumbnails by CAFU

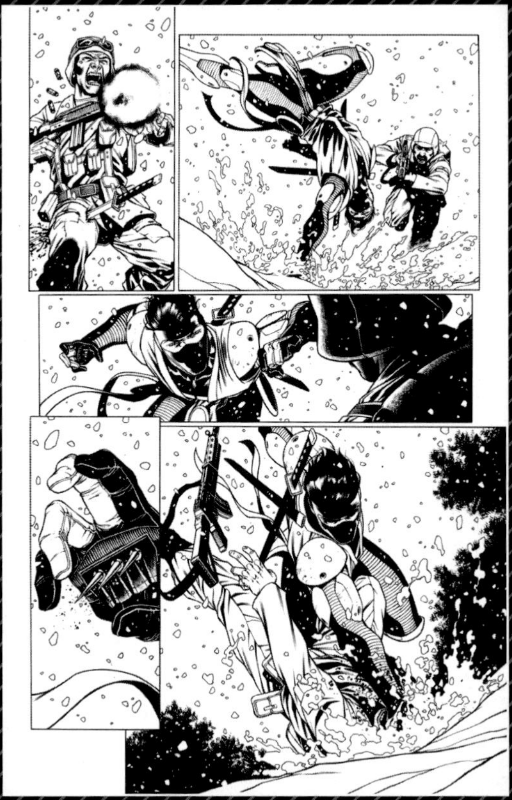

UNITY #7, p. 8
Art by CAFU

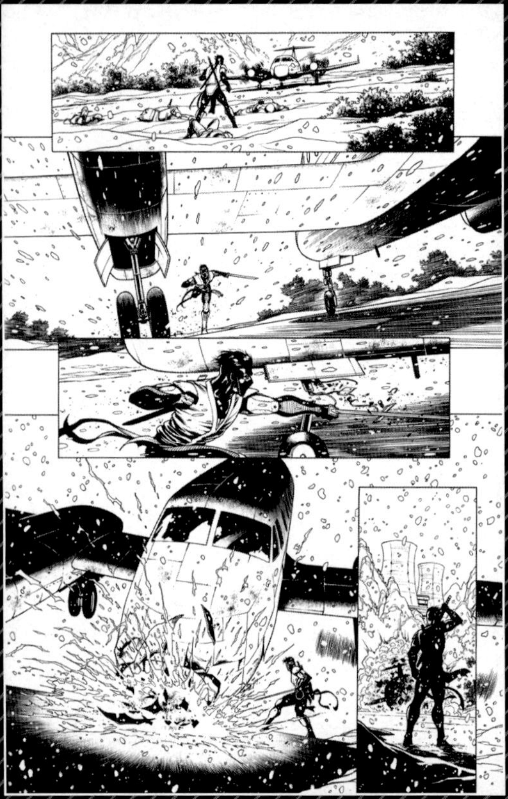

UNITY #7, p. 9
Art by CAFU

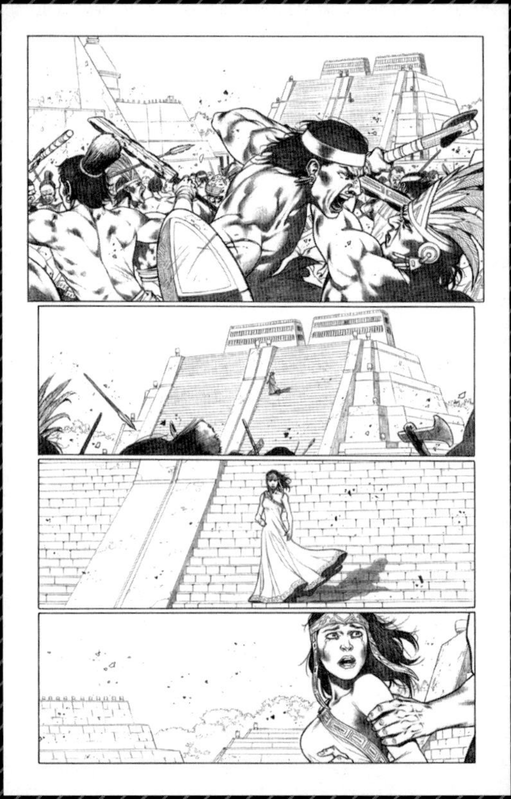

UNITY #7, p. 13
Pencils by CAFU

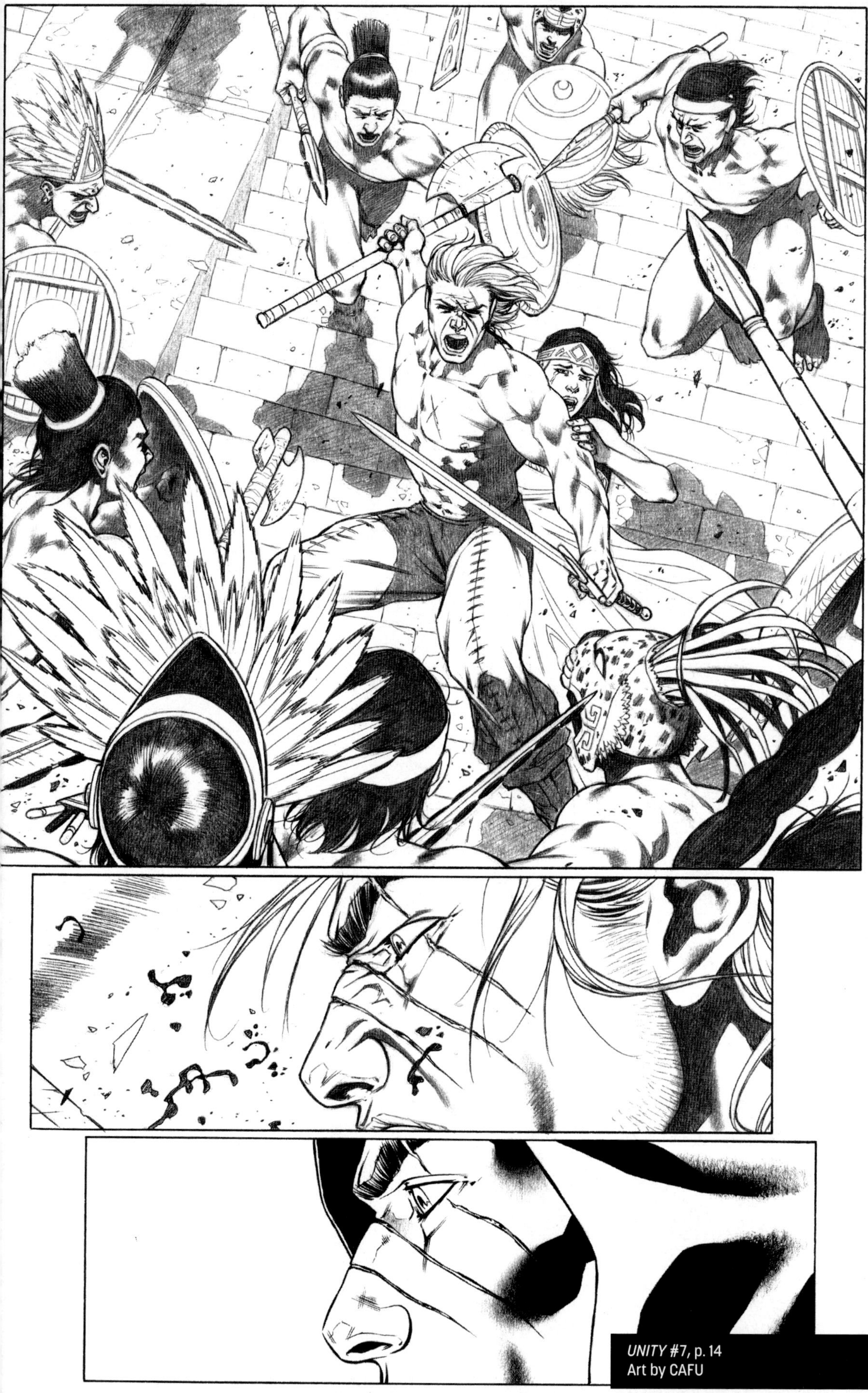

UNITY #7, p. 14
Art by CAFU

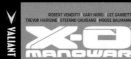

VALIANT® DELUXE HARDCOVERS

VALIANT
ROBERT VENDITTI | CARY NORD | LEE GARBETT
TREVOR HAIRSINE | STEFANO GAUDIANO | MOOSE BAUMANN
X-O MANOWAR
DELUXE EDITION 1

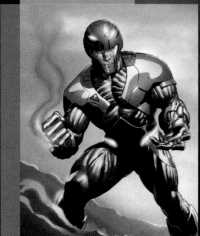

X-O MANOWAR DELUXE EDITION BOOK 1

Writer: Robert Venditti | Artists: Cary Nord, Lee Garbett, and Trevor Hairsine
ISBN: 9781939346100 | Diamond Code: AUG131497 | Price: $39.99 | Format: Oversized HC

Aric of Dacia, a fifth-century Visigoth armed with the universe's most powerful weapon, is all that stands between the Earth and all-out annihilation at the hands of the alien race that abducted him from his own time. Stranded in the modern day, X-O Manowar's battle against the Vine will take him into the shadows with the lethal operative known as Ninjak–and launch a quest for vengeance that will bring an alien empire to its knees. The Vine destroyed Aric's world. Now he will give them war.

Collecting X-O MANOWAR #1-14 and more than 20 pages of bonus materials!

VALIANT
JOSHUA DYSART | KHARI EVANS | TREVOR HAIRSINE
MICO SUAYAN | IAN HANNIN
HARBINGER
DELUXE EDITION 1

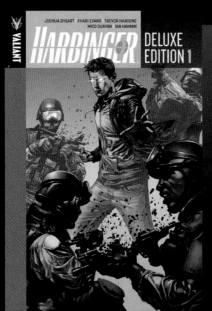

HARBINGER DELUXE EDITION BOOK 1

Writer: Joshua Dysart | Artists: Khari Evans, Trevor Hairsine, Barry Kitson, and Lee Garbett
ISBN: 9781939346131 | Diamond Code: SEP131373 | Price: $39.99 | Format: Oversized HC

Outside the law. Inside your head. You've never met a team of super-powered teenagers quite like the Renegades. Skipping across the country in a desperate attempt to stay one step ahead of the authorities, psionically powered teenager Peter Stanchek only has one option left–run. But he won't have to go it alone. As the shadowy corporation known as the Harbinger Foundation draws close on all sides, Peter will have to find and recruit other unique individuals like himself...other troubled, immensely powerful youths with abilities beyond their control. Their mission? Bring the fight back to the Harbinger Foundation's founder Toyo Harada–and dismantle his global empire brick by brick...

Collecting HARBINGER #0-14 and more than 20 pages of bonus materials!

VALIANT
DUANE SWIERCZYNSKI | MANUEL GARCIA
BARRY KITSON | ARTURO LOZZI | STEFANO GAUDIANO
BLOODSHOT
DELUXE EDITION 1

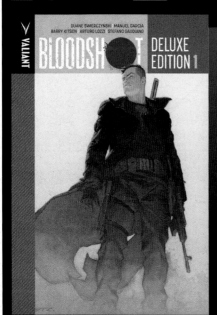

BLOODSHOT DELUXE EDITION BOOK 1

Writer: Duane Swierczynski | Artists: Manuel García, Barry Kitson, Matthew Clark, and Arturo Lozzi
ISBN: 9781939346216 | Diamond Code: JAN141376 | Price: $39.99 | Format: Oversized HC

You have no name, just a project designation. They call you Bloodshot, but the voices inside your head call you "daddy, "sir," "commander," "comrade"–whatever it takes to motivate you to get the job done. But after so many missions and so many lives, you're finally ready to confront your handlers at Project Rising Spirit and find out who you really are. You'd better move quickly, though, because your former masters don't like it when a billion-dollar weapons project goes rogue. And wherever you go, all hell is sure to follow...

Collecting BLOODSHOT #1-13 and more than 20 pages of bonus materials!

VALIANT® DELUXE HARDCOVERS

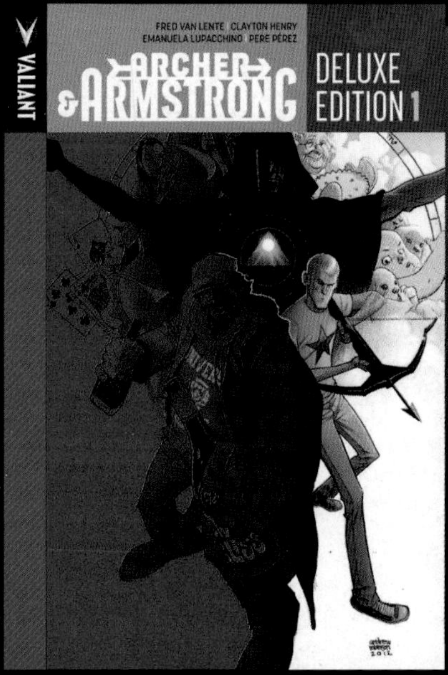

VALIANT
FRED VAN LENTE | CLAYTON HENRY
EMANUELA LUPACCHINO | PERE PÉREZ
ARCHER & ARMSTRONG
DELUXE EDITION 1

ARCHER & ARMSTRONG DELUXE EDITION BOOK 1

Writer: Fred Van Lente | Artists: Clayton Henry, Emanuela Lupacchino, Pere Pérez, and Álvaro Martinez
ISBN: 9781939346223 | Diamond Code: FEB141484 | Price: $39.99 | Format: Oversized HC

Join one of the most acclaimed adventures in comics as naive teenage assassin Obadiah Archer and the fun-loving, hard-drinking immortal called Armstrong unite to stop a plot ten thousand years in the making! From the lost temples of ancient Sumeria to modern-day Wall Street, Area 51, and beyond, Valiant's conspiracy-smashing adventurers are going on a globe-trotting quest to bring down the unholy coalition of cultists known as the Sect–and stop each of history's most notorious conspiracies from remaking the world in their own insane image.

Collecting ARCHER & ARMSTRONG #0-13 and more than 20 pages of bonus materials!

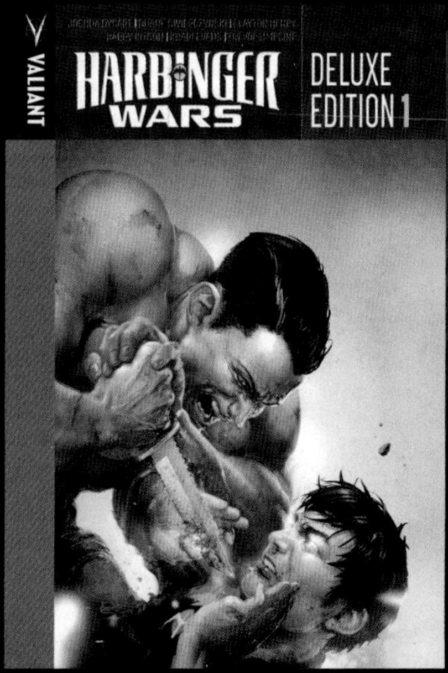

VALIANT
HARBINGER WARS
DELUXE EDITION 1

HARBINGER WARS DELUXE EDITION

Writer: Joshua Dysart & Duane Swierczynski | Artists: Clayton Henry, Pere Pérez, Barry Kitson, Khari Evans, Trevor Hairsine, Mico Suayan, and Clayton Crain
ISBN: 9781939346322 | Diamond Code: MAR141422 | **Price: $39.99 |**
Format: Oversized HC

Re-presenting Valiant's best-selling crossover event in complete chronological order!

When an untrained and undisciplined team of super-powered test subjects escapes from Project Rising Spirit and onto the Vegas Strip, Bloodshot and the Harbinger Renegades will find themselves locked in battle against a deadly succession of opponents–and each other. As the combined forces of the H.A.R.D. Corps, Bloodshot, and omega-level telekinetic Toyo Harada all descend on Las Vegas to vie for control of Rising Spirit's deadliest assets, the world is about to discover the shocking price of an all-out superhuman conflict...and no one will escape unscathed. Who will survive the Harbinger Wars?

Collecting HARBINGER WARS #1-4, HARBINGER #11-14, BLOODSHOT #10-13, material from the HARBINGER WARS SKETCHBOOK, and more than 20 pages of bonus materials!

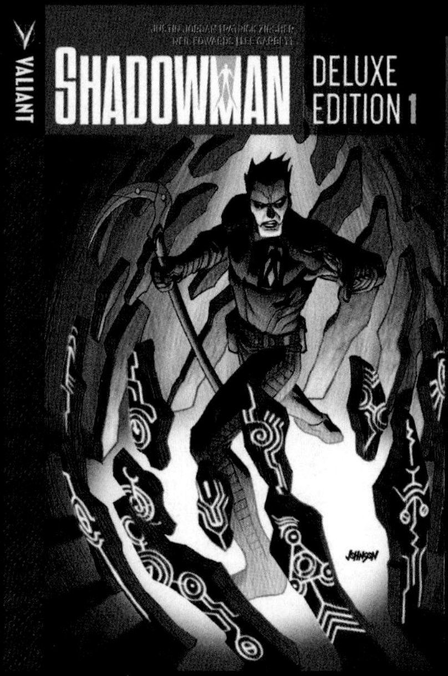

VALIANT
SHADOWMAN
DELUXE EDITION 1

SHADOWMAN DELUXE EDITION BOOK 1

Writers: Justin Jordan and Patrick Zircher | Artists: Patrick Zircher, Neil Edwards, Lee Garbett, Diego Bernard, Roberto de la Torre, Mico Suayan, and Lewis LaRosa
ISBN: 9781939346438 | Price: $39.99 | Format: Oversized HC | COMING SOON

There are a million dreams in the Big Easy. But now its worst nightmare is about to come true. As the forces of darkness prepare to claim New Orleans as their own, Jack Boniface must accept the legacy he was born to uphold. As Shadowman, Jack is about to become the only thing that stands between his city and an army of unspeakable monstrosities from beyond the night. But what is the true cost of the Shadowman's otherworldly power? And can Jack master his new abilities before Master Darque brings down the wall between reality and the otherwordly dimension known only as the Deadside?

Collecting SHADOWMAN #0-10 and more than 20 pages of bonus materials!

VALIANT®

TRADE PAPERBACKS

VALIANT
TO KILL A KING
UNITY

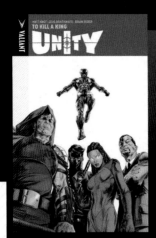

UNITY VOL. 1: TO KILL A KING
ISBN: 9781939346261 | Diamond Code: JAN141356 | Price: $14.99 | Format: TP

UNITY VOL. 2: TRAPPED BY WEBNET
ISBN: 97819393463461 | Diamond Code: MAY141658 | Price: $14.99 | Format: TP

VALIANT
BY THE SWORD
X-O MANOWAR

X-O MANOWAR VOL. 1: BY THE SWORD
ISBN: 9780979640995 | Diamond Code: OCT121241 | Price: $9.99 | Format: TP

X-O MANOWAR VOL. 2: ENTER NINJAK
ISBN: 9780979640940 | Diamond Code: JAN131306 | Price: $14.99 | Format: TP

X-O MANOWAR VOL. 3: PLANET DEATH
ISBN: 9781939346087 | Diamond Code: JUN131325 | Price: $14.99 | Format: TP

X-O MANOWAR VOL. 4: HOMECOMING
ISBN: 9781939346179 | Diamond Code: OCT131347 | Price: $14.99 | Format: TP

X-O MANOWAR VOL. 5: AT WAR WITH UNITY
ISBN: 9781939346247 | Diamond Code: FEB141472 | Price: $14.99 | Format: TP

VALIANT
SETTING THE WORLD ON FIRE

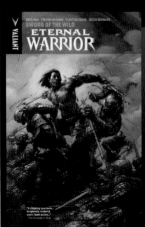

BLOODSHOT VOL. 1: SETTING THE WORLD ON FIRE
ISBN: 9780979640964 | Diamond Code: DEC121274 | Price: $9.99 | Format: TP

BLOODSHOT VOL. 2: THE RISE AND THE FALL
ISBN: 9781939346032| Diamond Code: APR131280 | Price: $14.99 | Format: TP

BLOODSHOT VOL. 3: HARBINGER WARS
ISBN: 9781939346124 | Diamond Code: AUG131494 | Price: $14.99 | Format: TP

BLOODSHOT VOL. 4: H.A.R.D. CORPS
ISBN: 9781939346193 | Diamond Code: NOV131275 | Price: $14.99 | Format: TP

BLOODSHOT VOL. 5: GET SOME
ISBN: 9781939346315 | Price: $14.99 | Format: TP | COMING SOON

VALIANT
SWORD OF THE WILD
ETERNAL WARRIOR

ETERNAL WARRIOR VOL. 1: SWORD OF THE WILD
ISBN: 9781939346209 | Diamond Code: NOV131271 | Price: $9.99 | Format: TP

ETERNAL WARRIOR VOL. 2: ETERNAL EMPEROR
ISBN: 9781939346292 | Diamond Code: APR141439 | Price: $14.99 | Format: TP

VALIANT® TRADE PAPERBACKS

VALIANT
OMEGA RISING
HARBINGER

HARBINGER VOL. 1: OMEGA RISING
ISBN: 9780979640957 | Diamond Code: NOV121345 | Price: $9.99 | Format: TP

HARBINGER VOL. 2: RENEGADES
ISBN: 9781939346025 | Diamond Code: MAR131332 | Price: $14.99 | Format: TP

HARBINGER WARS (MINI-SERIES)
ISBN: 9781939346094 | Diamond Code: JUL131325 | Price: $14.99 | Format: TP

HARBINGER VOL. 3: HARBINGER WARS
ISBN: 9781939346117 | Diamond Code: JUL131326 | Price: $14.99 | Format: TP

HARBINGER VOL. 4: PERFECT DAY
ISBN: 9781939346155 | Diamond Code: DEC131331 | Price: $14.99 | Format: TP

VALIANT
THE MICHELANGELO CODE
ARCHER & ARMSTRONG

ARCHER & ARMSTRONG VOL. 1: THE MICHELANGELO CODE
ISBN: 9780979640988 | Diamond Code: JAN131309 | Price: $14.99 | Format: TP

ARCHER & ARMSTRONG VOL. 2: WRATH OF THE ETERNAL WARRIOR
ISBN: 9781939346049 | Diamond Code: MAY131314 | Price: $14.99 | Format: TP

ARCHER & ARMSTRONG VOL. 3: FAR FARAWAY
ISBN: 9781939346148 | Diamond Code: OCT131350 | Price: $14.99 | Format: TP

ARCHER & ARMSTRONG VOL. 4: SECT CIVIL WAR
ISBN: 9781939346254 | Diamond Code: DEC131317 | Price: $14.99 | Format: TP

ARCHER & ARMSTRONG VOL. 5: MISSION: IMPROBABLE
ISBN: 9781939346353 | Diamond Code: APR141438 | Price: $14.99 | Format: TP

VALIANT
BIRTH RITES
SHADOWMAN

SHADOWMAN VOL. 1: BIRTH RITES
ISBN: 9781939346001 | Diamond Code: FEB131168 | Price: $9.99 | Format: TP

SHADOWMAN VOL. 2: DARQUE RECKONING
ISBN: 9781939346056 | Diamond Code: AUG131482 | Price: $14.99 | Format: TP

SHADOWMAN VOL. 3: DEADSIDE BLUES
ISBN: 9781939346162 | Diamond Code: NOV131282 | Price: $14.99 | Format: TP

SHADOWMAN VOL. 4: FEAR, BLOOD, AND SHADOWS
ISBN: 9781939346278 | Diamond Code: MAR141410 | Price: $14.99 | Format: TP

VALIANT
THE WORLD'S WORST SUPERHERO TEAM
QUANTUM AND WOODY!
KLANG.

QUANTUM AND WOODY VOL. 1: THE WORLD'S WORST SUPERHERO TEAM
ISBN: 9781939346186 | Diamond Code: SEP131374 | Price: $9.99 | Format: TP

QUANTUM AND WOODY VOL. 2: IN SECURITY
ISBN: 9781939346230 | Diamond Code: JAN141365 | Price: $14.99 | Format: TP

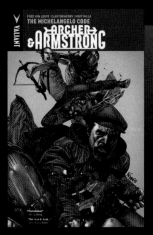

VALIANT®

ARMOR HUNTERS®

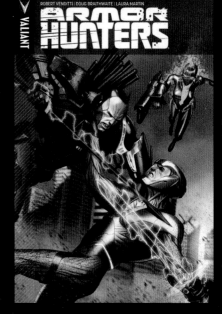

EARTH WILL BE THE GREATEST HUNT OF ALL!

VALIANT
ROBERT VENDITTI | DOUG BRAITHWAITE | LAURA MARTIN
ARMOR HUNTERS

When Aric of Dacia returned to Earth with the stolen X-O Manowar armor of an alien race, he thought he'd finally found a weapon to guard the peace and kingdom he'd struggled so long to secure. But now, a relentless and surgical strike team from the farthest reaches of space - sworn to exterminate the armor and all like it - have found their final target. The ARMOR HUNTERS are coming. They will hunt. They will trap. They will kill. And they will rid the universe of the X-O Manowar armorø's incalculable destructive power...even if it means taking the Earth with it.

In the tradition of the universe-shaking HARBINGER WARS, be here when New York Times best-selling writer Robert Venditti (*X-O Manowar, Green Lantern*) and superstar artist Doug Braithwaite (*Unity, Justice*) launch Valiant's biggest heroes into the year's blockbuster crossover event - ARMOR HUNTERS! Collecting **ARMOR HUNTERS #1-4** and **ARMOR HUNTERS: AFTERMATH #1**.

TRADE PAPERBACK
978-1-939346-45-2

UNITY®

VOLUME THREE: **ARMOR HUNTERS**

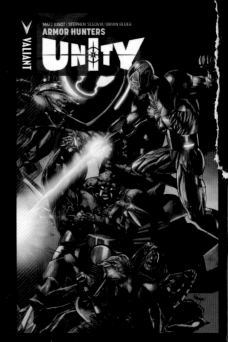

IN BATTLE WITH THE ARMOR HUNTERS!

VALIANT
MATT KINDT | STEPHEN SEGOVIA | BRIAN REBER
ARMOR HUNTERS
UNITY

When an ultra-powerful threat from deep space begins brutalizing Earth, humanity's first response is - who else? - the fearless team of heroes, soldiers, and short fuses called Unity! Now it's down to X-O Manowar, Ninjak, Eternal Warrior, and Livewire - plus some special surprise recruits - to lead the assault on the ARMOR HUNTERS' frontline...even if they die trying!

Valiant's unbreakable all-star superteam leads the resistance against the Earth's first all-out extraterrestrial incursion right here in an all-new, standalone story arc from New York Times best-selling writer Matt Kindt (*Mind MGMT*) and red-hot artist Stephen Segovia (*Superior Carnage*)! Collecting **UNITY #8-11**.

TRADE PAPERBACK
978-1-939346-44-5